Heart of Steel

Based on a True Story

By Kevin D. Miller

To my Grandfather Stanley William Miller, the Patriarch who gave us our family name and our legacy. To my father who encouraged me to write his story.

FORWARD

All sons think their fathers are the strongest, fastest, smartest and greatest and I am no exception. However, every now and then a father's story must be told. I thank my son Kevin Miller for telling my father and his grandfather's. I trust you will agree it is most compelling in terms of love for family, dedication and personal sacrifice. I am proud to be the son of Stanley William Puchalski, better known as Stanley William Miller.

Robert J. Miller (Second son)

ACKNOWLEDGMENTS

Writing this book presented many challenges from research and filling in the unknown to learning how to write and accepting critique. I want to thank my father for encouraging me to take on this endeavour. His faith in me allowed me to reach the finish line. I want to thank my sister Tari for helping me properly title the book. A special thanks to my wife Annette for her patience and dedication as a wonderful critique partner who provided me with much-needed inspiration and ideas. A big thank-you to my brother Craig for his support. I want to thank my two grandsons Kaleb Rhoten and Joel Miller for providing the photography and modelling for the book cover. Lastly, I want to express my appreciation for my daughters Emily and Gracie for their patience and selflessness in allowing me time away from them to write this story.

PART I - CHAPTER ONE

MONDAY, SEPTEMBER 13, 1920 – Twelve-year old Stanley William Puchalski runs for his life along a dusty country road. His mother's pleas for him to fetch the sheriff echo through his mind. How did she escape her bindings? Who are these men, and what did they want with Papa?

The rhythmic pounding of his boots against the road are the only sounds now. His throat is raw from gasping icy winds. Sweat and tears blur his vision. His heart pounds. Excruciating spasms cramp his calves and thighs, causing him to stumble and limp. He pushes on until the sheriff's office comes into view, revealed by early morning sunlight.

He presses his hand against a painful cramp in his side stopping only long enough to catch his breath. With hands braced on his knees, he lifts his eyes towards his destination. Heaving a final breath, he rushes to the entrance and bursts through the door.

***

FIVE DAYS EARLIER - The morn is clear and cool in Southington, Ohio. The Puchalski farm is a splendid, robust farm. Acres of crops are bathed in sunlight. Corn, cabbage, watermelon, and more, ready for harvest. Cattle and horses graze in lush grassy fields. A large orchard produces red plump apples, cherries, peaches and green crab apples. A small field of strawberries, raspberries and blackberries grow wildly behind the family farmhouse.

Stanley sits on a sturdy wooden fence in faded worn overalls. Both knees are exposed from shredded holes in the denim. The sleeves to his grungy-white cotton shirt are rolled to his elbows. Laces from his weathered leather boots dangle loosely and untied. His deep-set icy-blue eyes squint in protest from the rays of sunlight, having just peeked over the horizon. He removes a straw cap from his dirty blonde hair and brushes away beads of sweat from his brow. Chores begin early on the farm. He stretches his right arm into the air, arching his back, inhaling a deep yawn.

He tosses corn cobs to fat pigs as they roll around in the brown rich mud of their pigsty. "Here pig. Piggy piggy. Here, ya go pigs." *Dang, now I know why they call you pigs.*

He hops off the fence and darts inside the family's spacious barn. The oaken boards are weathered and stained red. A sturdy tin roof sits atop its walls. "Hey Maggie. What do you have for me this morning, girl?" He slides a bucket under his favorite Holstein and tugs on her udders, creating a steady stream of milk and warming his hands at the same time. He patiently transfers and distributes each full bucket of milk into several two-gallon milk cans.

"Damnit, I'm starving. Hope Mama's cook'n up something good. Hurry up, Maggie. I gotta go eat." The Holstein snorts then bellows, lifting her rear leg, then setting it back down.

He sets aside four full milk cans marked for delivery after breakfast. A daily task he enjoys. It gives him a break from the more demanding chores around the farm. Sometimes his big sister Sophie gets to tag along and the two talk about life and share their dreams for the future.

Stanley fills a small pail to the rim with fresh milk for the breakfast table. He walks outside the barn, setting the pail on the ground, allowing himself a moment to transfer the grime from his hands onto his overalls. He gazes as wagons, tractors, horses, plows and dozens of farmhands are hard at work, harvesting and tending to the vast, rich farm.

Grasping the pail, he walks toward the family farmhouse, a sizeable two-story Dutch Colonial building painted entirely white. A gray squirrel pops his head out of one of many giant shade trees surrounding the home as if to greet him or beg for food.

"I don't have anything for ya. Better scram, or I'll turn you into breakfast." He climbs the steps to a massive porch and sets the pail next to the front door. He plops onto a weathered wooden rocker. "I need a break." He spots a green mantis crawling along one of the sturdy white pillars that line the porch. His eyes follow the insect's journey until he's distracted and refocuses his attention on the far-reaching apple orchard being harvested by dozens of farmhands.

Wow. Look at all those apples. Twenty, thirty baskets, and the trees are still full. Mm, Mama's hot apple pie, topped with vanilla ice cream.

The smoky aroma of bacon fills his nostrils, triggering his gut to grumble and churn and alerting him, breakfast is ready. He snatches the pail and slips through the screen door allowing it to slam behind him.

Mama cracks fresh eggs she gathered early this morning, dropping them one by one on a hot skillet. They sizzle the second they hit the iron. "Here's the milk, Mama. What's for breakfast? I need food for my belly." She smiles. "Wash your hands first. Then you can eat."

"Hey Sophie, don't burn my bacon this time. Mama, don't let Sophie burn the bacon."

Sophie wrinkles her nose and sticks out her tongue. "Do what Mama told you to do. Go wash your filthy hands."

There he is. Papa. Sitting at the table in his neatly-pressed overalls. Always wearing that same stupid T-shirt with the torn collar. His cold-blue eyes are mean and piercing. You don't want to look him directly in the eye for too long. Not if you know what's good for you.

Papa isn't a particularly large man, he's of average height, but he's lean, broad-shouldered and muscular and he can outwork any man on the farm. Mama always said his thick chestnut mustache and square chin were handsome. But I don't see it. All I see is an angry face. Angry all the time. Unless he's going to the bar or kicking someone's ass. The good ole boy of Southington. George Puchalski. My Papa. Maybe he won't notice me since his face is buried in that newspaper.

"Stanley. Sit down at the table, boy"

"Yes, sir." *Why do I always have to sit next to him?*

"Ha-ha, Billy. You're getting more of that oatmeal on your head than in your mouth. Eat it. Don't wear it. Mama, when does Billy get to sit in a regular chair? He don't look too comfortable."

"Billy! Stop playing with your food and eat right, boy."

Great. Now I got Billy hollered at.

Seems like Billy gets most of the attention from Mama and Sophie. His round soft-blue eyes and rumpled white-blonde hair are hard for them to resist. He's only three, but he's a big kid. Way too big for that high chair. He can't sit still for a second. And he can't seem to find his mouth with that oatmeal.

Tap, tap, tap. Stanley reaches across the table and grabs Frank's fork and whispers. "Frank, stop." Frank frowns and stops tapping. Thirty seconds later. Tap, tap …

The newspaper lowers. Papa slaps Frank in the back of the head. "Put the fork on the table where it belongs. Leave it there." Frank's eyes well. He glances at Stanley. Stanley mouths the words, "I told you."

Papa's voice is acrid and harsh. Its deep, raspy tone makes us all want to withdraw and hide. Frank gets really nervous around Papa. He's only two years younger than me, but he's almost as tall. He's built solid and stout for a ten-year old kid. His beefy thighs are held up by two man-size feet. I swear his toes look like fingers. His straight nut-brown hair always seems to look a bit oily and a few strands usually dangle in his face.

Six-year-old Annie fidgets in her seat. "When will breakfast be ready, Mama?" Papa pounds the table with his fist. "Quiet at the table!" And there that is. Papa's terrifying glare. Cold, dead silence is the temperature of the room now.

Annie's lower lip and chin tremble and her eyes well. She's frozen to her chair clutching an old rag doll she loves so much. She's wearing her favorite dress. A faded yellow cotton dress Mama made just for her. Her thick sandy-brown hair is pulled tight into two perfectly braided pigtails. Her chubby cheeks quietly glisten with silent tears.

Billy breaks the silence and wails, reaching his arms towards Mama and flexing his fingers in a grabbing motion, begging Mama to pick him up. Frank hides under the table.

Sophie stares at Mama, mouth agape. She's only fifteen, but she bears the burden of a lot of responsibility. Papa expects so much from her. Too much. Maybe because she's the eldest.

Sophie routinely keeps her long chestnut brown hair pulled back into a tight bun. A few of the strands work their way out and hang over her cheeks. Her round olive-green eyes always seem to be looking downward. She purposely wears oversized clothes and her shoulders often droop. Probably from trying to hide her developing body and large bosom. It makes her look awkward. But Sophie has the sweetest heart and is the kindest, gentlest and most thoughtful person I know. She looks out for me and I look out for her.

Papa continues to glare. His brow furrowed. He wears a tight-lipped frown. So much anger in his eyes. Where does it come from? Maybe he didn't want a family? Are we that much of a burden on him?

Why are you so damn mean? Stanley's arms shake. He clenches his fists beneath the table. His throat tightens. *Just leave everyone alone.*

Stanley glances at Mama. Her gentle eyes smile, crinkling at the corners. She presses her index finger to her lips. "Sh."

Mama. George's wife, Stella. Always trying to make peace with the Devil. To keep the flame of his fiery temper on low. And to keep us all safe from his cruel wrath.

Mama is ten years younger than Papa. I think their marriage was arranged years ago in Poland when Mama was only thirteen. She keeps her full wavy brown hair pulled back into a perfect bun. Her amber-green eyes are round and doe-like and deeply set into her full round face. A face delicate and symmetrical in its beauty. Mama is slender, even after bearing five kids. The daily hard work on the farm keeps her fit. Or so she says. I tease her because she has to look up to talk to me now. Mama's voice is soft and pleasant. Her Polish accent is always evident and sometimes when she prays, she chooses to pray in Polish instead of English. She's never without her silver crucifix around her neck.

Mama serves Sophie, Frank and I scrambled eggs, bacon, potato pancakes and a tall glass of milk. She serves Annie eggs, bacon and a slice of buttered toast. She places a plate of steak and eggs Sophie prepared earlier in front of Papa. She accidently slams his coffee cup on the table, spilling a few drops onto his T-shirt. He grabs her arm.

"Suka. Clean it up. Why are you so clumsy, Stella?"

Mama cowers, but yanks her arm away. Her brow raises and her jaw tightens. Her eyes are filled with pain and dark with anger. Is that a bruise on her left cheek?

Why does she let him treat her like this? Why does she let him treat us like this? Stanley clenches his jaw, staring at his food. He grasps his fork. *I swear if he touches her…*

Mama sits at the table and folds her hands in front of her. "Lord, please bless this meal and bless our family. We thank you for all our bounty. In Jesus name, Amen."

Frank clutches his fork, eyes darting between Mama and Papa. Annie plays with her food, breaking her bacon into tiny bits and mixing them with her eggs. Mama sits next to Billy who continues to fuss and sob. His whining is getting annoying.

She spoons the remaining oatmeal from his bowl into his mouth. "Open up, baby cakes. Eat like a big man." Billy has so much oatmeal on his head you can barely see his hair.

Sophie sits quietly, politely wiping her mouth with her napkin and occasionally glancing at Papa's steak. She spent the morning meticulously grilling Papa's steak to just the right temperature and prepared medium-rare.

Papa cuts into his steak. Blood squirts and runs thick across his plate mixing with his eggs. He grabs the steak and hurls it at Sophie, hitting her in the chest, leaving a bloody stain on her white nightgown. She cries out. Her eyes always flutter when Papa frightens her.

"Goddammit Sophie. I said rare, not raw. Make me another steak, girl. Rare this time." Mama uses a napkin to wipe a trickle of blood from Papa's right temple.

Sophie's eyes rapidly blink and water. She places another steak in the skillet. Mama glares at Papa, then looks away. She stands and takes a step towards Sophie, but Papa shouts, "Let her do it, Suka. She needs to learn how to cook a proper steak."

Stanley locks eyes with his father. "Stop it Papa. Leave them alone."

A slap across the mouth is followed by the taste of blood. "Enough out of you, boy." The tingling burn on his cheek, ignites rage inside his heart. The fire soon dissipates at the threat of Papa's scowl. Stanley looks away. *Why do I have to be so afraid of him?*

Sophie serves Papa the freshly cooked steak. She trembles and stands meek and quiet, hands folded in front of her, eyes still rapidly blinking. Everyone but Billy is holding their breath.

Papa cuts into the steak. He bites, then chews. He nods and points to Sophie's chair. Sophie's sigh brings the air back into the room. She returns to her seat.

Breakfast continues in dead silence. Papa slides his empty plate towards the center of the table. "Annie, help your mother clear the dishes. Stanley, take Sophie with you when you deliver milk this morning. Make sure you collect all the money. Frank, I want you to fill a dozen baskets of berries from the raspberry patch so your mother can make her jam."

Sophie dashes upstairs to change clothes. Annie plays with her pigtails, staring at the table for a moment, then rises and collects dirty dishes placing them neatly by the sink. Frank slides his chair out from the table, making a godawful screech. He bolts out the door.

Chores are a welcome activity around here. Just to get out from under Papa's roof and all his cruelty and the tension it brings. Stanley wipes his mouth with his sleeve. "I'll be outside loading the milk cans."

The old rusty Radio Flyer makes the milk haul a manageable chore. Four milk cans and the wagon is loaded. "Come on Sophie. I don't want to spend all day delivering milk."

Sophie steps outside and follows him. He's already started walking pulling the wagon behind him. "Hold your horses. Geez. Wait up."

The morning is cool and the air moist as they make their way along an old country road headed towards their first delivery about a half mile away. The smell of the onset of Fall lingers in the air. That earthy smell of leaves on the ground mixed with the cidery scent of decaying apple.

The wagon bogs as it hits several potholes along the way. They enjoy the peacefulness and openness of the farm fields surrounding them, listening to the high-pitched chirps of Carolina Wrens and the intermittent knocking of a woodpecker in the distance. A soft breeze whisks across the tall grasses and bushy trees that line the well-traveled dirt road in the Ohio countryside. They look out across miles of green rolling hills and blue skies filled with an occasional fluff of white clouds.

"I'm really sorry Papa hit you with that steak. He's so damn mean. I wish I was grown up. I'd sock him right in the nose."

"It didn't hurt that bad. I just don't understand why he's always so angry with me. I always seem to upset him. Maybe he just has so much on his mind that he needs to take it out on me?"

Stanley stops walking. Hearing Sophie take the blame for Papa's temper doesn't sit well. "No. He has no right to treat you like that. You do everything you're supposed to and still he hurts you. It won't be like that, when I grow up. I promise. I'll always take care of you. I'll stop him from hurting you ... and Mama ... for good."

"Well good morning Stanley. Good morning Sophie. How's your mama?"

Sophie smiles. "She's doing very well, Mrs. Winfield. Thank you."

Stanley lifts a milk can from the wagon and empties some of the contents into the Winfield's billycan sitting on the front porch.

"Wow, Stanley. You are growing into such a strong young man. Here you go."

He pockets two quarters. "Here are two extra nickels for the both of you." Sophie's eyes beam. Tips go into the other pocket.

They continue on their route, working their way along the road to the next stop. Stanley examines the nickels. "Hey, one of these is a Liberty nickel. See, look at the 'V' on the back."

"Um ... that's swell. We need to add them all to our stash under the old rock back home. How much money do you think we have?"

"I figure ... around seven or eight dollars. We can never let Papa know we have it, Soph, or that cheap old bastard will take it all. What are you going to do with your share? Donate it to me?"

"Uh, no...." Sophie pauses and speaks in a softer tone. "Don't laugh. I really want to be a nurse someday. I want to help people. So, I'm going to use my half to go to nursing school. How 'bout you, little brother? What do you want to do?" She glances at the holes in the knees of his pantlegs. "Maybe you should consider buying some new overalls."

He glances at his overalls and frowns, then glances at Sophie. "Very funny."

Stanley steers the wagon to avoid a small pothole in the road. "I don't know. I think I want my own farm. I don't want to work for Papa all my life. I want to work with my hands. Build stuff, ya know? Make lots of money, so I can take care of you and Mama and everyone. You all can come live with me. We'll get away from Papa, for good. Leave that old bastard to drink himself to death."

Another extra dime from the Johnson farm and two more nickels from Mr. Patterson. Time to turn the wagon around. Stanley grins. His eyes suspiciously glint. "Get in, I'll pull you."

Sophie crosses her arms, slightly shaking her head. "I don't trust you. Last time you hit every pothole on purpose. Nope. I'll walk thank you."

"Oh, come on. That was an accident. You can trust me."

"Sure, it was. Forget it…. Hey, let's head over to the cornfield and count our stash."

The cornfield has grown tall. Plump ears dangle from its thick stocks. This part of the field has yet to be harvested. "There it is." Stanley turns over a flat gray sandstone about the width of a frying pan. He pulls a small leather pouch from a hole in the ground beneath the stone. The leather is cracked and dry and the pouch sealed by a drawstring.

"Count it. How much do we have?"

Stanley pours the coins onto the flat stone, separating them into piles of similar denominations. "Nine dollars and forty-five cents."

He returns the coins to the pouch and places the pouch in its original hiding place under the rock. Sophie hugs him. "Ah. Get off me." They continue to make their way back to the farmhouse where Stanley parks the wagon.

The heavy rusted handle of the well pump squeals and rumbles, sucking ice-cold water from a well deep within the earth, up through pipes and out of a large iron faucet. The cold water is a shock at first, but it washes away the sweat and grime from his blonde head. "Ah, that feels good." The frigid water quenches an arid thirst, leaving a dull ache in the back of his throat and a light throb in his temples. "So cold. But damn good."

"Ahem." Sophie stands behind him, arms crossed, tapping her foot. "Save some of that for me. Move." She shoves Stanley aside.

Papa stands on the porch dressed in pressed high-waisted tan suit pants, a crisp white long-sleeved shirt and vest. He's headed to town again.

Stanley shakes his head. "Why doesn't he put his jacket on instead of carrying it on his arm? He thinks he's an important politician or something, the way he acts. Ah, rhatz. He spotted us."

"Stanley, Sophie. Come here." They hurry to reach the porch.

Sophie snuggles next to Mama on a large porch swing. Mama places Billy in Sophie's lap. Frank sits on the porch floor next to the porch swing. Annie rocks back and forth in the old rocker fiddling with her dress. She's still clutching that silly rag doll. The best view of all though, is right here on the porch rail.

Here comes the speech, before he goes to town to get drunk.

"Attend to your chores today. No excuses. Be thankful for the roof over your head and the food I put on my table."

Papa eyeballs Mama. That wicked glint in his eye always fills the air with tension. "Wife, handle the farmhands and let me know if anyone slacks on their work. Clean my house before I return. I better not come back and find everything a mess."

Papa beams as he looks out across his farm fields. He juts his chin. There's a twinkle in his eye as he watches his farmhands busy at work. Placing a derby on his head he steps off the porch and drives away in his 1919 Royal automobile. No doubt he's headed to his favorite local speakeasy. *The Vine.*

***

"We have to tie the stacks of haybales together by weaving them crisscross like this to keep them from falling over. Grab the wires like this and use your knee to help throw it on top of the stack. You got all that, Frank? Give it a try. Put your fat ass into it."

Frank grips a haybale by the wires and using his leg he attempts to swing it to the top of the stack. "Whoa, that was close. Ha-ha. Nice try. Get up off your butt and try again."

The sound of an automobile approaching creates a churn of uneasiness in Stanley's stomach. *What? He's already drunk? He's only been gone a couple hours.* The inside of the open barn door frames the scene. Papa staggers toward the house. "Frank. We'll finish this later. Go play with Annie, okay?"

Sophie fills feed bags with oats for the horses. Frank and Annie slip and slide in the mud by the water pump. They all stop what they're doing and freeze when they see Papa approach.

Please just pass out today. Just go inside and pass out.

Upstairs Mama puts Billy down for a nap. She pauses when she hears the front door squeak then slam shut.

Dirty dishes from breakfast sit piled by the sink. There wasn't enough time to get to them. Dried oatmeal is stuck to the floor and to Billy's highchair. Toys are scattered around the living room floor. He steps on one.

"Stella!"

An icy chill travels up her spine. She lays Billy in his bed and closes his bedroom door behind her.

Papa stands in the living room with fists clenched. His brow is furrowed and his eyes are dark. His jaw is tight and veins swell in his neck. He glares up the stairs at her. A menacing glare she is all too familiar with.

Nowhere to run. Push past him. Run for the door!

He grabs her by the wrist. Whiskey, cigar smoke and stale perfume reek from his breath and his clothes.

"Let me *go*. Get *away* from me."

She can't breathe. The pressure on her neck is too great. "Don't *ever* talk to me like that, bitch. You're not even good enough to wipe the shit off my shoes." Fingers dig into her shoulders. He shoves her. She stumbles backward slamming her head onto the hard, wooden floor. A white flash and loud ring follow a throbbing ache in the back of her skull. The room is blurry. Her heart races.

"I'm sorry. I'm sorry. Please don't hurt me, George." A blow crushes her ribcage. She gasps for a breath, moaning. He yanks her hair; lifting her off her feet. Her scalp burns. She attempts to grip her hair to prevent it from being ripped out of her head.

"You want more of this?"

Everything is surreal. She hears herself scream. The warmth of adrenaline coursing through her veins. She kicks and flails her arms digging her nails deep into the flesh of his forearm.

Sophie rushes into the house. "Leave her *alone*."

Papa allows Mama to fall to the floor. He grabs Sophie by the hair dismantling her neatly groomed bun and yanking her towards him. He slaps her repeatedly. She cries and winces. Blood runs down her face and into her mouth.

"You don't know what's good for you, butting in where you don't belong. He hit her again and again. How do you like that? You like it? Do you?"

Sophie hits the floor in a thud.

She curls into a ball, but she can't protect herself from the kicks to her back. Each blow pounding her ribcage.

Stella punches and scratches at George's back. "Don't touch her."

Solid knuckles smash into her cheekbone. She stumbles backward and collapses to the floor in a heap. Sounds echo and fade as she tries to reach for Sophie. She can't make herself move, can't make herself do anything.

Everything turns black.

Sophie attempts to run out the door, but he grabs her, ripping her dress and exposing her large breasts. She desperately attempts to cover herself.

The sight of Sophie's exposed bosom sets Papa into a rage. He slaps her in the face, then lifts her and slams her into the sofa. "You think those bubs are going to save you? You're going to have some sweaty pimple-faced boy touching you?"

Sophie cowers on the couch. He fumbles with the buckle of his leather belt. "No, Papa, no." Sophie flinches from vicious lashes to her face and body. His curses become muffled. All she can do is curl into a ball, make herself as small as she can.

Papa wears down and stands over them, breathing heavy, sweat pouring from his reddened face. He slides his belt through the loops in his trousers and walks toward the front door.

Stanley blocks the doorway. "Get away from them." He grips the wooden handle of a spade visibly shaking. He heaves a breath, ready for what comes next.

"Put it down boy. Put it down, or you'll get the same."

Backing down the porch steps, Stanley's throat tightens. His heart pounds. His grip begins to slip from beads of sweat forming on his palms. Papa lunges. Stanley's grip on the handle gives way. The spade flies harmlessly through the air. Papa's open hands slam into his chest with a powerful shove. He can only watch as Papa steps over him.

Sophie covers her breasts, tucking the torn material of her dress into her bra. She crawls to reach Mama. Mama isn't moving. "Wake up. Please. Mama please, wake up."

Sophie's muffled voice calls to her from a distance. Shades of light and dark swirl in front of her eyes, eventually coming into focus and forming the face of her terrified daughter. A face swollen and bruised with welts. Her left eye bloodshot. Blood congealing on her upper lip. The horrific sight causes Mama to weep.

Frank and Annie stand covered in mud, frozen with fear and hugging each other. They watch as Papa's automobile disappears into the countryside. "C'mon Annie."

The screen door creaks. Mama flinches from the sound, then sighs. "Come here children." Covered in patches of wet and dry mud they rush to her side. Billy stands atop the stairwell crying. "Come here Billy. Come to Mama." He waddles his way down the stairs whimpering and clutching a teddy bear.

Frank, Annie and Billy sit on the floor next to Mama and Sophie. Mama's arms tremble with pain as she attempts to cradle them. The beatings are happening more often now, and with greater ferocity. Sophie has become a main target just like Mama. *Why can't I stop this?*

Mama lifts herself from the floor, and helps Sophie to her feet. A wave of nausea overcomes her after seeing the full extent of Sophie's injuries. They make their way into the kitchen. Mama splashes water onto her own face, then uses a wet towel to dab the blood off of Sophie's face. "I promise. You will never have to go through that again my sweet girl. I'm so sorry."

Mama points to the front door with a trembling hand. "Frank, take Annie outside and the two of you wash off by the well pump. Leave your clothes out there."

Sophie whispers. "Mommy." She buries her face in her mother's bosom, wishing she could be small again; wishing to be safe in her mother's arms.

With Billy on her hip, Mama takes Sophie by the hand and leads her upstairs. "Change into another dress." She pulls a small valise out of a closet and packs it full of her daughter's belongings.

Mama cradles Sophie's face, her hands still shaking. "I'm taking you to Aunt Mary's in Lisbon for a few days." Sophie nods. Mama's words carry hope and encouragement even in the face of such horror.

"Mama, what about you and Annie and the boys? Shouldn't you leave too? He's getting worse. What if he starts hurting them too?"

"We'll leave soon enough. For now, we have to get you out of here. I'm afraid of what he might do next. You'll be safe at Aunt Mary's. He can't hurt you there."

Mama and Sophie cautiously peek outside. "Billy, go with Frank and Annie." Billy toddles his way over to the water pump.

Stanley sits on the porch railing sobbing. "Mama, I couldn't protect you and Sophie. I tried, I'm sorry." Tears roll off his cheeks. "I'm not big enough. When I'm a man, I'll beat the tar out of him. I promise." His eyes lower. *Why am I so afraid of him?*

Mama does her best to place her battered arms around him. "It's okay, son. Stay here and take care of Annie and the boys. I'm taking Sophie to Lisbon, to stay with Aunt Mary for a few days. I'll be back soon."

Powerless to do anything, he wipes his eyes and hugs them both. "Be careful, Mama."

Mama grabs the valise and takes Sophie by the hand. They lean on each other as they walk along the dirt road to the bus station. They struggle with each step, fighting through immense pain and dizziness. The bus station is a mile away from the farm. It may as well be twenty-five miles away. They'll have to pass *The Vine* along the way.

"Mama, what if he's there? … at The Vine. What if he sees us?"

Stanley watches from the road, helpless as Mama and Sophie fade into the distance. Tears well in his icy-blue eyes, creating tiny streams of mud along his dirty cheeks. Grief crushes his soul like a sledgehammer pulverizing stone into sand.

CHAPTER TWO

THURSDAY, SEPTEMBER 9, 1920 – Activity begins to stir in the early shadows before dawn breaks on the farm. The morning's chores aren't enough to provide an adequate amount of distraction for Stanley. Focusing on simple tasks seems near impossible. Yesterday's horrific events echo over and over in his mind, the way hands on a clock spin around and return to the place where they started, only to repeat the cycle again and again. *I miss Sophie.*

"C'mon Maggie, hold still. I need more milk, girl." Stanley keeps the stream of milk flowing into the metal pail with his hands while his mind focuses on Papa. *How about I punch you in the face? Stomp you with my boot. Maybe when your sleeping, I'll hit you with a bat and split your skull wide open.* "See how you like it."

The Holstein grunts and kicks her leg. "Sorry Maggie. Settle down now, girl." He snatches the pail of fresh milk and dashes to the farmhouse.

Inside, Mama prepares a breakfast of ham steak, eggs and fresh apple slices. Stanley fills two glass bottles with fresh milk from the pail. He sets one on the table and places the other in the icebox. Annie tugs at Mama's dress. "Where's Sophie?"

"She's visiting. Eat your breakfast, sweetheart."

Stanley joins Frank, Annie, Billy and Mama at the table. Papa's seat is empty along with Sophie's. Mama seems lost. She looks distant. Staring at the wall, barely eating, rubbing her temples. Her hands feel cold to the touch. Patches of purple and yellow cover her arms.

"Are you okay, Mama?"

Her far-away stare fades. Her round eyes focus on mine. Sunlight reflects within her loving amber eyes revealing tiny flecks of green. Never noticed those before. Her eyes sparkle and crinkle at the corners as she smiles. It's hard to describe, but there's a sadness that lives deep behind them. She tries to hide it, but it's always there.

"I'm okay, son. I'm just thinking about Sophie. And I have this constant ringing in my ears that just won't go away." She can barely chew. She sets her fork on the table.

Papa didn't come home last night. Mama has no idea where he went. Seems like she's worried about him too. Mama once said he's the only man she's ever loved. How can she love someone so cruel? I'll never understand that.

After breakfast, Mama sends Frank, Annie and Billy outside to play. Stanley wipes his mouth and gives his mother a gentle hug. "Everything will be okay, Mama." A single tear runs down her left cheek. She pats his forearm. "Tend to your chores, son. I'll bake you an apple pie later."

"Ah ... I've been craving your apple pie for days. Can I have a whole pie of my own?"

Her short laugh mixes with a sob. "Of course, you can. I'll make one special, just for you."

The farm is quiet today. Some of the farmhands are off or working other farms. A few female farmhands balance on ladders in the orchard as they pick apples, filling their aprons with fruit and emptying them into wooden baskets.

Frank, Billy and Annie run around the property, throwing mud balls at each other until Billy gets hit in the head with a hard clod. He wails, and Frank and Annie try to shush him. Mama rushes onto the porch and discovers them attempting to cover little Billy's mouth. She cradles him, kissing him on the head.

"Come inside now children. It's time for naps."

The old rocker makes a comforting sound as it creaks and rocks back and forth. Stanley whittles a wooden figure out of a piece of basswood with his pocket knife. Mama sits on the porch swing, content to have a moment to herself.

The soft breeze lulls her mind to sleep, only to be interrupted a few moments later by the sound of an automobile in the distance. Her chest tightens and her stomach churns. Her palms become moist. Body heat flushes her face forming salty droplets over her brow that trickle down her temples. Papa steps out of the automobile. Tension mounts with each approaching step. His suit is crumpled and dirty. His sleeves are rolled to his elbows. He looks like he slept in the woods all night. Her pulse throbs in her neck and the swish of blood resonates in her ears. She raggedly breathes.

Stanley stops rocking, but continues to whittle. *Touch her and I'll stab you.*

Papa stands on the porch before them. His head lowered, his eyes bloodshot and sorrowful. He sits next to Mama and takes her by the hand. His voice is raspy but soft in tone. "I'm so sorry, Stella. I don't know what came over me. I didn't mean to hurt you and Sophie. Can you forgive me?"

We've heard this apology a thousand times. It's part of the cycle and always predictable. She catches her breath as her heart rate slows. She meekly nods her head, absently rubbing her belly. Papa gives her a quick hug and walks towards the door. He pats Stanley on the shoulder. The spring of the screen door squeaks as Papa opens it, followed by a slam as it closes behind him.

She trembles. Her clothes are fitting tighter than normal. Her breasts are tender. She feels bloated and crampy. She closes her eyes and whispers The Lord's Prayer in Polish. With Papa passed out, the rest of the evening is uneventful and quiet.

***

Around nine o'clock at night, Papa emerges from his bedroom wearing faded Levi's and a white tank-top T-shirt. Frank, Annie and Billy are asleep upstairs. Mama sits at the kitchen table reading a newspaper. Stanley sits outside on the rocker. His whittled figure has come to life in the form of a squirrel. "Looks pretty darn good, if I say so myself."

Papa steps out onto the porch. "Son, let's go to the barn. I haven't given you a lesson in a few weeks. Get up. Let's go."

Swell. These lessons usually end up with me getting a bloody nose.

Papa lights a lantern on a work bench and grabs two pairs of old leather boxing gloves from the top of a haybale. He takes great pride in the glory of his boxing days back in Poland as a young man. He throws a pair to Stanley. "Put 'em on. Show me your stance."

Papa pulls off his shirt and slides his gloves on. He smacks the worn leather together, rolling his broad shoulders, and snapping his neck side to side making a loud crunch. Sweat glistens off the coarse hair of his solid square pectorals. He shakes his arms out, flexing the muscles of his thick forearms.

"Your stance looks good, boy. See if you can hold it." The smack of leather stings Stanley's left cheek. Papa points at him with his right glove, waving it up and down to draw attention to his lecture.

"Always keep your eye on your opponent. Don't ever look away. Even for a second. Let him know, you're not afraid."

Two body shots. Stanley's ribs burn and he struggles to breathe.

"In a street fight, there are no rules, son. Attack first. Don't wait. Take your opponent down quickly. Kick him in the balls. Use the heel of your hand like this. Up through the nose. Use an open hand like this, across his face. And never, ever hit a man on the crown of his head. You'll break your hand. Now, you come at me. Try to hit me in the face."

A swing and a miss. Papa ducks. Another swing and miss. Leather smacks Stanley in the nose. He wipes his nose with his glove. Blood smears across the laces. *Never fails.*

"You're hurt. What are you going to do? Gonna quit? Gonna cry? Or are you gonna be a man?"

The stinging on his cheek lights a fiery rage in his heart. He charges swinging wildly, landing punches to Papa's rippled abs and ribs. Papa laughs. "Those are good punches, son. Okay. Okay. Very good punches. We're finished for the night. Nice work, boy."

Papa lowers his hands. *Now's my chance. There are no rules, right?* Stanley smacks him in the jaw with a solid left hook. Papa's head snaps backward.

"Boy. I said we were done." Papa's steely blue eyes grow dark. His brow lowers.

Stanley's head explodes. White lightening rips through the back of his eyes. *Why am I looking at the rafters?* Papa's voice echoes in the distance. "Now, we are done."

Stanley gathers himself and dusts off the dirt and hay from his clothes. He wanders back to the farmhouse. As he approaches the steps, he finds the wooden squirrel he spent the afternoon whittling with so much patience and care, lying on the ground broken.

***

Early the next morning, Mama steps out of the house and walks towards the main road leading to the bus station. Papa must have left in the middle of the night.

"Mama. Wait up. Where you going?" Stanley rushes to meet her on the road.

"I'm going to check on Sophie. I'll be back shortly. There're some flapjacks in the kitchen. Make sure you save some for everyone."

"Can we come? I'll grab Annie and the boys. We miss her too, Mama."

She pauses and stares for a moment. "Okay. But hurry. We must be back before your papa returns."

Stanley sprints to the barn. "Come on Frank, we're going to see Sophie." Frank drops a hammer he was using to secure a loft beam and follows.

Annie and Billy are attempting to pump water from the well along with stomping in the mud as usual. "Come on Annie. Take Billy's hand. Let's go see Sophie." Annie's eyes widen and her tiny plump lips pucker. They follow Stanley and Frank to the road to meet Mama.

There's a cool breeze this morning. White billowy clouds form in the eastern sky. Mama holds Annie's hand as they make their way along the country road. "Billy. Stop farting on my neck, or I'll put you down." Billy giggles, holding onto Stanley's ears as they follow Mama on their way to the bus station.

Mama has no automobile of her own, and she wouldn't know how to operate one if she did. And if they had the luxury of a telephone, she could simply call Sophie. Electricity hasn't found its way to most of the farms in rural Southington yet, let alone a telephone.

***

The bus ride was uneventful. They step onto a gravel road in Lisbon. Mama glances at the sky. "Hurry. Let's walk fast before we get caught in the rain."

Aunt Mary's home is modest. A yellow clapboard exterior with white trim. A small front yard with a three-foot embankment. A path of flat slate stones leads to the porch, lined on either side with beds of red, gold and orange marigolds. The porch floor is painted white with a variety of flower pots decorating the porch in a display of greenery and colorful autumn flowers. Aunt Mary has a knack for making the simplest of things beautiful and eye catching.

Stanley sets Billy by the front door. "Mama, let's have Billy knock." Sophie answers. "Oh, my goodness, Billy." She swoops him into her arms and steps out onto the porch. "Mama." Annie hugs Sophie's legs. Frank, Stanley and Mama complete the group hug. Mama caresses Sophie's cheek, gently examining her bruises.

Sophie partially smiles. "Come inside. Aunt Mary will be so surprised.

"Aunt Mary. Look who's here."

Aunt Mary places her hands on her cheeks. Her eyes pop open. "Oh, my gosh. What a nice surprise. Come in. Sit."

Stanley and Frank plop onto a flowery colorful sofa, while Annie and Billy sit on a blue and cream rag rug next to them. Sophie sits in an easy chair across from her family. Mama stands behind the sofa with her hands resting on Stanley's shoulders.

Aunt Mary smiles, running her fingers through her long dark brown curls. She places her hands on her hips. "Well. How is everyone doing?"

"We're doing okay, I guess. We just wanted to visit and check on Sophie. We can't stay long. I have to get back before George returns. I have no idea where he went, but we can't be gone too long."

Aunt Mary wipes her hands on her apron. "Can you at least stay long enough for some coffee? I baked a yummy cherry coffee cake yesterday."

Annie glances at Mama. "I'm hungry Mama. I want some cake."

Billy chimes in. "Me too, me too."

Mama perks up. "That's sounds delicious. Okay, we'll stay. But for just a little bit."

"Great. Follow me into the kitchen. Who wants watermelon? Sophie, can you cut up some watermelon for your brothers and Annie and take them out back?"

Billy frowns. Annie protests. "I want cake, Mama."

Stanley pokes Annie's stomach. "You don't need any cake, Annie. Besides, watermelon is good for you. You too, Billy. Let's go out back."

Annie and Billy run around the backyard slurping watermelon and spitting seeds at each other. Frank plays with Mary's dog, Brutus. A small, feisty Jack Russell terrier starving for attention. Stanley sits on the small porch steps near the backdoor. Sweet sticky juice drips from his chin. Spitting watermelon seeds is an art. You have to hold the seed on the tip of your tongue with just the right amount of air pressure and let it fly precisely at the right time.

Mary's husband, Syski steps off the living room stairway and enters the kitchen. "Stella, how are you feeling? You ever going to leave that crazy son of a bitch you're married to?"

"I'm doing much better but, how can I leave him? Maybe paying someone six-hundred dollars to shoot him would be easier. Know anyone interested?"

"That much? Hell, I'd shoot him for eight bits."

Syski chuckles and pats Stella on the shoulder. He walks onto the front porch and sits in his rocker. He lights a cigar and blows circular puffs into the air. Stanley sits quiet on the rear porch. He can't help but hear the conversations through the screen door.

Yeah, sure Uncle Syski. Your skinny butt would be too afraid to shoot Papa. Your ass would be shaking and scared. He'd bust that big nose across your cocky face.

Mama, Mary and Sophie spend the next forty-five minutes sharing coffee, cake and small talk.

Mama slides her lips across her fork to savor the last piece of her coffee cake. "Mm … I want the recipe for this. We really have to go now. Sorry we can't stay longer, Mary."

Mary nods and pats Mama's hand. "I understand. You know I'm here if you need me. Sophie has been a tremendous help around the house. She's such a good girl."

Mary glances through the screen of the rear door. "It's probably a good idea you get going, anyway. Looks like a storm is blowing in."

Mama gathers Annie and the boys. Together, they hurry back to the bus station.

***

When they arrive home, Papa is shaved and looking dapper. It's apparent he's been waiting on the porch swing for a long while. He storms down the porch stairs to meet them. "Where have you been? Where's Sophie?"

Her heart pounds against her ribs. Her stomach twists and cramps. She stammers. "I-I went to check on Mrs. Winfield and take her another dozen apples. You know ... she asked for three dozen but I-I ... just forgot. We only gave her two. I took the children with me ... and ..."

"And Sophie?" He pinches her arm.

She winces, then jerks her arm away. "I sent her away."

He clenches his teeth as he speaks. "Where did you take her? You need to bring her back home, now. She needs to be here working on the farm."

She places her hand on Stanley's shoulder. "Take Annie and the boys inside the house. Go."

"Mama, I don't want to leave you here."

"Do what I say. Go right now."

"Come on Frank. Grab Billy. Annie, let's go." Stanley herds his siblings into the house. He watches the scene through the screen door. *Don't you touch her, you asshole.*

Mama stands her ground. "I needed to keep her safe because of what you *did* to her, George."

He backhands her across the face.

She stumbles backward. "No! No more of this."

He grasps a handful of her hair and slaps her again and again. She drops to the ground in a fetal position hoping he'll stop.

He kicks her in the stomach, knocking the wind out of her. She gasps, struggling to breathe. A warm wet sensation trickles between her thighs. She grasps her dress, then looks at her hand. Blood.

She writhes and moans in pain, whimpering. *My baby. Please God, no. Please don't take my baby. Not another baby, Lord please ...*

"I can't watch anymore of this. Mama!" Adrenaline surges like hot fire through his veins. Leaping off the porch Stanley sprints toward his mother. "Leave her alone. Stop it." Papa turns to meet his charge. The face of a demon stares back at him. Eyes black and piercing. Teeth clenched. A sadistic evil grimace almost welcoming the confrontation.

Stanley flails his arms and manages to bust his father's lip. A flash of colors followed by intense pain rips through his skull like cherry-red iron. A loud buzzing fills his ears. Voices muffle and echo. Clouds rumble and roil above him. Raindrops begin to tap his face in soft sprinkles. The sky fades in and out of focus.

George stands over her. Staring at the pooling blood. He should just leave her there. He uses a hanky to wipe a drop of blood from his lower lip.

A farmhand hears the commotion and sees Mama lying on the ground. "Mr. Puchalski, your wife is hurt. If you don't take her to the doctor right now, I will."

"Mind your own damn business."

He steps closer. "I won't stand here and watch you beat this woman. Can't you see she's bleeding?"

"This woman is my wife and I'll do as I damn well please. Now get your black ass off my farm. You're fired."

The farmhand drops a spade he was clutching and stands defiant.

Papa doesn't say another word to the farmhand. He ignores him. He doesn't view any farmhand as his equal and won't waste anymore words on him. He lifts his bleeding wife and places her into his automobile. He yells to his foreman. "Get this black bastard off my farm. Don't pay him."

"You brought this on yourself, woman. Look what you made me do. How are you going to do your work now? A wife is supposed to obey her husband. When are you going to learn that?" He speeds away leaving a cloud of dust in his wake.

***

Thunder rumbles in the heavens, warning of the impending storm. Black clouds boil ready to burst. *Why am I in the grass? How long have I been here?* "Frank?"

"Stanley. Come on. Wake up. Why are you laying on the ground? It's starting to rain. Hurry." Frank helps him to his feet. Cold rain explodes from roiling dark clouds above. They're soaked when they reach the porch. "Take off your shoes and britches out here, Frank."

Thunder explodes, shaking the farmhouse. Bright flashes of light illuminate the walls. Billy screams and buries his head in the sofa. Annie runs to Stanley. "Pick me up. Pick me up."

"It's just thunder, Annie. Stop being such a crybaby." Annie's large hazel eyes water. Her full round chin, trembles. Her cute little pigtails are too hard to resist. "Okay, okay. Come here." He lifts her. She squeezes his neck, hiding her face in his chest. "Jeez, Annie. When did you get so heavy? Frank, sit with Billy. Make him stop screaming. He's making my head hurt worse than it already does."

"Billy, get under the blanket with me. It's safe under here." Billy scrambles beneath the blanket with Frank.

"Let me in too." Stanley drops Annie on the sofa and she disappears under the blanket like a bug. He plops on the sofa. They listen as the sky crackles and booms. White flashes light up the room, followed by rumbling that rolls and fades into the distance. Strong winds and heavy rain pound the farmhouse, rattling windows and sending howling shrills through its walls. *What happened to Mama? Where did Papa take her?*

* * *

Hours later the storm has quieted. The screen door creaks open. It's Papa. He's holding Mama in his arms. He carries her to their bedroom up the hallway. He sets her on the bed and lays a blanket over her, then shuts the door behind him.

"What happened to my mother?"

Papa shoves him into the wall, out of his way.

He grabs Papa's arm. "What did you do to my mother?"

His arm is slapped away. Stanley is face-to-face with clenched teeth and a menacing grimace. His air cut off from the pressure on his throat. Stanley's blood boils. He glares into the eyes of evil in complete defiance. Fear leaves his heart, replaced by fury and a level of courage he's never experienced before. He's not afraid anymore.

Papa releases his grip and shoves Stanley backwards, then leaves the house. Stanley sighs at the sound of Papa's automobile fading into the distance. *Yeah, stay gone. Don't come back.*

He sits on the bed next to Mama. He gently squeezes her hand, willing her to be okay. Mama slowly peers through bloodshot eyes. She smiles a feeble smile. His heart aches from the pitiful sight of her condition.

"Are you okay, Mama? What happened?"

She whispers. "I'm sorry son. I lost the baby. I just need to rest. Tomorrow we'll go to Mass and pray for God's blessings on our family. How are you feeling, precious boy? My brave boy."

"I'm okay Mama. But … you were having another baby? Why didn't you tell me? Did Sophie know?"

"Sophie was the only one who knew. I wanted to wait a little longer before I told you. I'm sorry, son."

"It's okay. Just get some rest Mama. I'll check on you later." He kisses her on the forehead, then closes the door and walks to the living room.

"Frank, keep an eye on Annie and Billy for a few minutes. I gotta do something."

The air is damp and fresh. An occasional rumble can be heard in the distance. He walks into the barn. He slings a stone against the wall listening to the ricochet through the rafters. *Why are you so damn mean? Why do you have to hurt everybody?* "I hate you." He throws a flurry of punches at a bale of hay. "How do you like that, huh? I'll break your damn nose. Hurt her again, you bastard. See what happens." He swings and punches the haybale until his arms and shoulders burn and twitch with exhaustion.

He stands there, out of breath, his knuckles bloodied and stinging. He stares, panting at the haybale like a prize fighter taunting a defeated opponent. It's no use, though. His father is so much bigger, so much meaner. He can't protect his mother or his sister or anybody.

He climbs a wooden ladder into the loft and weeps. Ten minutes go by. He dries his tears and descends the loft and walks back to the house, emotionally drained.

"Come on. Let's go outside and play." Stanley gives his siblings each a turn on the tire swing until the sun sinks in the western sky and daylight fades.

"Frank, Annie. Grab Billy. Let's go inside and get something to eat."

Annie pleads. "Come on. Just one more turn, okay?"

"No Annie. You need to eat dinner and get ready for bed."

He points to the front porch. "Last one in is a fat hog." Frank and Annie push Billy out of the way and rush up the porch stairs battling to be the first into the house. "Come on Billy. It's just you and me now." Sharp kick to the shin. "Ouch. Cheap shot, Billy." Billy darts up the porch steps. "I'm coming Billy boy."

Billy screams. "You da fat hog! Not me."

"Ha-ha. You win. I'm the fat hog, and this fat hog is going to eat you."

Billy shrieks and hides under the table. Annie jumps on the sofa giggling. Stanley presses his index finger to his lips. "Shh. You'll wake Mama. Frank help Billy get in his highchair. Come on Annie. Come eat."

The snap of a match and the smell of sulphur. He drops the tiny flame into the kindling inside the stove. He places a pot of left-over beef stew over the flame and sets homemade bread on a flat pan to warm.

Frank taps his spoon on the table. "When is Sophie coming home?"

Stanley shrugs. "I don't know. Maybe when she's feeling better. Finish eating so we can go to bed."

The light in the house grows dim as the sun fades. Stanley descends the stairway into the living room after tucking his siblings in bed. He strikes a match and lights an oil lamp sitting on a vanity near the front door. The lamp illuminates the room with a soft yellow glow.

Stanley plops on the sofa and lays his head on a pillow and closes his eyes.

The front door screeches. Papa stumbles into the house grasping a bottle of whiskey. His eyes are bloodshot. He stares and sways, mumbling in Polish.

The pathetic sight softens Stanley's heart. He helps him to the sofa and removes the whiskey bottle from his hand and sets it on the coffee table. Papa stretches out, continuing to mumble. "Stanley. I love you, son … love you son. Where's my Sophie? Gimme my whiskey damnit …" Papa closes his eyes and passes out.

Stanley removes Papa's shoes and covers him with a blanket. "The rest of this whiskey can go down the sink where it belongs." He tosses the bottle into the garbage.

He pulls a towel from a kitchen drawer to wipe his hands, revealing a .25 caliber revolver hidden beneath the towels. It's loaded. The weight of it feels light. He stares at the revolver, then stares across the room at his sleeping father.

CHAPTER THREE

SATURDAY, SEPTEMBER 11, 1920 - Papa took the flatbed and left early this morning to buy feed and hay from some neighboring farms. He loaded several jugs of hooch and concealed them under a canvas. He uses them to barter or sweeten one of his deals. Papa tries to keep all us kids far away from the cellar. He has a still set up for making moonshine and he doesn't want us going anywhere near it. His recipe usually consists of sugar, yeast, rye, corn and some fruit. Either prunes, raisins or apricots. His concoction sits and ferments for days before he cooks it. The contraption is made of a copper boiler with a gooseneck. A coil runs through a barrel of cold water and out a tap, where clear alcohol drips into a ceramic jug.

Frank and I have been down there a couple times to look over the operation and one time, we even snuck a swig of the brew. Nasty shit. Why anybody would want to sit and drink that horse piss is beyond me.

One of the hopper windows has a broken latch Papa has neglected to fix. Frank and I slip through it occasionally and climb into the cellar. There's nothing of interest down there, really. The idea of disobeying Papa and snooping around, knowing we aren't supposed to be in there, has a certain thrill and excitement to it. Papa would tan our hides if he ever knew we were down there.

Mama leads us on a peaceful early morning walk to our local Catholic church to receive communion. With Papa gone all day the afternoon is peaceful and restful and quietly passes.

Daylight fades. Mama sits on the sofa tatting a pattern of lace. She works her needle in and out forming perfect knots and loops using the light from a single lamp.

Stanley sits next to her. "The little ones are asleep, Mama. Frank just went to bed. What's the lace for?"

"Well, I'm going to attach this to my tablecloth to use for Thanksgiving and Christmas. Tatting relaxes me. I enjoy it." Mama places the tatting in her lap and smiles. "I made you something special. Look on the windowsill in the kitchen."

"What? Really? Let me see." He walks into the kitchen and catches the sweet aroma of cinnamon and apples permeating the air. Two round apples pies sit in the windowsill, steam rising from the golden-brown crust. "Ah, Mama. I thought I smelled something when I walked in. Which one's mine?"

Mama giggles. "Pick one. You better hide it, though. I saw Frank and Annie sniffing around earlier."

He gouges out a quarter of the pie, scooping it onto a plate. He sits staring at the warm plump mess of apples, crust and goo spreading out to the edges of the dish. His mouth waters. He scoops a perfect balance of crust and apples with his fork. His taste buds burst from the warm sweet spices. Tender apples come apart and mix with cinnamon and dough as he chews. The bite slides down his throat. Pure heaven all the way to his stomach.

Papa's home. He unloads bags of feed into the barn and carries a large block of ice to the icebox. "Where are my children?" Mama stops tatting. "The little ones are in bed. Stanley is in the kitchen."

"Come to bed with me, wife." She locks eyes with him taking in his sneer, daring her to deny him. She looks away and continues to work on her tatting piece. He takes a step closer, fondling a few strands of her hair. "I said, come to bed with me woman." She recoils from his touch. "I'm still in pain, George. I lost a child. Remember?"

You just can't keep your filthy hands off of her, can you? Stanley places his empty dish by the sink and hides the remainder of his pie in the bread box on the counter. He climbs the stairs. "Goodnight, Mama. Goodnight … Papa."

Liquor from his breath and the faint scent of another woman fills the room. He isn't taking no for an answer. The dead glare in his eyes stay fixed on her. His presence is unmoving and intimidating. His jaw tightens and he wiggles his fingers like he's about to draw a six-shooter from a holster any minute.

His voice deepens and becomes raspy. "I'm only going to tell you one more time, wife. Come to bed." Her heart rate rises from his tone. She abides and follows him to their bedroom.

She swallows two of the codeine pills Doctor Johnson gave her in the hopes it will numb her discomfort and her disdain for him.

***

Stanley sinks into his bedding and cushy down pillows. The room is dark as pitch. Barely a sliver of crescent moon glints off the window pane.

He fades in and out of sleep. Walls creak. His mind focuses on the rhythmic tic-toc of a clock in sync with the soft whistle of wind against the trees outside his window. The faint hoot of an owl randomly interrupts the chorus of the night. Fading into deep relaxation now. Gone into restful bliss.

What was that? Someone's in the kitchen. My pie ...

He slips out of bed and peers through his doorway. A shadow moves around in the kitchen downstairs and removes something from a kitchen drawer. It looks like Mama. She walks out the front door.

He steps down the stairs and tiptoes to the door. It's open. He peeks through the screen. *What the heck is Mama doing out here in the middle of the night? Why is she waving a flashlight around?* He opens the door. "Mama?"

"Oh. Stanley. You scared me. What are doing awake, son?"

"I was going to ask you the same question. Why are you waving that flashlight around?"

"I thought I saw something in the woods. It's so dark out here, I wanted to see what it was. Probably a coon or a fox. Go back to bed. Get some sleep."

"Okay. Are you sure you're alright?"

"Yes, I'm sure. Go back to bed, now. Goodnight."

"Goodnight, Mama." He ascends the creaking stairs and climbs into bed. Thoughts dissipate into emptiness, replaced by images of dreams.

***

SUNDAY, SEPTEMBER 12, 1920 - It's a cool, clear day in Southington. Stanley walks alongside a horse-drawn wagon helping to shuck corn and tossing the ears against the bang board inside the wagon. Two young men approach the farmhouse on foot. They're met by Mama. She's carrying a tray of sweetbread, milk, several packs of cigarettes and a jug of raisin jack moonshine. Probably one of Papa's home brews. Mama has been serving the farm hands snacks and smokes most the morning.

Wonder what they're talking to her about? Mama hands the men food, cigarettes and the jug and points them in the direction of the woods. "What? Are they bums looking for a free meal and cigarettes? Get lost, bums." *Hey. That guy kind of looks like Uncle Syski. It can't be. What would he be doing all the way out here?* The men disappear into the thickets of the woods off the property.

"I'll be back fellas. I have to check on something."

Frank, Annie and Billy go about their business finishing chores and playing on the farm. Mama sets her serving tray on one of the unused wagons and fills feed bags full of oats for the horses.

"Mama, who were those men you were talking to? Was one of them Uncle Syski?"

"No, no. Just a couple of drifters looking for work. Uncle Syski wouldn't be wandering around in Southington, silly boy."

"Well it sure looked like him. Why'd you give 'em food?"

"Never mind that. Can you take Mrs. Johnson a bushel of cabbage?"

"Sure. I need a break from shucking, anyway. My fingers hurt."

Mama's mood turns solemn. "You're a good boy, Stanley. I don't know what I'd ever do without you." She pauses. "You're the man of this family. A *real* man." She blankly stares off into the distance. "If anything happens to me son, promise me you will look after your brothers and sisters."

"What? What are you talking about? Nothing's going to happen to you."

"Promise me, son."

"Well, of course … I'd take care of 'em. You know I would." Her kiss on his cheek carries a sadness in its touch he can't quite understand. It's troubling.

Stanley fills a flat crate with around thirty pounds of cabbage and lays it in the Radio Flyer. He draws the wagon along the dirt road to the Johnson farm. The trip takes over an hour. When he returns, he catches up with the wagon and continues to shuck corn the rest of the day. The sun begins its descent marking the end of a tiresome workday.

Another dinner without Papa or Sophie. Stanley helps Frank, Annie, and Billy retire to their rooms. Mama continues to work on the tatting piece from the night before.

Hours later, Papa arrives home. He stomps up the porch stairs and stumbles into the house. Mama avoids eye contact. "Where's my children?"

Mama continues to tat. "They are all in bed asleep, George."

"Where's my Sophie?"

"Sophie is visiting my sister Mary. Remember?"

Papa grumbles, slurring his words, "How long is she going to stay there? Get her ass back home. I need her on the farm, Goddammit."

Mama raises a finger to her lips. "Shush. Please keep your voice down, George. The kids are sleeping." He staggers towards the hallway. "Let's go to bed woman." She sets the tatting piece neatly on the coffee table and follows him into the bedroom, expressionless and without protest. Their bedroom door shuts.

Stanley lies in bed. He's listening. *Please just go to sleep.* Nearly an hour passes and his mind fades into deep slumber.

"Again? Who's downstairs? My pie ..." Stanley peers out his door. He observes Mama walking around the kitchen. She takes something from the kitchen drawer again tonight. *Am I dreaming this?* She opens the front door and steps out onto the porch and sits in the rocker.

I swear these steps wait until nighttime to creak so dang loud. He peers through the screen door. Mama is waving a flashlight again tonight. *What the heck's going on?*

"Mama? Why are you out here again tonight? ... And why are you waving the flashlight again?"

"Oh! You startled me. Did I wake you again? I'm sorry. Go back to bed. I'm just going to sit out here for a while. You need your rest, son. Don't worry about me."

"Mama, are you hurt? Why are you sitting like that? Did Papa hurt you again?"

"I'm okay. I promise. Still having pain from the miscarriage. But it'll heal in time. Goodnight, son. I love you."

"Goodnight, Mama. I love you too." He shakes his head as he leaves her. This is the second night in a row she's sitting out there.

I'm so tired. Just get me up these stupid creaky steps and back into my bed. It's cold as shit. The warmth of his covers and the softness of his pillow soothes and lulls his busy mind. His breathing slows to deep sighs and an occasional snort.

CRACK!

Stanley's eyes pop open. "What the heck was that? Was that real?" *I must have been dreaming ... too damn tired for this crap.* He rolls over and closes his eyes and drifts off.

CHAPTER FOUR

MONDAY, SEPTEMBER 13, 1920 – "Stanley. Wake up." A familiar voice pierces the silence of the early morning. A soft hand presses on his shoulder gently shaking him. Peering through sleepy eyes, his mother's round face comes into focus among the shadows. "Mama? What's going on?"

"Put your clothes on. Come downstairs, right now. I'll wait for you in the kitchen."

Why do I have to get up? I just wanna sleep. "It's too cold."

Where's my overalls? Dang it, wrong foot. Missed a button ... shit.

"Ouch. What the hell? Why can't Frank pick up his crap?"

The soft glow of an oil lamp emanates from downstairs, reflecting off the mahogany stairway and illuminating the sizeable living room. Something doesn't feel right. There's a stillness in the air. A foreboding silence.

"What are you doing up so early, Mama? What's that rope for?"

Mama breathes raggedly. "Son. Listen to me carefully. Three negroes burst into our house last night around one in the morning. They shoved a pistol in my face and told me to stay quiet. They tied me up with this rope and gagged me."

She pauses. Her eyes widen and well with tears. She whimpers. "They shot and killed your father. They stole six-hundred dollars from the kitchen and ran out of the house."

"What? Papa's dead?" His heart races. He can't catch his breath. Tears well, blurring his vision. The back of his neck prickles all the way down his spine with nervous electricity. His twelve-year old mind swirls with confusion. *Did she really just say that?*

"Stanley. Run and fetch the Sheriff. Hurry ... they might come back any minute."

"But what about Annie, Billy and Frank? What about you?"

"Just go. Quickly. There's no time to waste."

**

Out of breath and exhausted, Stanley bursts through the front door of the sheriff's office. A startled Sheriff Thomas leaps from his chair, coffee mug in hand. A swirl of coffee splashes over the rim of the mug and soaks into the sleeve of his crisp clean uniform.

"Damnit son. What's the emergency?"

"Sir, we were robbed last night at our farmhouse. The men tied up my mother and shot my father ... They stole six hundred dollars ... I-I'm afraid they might come back."

"Okay, okay, calm down. Where do you live?"

"Southington." He heaves another breath. "The Puchalski farmhouse"

Sheriff Thomas nods and places his coffee mug on his desk. He attempts to wipe his sleeve with a napkin to no avail. "Are the men still there? Is anyone else in danger?"

"No sir. They left last night, but what if they come back? I think my father is dead. My little brothers and my sister were sleeping upstairs when I left. Please hurry."

Thomas places his hand on Stanley's shoulder. "It's okay, son. Follow me."

"Deputy Moser. Can you follow me to the Puchalski farmhouse in Southington? We have a possible homicide and the suspects are at large. I may need your help."

"Right behind you, Sheriff."

The soft leather front seat of the Model T patrol vehicle provides relief to his tired legs from the two-mile run. The vibration of the engine travels through the seat and penetrates and relaxes his weary thighs. *Ah, that feels good.* He rubs the cramps from his thighs and calves as the truck turns onto the gravel country road headed toward the farmhouse.

"Where exactly is your home, son?"

"Just go straight up Robinson Road towards Southington past the railroad tracks, sir. It'll be the large white house on left hand side of the road."

"What's your name? How old are you, boy?"

"Stanley. I'm twelve. But I'll be thirteen in a couple months."

"I'm going to get you home son, and we'll get your family to safety. Don't you worry about that. You just try and relax."

"Thank you, sir." He sighs, slouching into the seat and staring out the window. Grassy hills and thick bunches of trees showing signs of Autumn fly past the window in a blur of fall colors. *Papa can't be gone. What's going to happen to us? What if they come back?* His eyes close. The hum of the engine and the sound of gravel beneath the tires distracts and numbs his restless mind for the moment.

"Is this the place, Stanley?" Stanley's stomach tightens as the farmhouse comes into view.

"Yes, sir. This is it."

"Okay, wait here until I tell you it's okay to come in." Sunlight breaks through the horizon casting a golden hue on the white clapboard farmhouse. Sheriff Thomas and Deputy Moser pull their service revolvers from their holsters and cautiously approach the front door.

Shivers of nervous energy surge through Stanley's veins. Minutes pass. *Why is it taking so long?*

The front door opens. Sheriff Thomas pops his head out and motions for Stanley to come inside. He leaps from the truck, landing on his feet. Thomas holds the door open until he enters. "Have a seat next to your mother on the sofa, son."

Mama's hands feel cold. She's trembling. Stanley slides his body against hers and wraps his arms around her. Nobody is going to hurt her. Nobody. "It's okay, Mama."

Deputy Moser roams the house looking for clues. He enters the bedroom where Papa's body lies. Thomas sits in an easy chair facing them. He strokes a coarse black mustache and leans forward, speaking in a soft tone. "Ma'am, can you tell me what happened here last night?"

"I'm not sure. Around twelve or one o'clock last night three negroes parked a big car in front of our house and forced their way in. One of them was tall and the other two were short. They must have known we always leave our door unlocked. George was asleep in the other room.

They shoved a pistol in my face and said if I made a sound, they'd shoot me. Then, they tied me up and gagged me and made me sit in a chair. They went into our bedroom and shot my husband. They tore through our house and found six-hundred dollars George hid in a cookie jar in the kitchen. Once they had the money, they ran out the door and drove away. I was able to get loose around six this morning. That's when I went upstairs to wake my son, Stanley. I-I sent him to fetch you."

"Ma'am, the bedroom down the hall is where your husband was killed, correct?"

"Yes." She sobs.

"Wait here with your son while I check on things."

"Can I wake up my other children and bring them downstairs?"

Thomas places his hand on her shoulder. "Please wait here with your son and let me check the bedroom first … to see what the deputy's found."

Thomas eases the door open and enters the room. The body lays face-up on the bed. A pool of brown sticky blood surrounds the head. Specks of brown and gray brain matter, mixed with dried blood create a pattern of spray across the bed sheet—some stuck on the far wall. A small bullet hole, the width of a pencil eraser can be seen in his right temple, along with a congealed clot. Rigor mortis has set in.

Moser is kneeling by the far wall. "Here's the slug, Sheriff … embedded in the wall." Moser uses a pocket knife to carefully remove it, placing it into a paper bag. "The old man never knew what hit 'em. Probably died instantly. Judging by the powder burns I noticed on his temple earlier, he was shot at very close range."

"Nice work Deputy." Thomas walks back to the living room.

"Ma'am, I'm very sorry to have to tell you this but your husband received a fatal gunshot wound to the head." Stanley tightens his hold on his mother. Her body shakes and sobs. Tears fill Stanley's eyes. "Papa? Why?"

The finality of losing someone close generates a flood of emotions. Horror, sorrow, anger and fear, loss and uncertainty. Sometimes he hated Papa. Hated his cruelty towards Mama and Sophie. Hated his harshness and nasty temper. Hated how he seemed to care more about his money and property and status in the community than he cared about them.

Being the eldest son, Stanley also saw another side to Papa. A father who taught him to fish; taught him to hunt; taught him to farm and to work hard. He taught him how to fight and persevere, planting the seeds of an inner toughness that will carry him far in life.

Papa would lose his temper and unleash a firestorm of hell over the most insignificant of things. Yet, there were times when serious events occurred where Papa should have lost his temper, and didn't. A few months back, Stanley ran a tractor through a fence and into a ditch. Papa used one of the plow horses to pull the tractor out and repaired the fence himself. He never said a word about it.

Moser exits the bedroom and shuts the door behind him.

"Deputy, can you take a look around the property outside? Check the woods. Holler if you find anything. Or anyone."

"Sure thing." Moser tips his hat. "Ma'am."

"Mrs. Puchalski, let's get your children and bring them downstairs."

Stanley sits frozen. Numb from the disbelief of the events around him. Sheriff Thomas escorts Mama up the stairs. Moments later, Annie and Frank groggily bumble down the stairs and plop onto the sofa next to him. Annie lays on top of Frank hugging him. Frank pushes her off. "Get off me Annie. You're too fat." Stella carries Billy in her arms.

"Here Stanley, take him."

"Ma'am, are all the children accounted for?"

"Everyone but my fifteen-year-old daughter Sophie. She's visiting my sister Mary in Lisbon."

"Son, can you keep an eye on your brothers and sister while I speak with your mother in the kitchen?"

"Yes sir. I can do that." Thomas nods and winks.

I have a few questions I need to ask you." Thomas pulls out a chair from the table for Mama. He sits across from her and removes a notepad and pencil from his shirt pocket.

Frank shoves Annie with his feet. Billy giggles.

Stanley grabs Annie's calf. "Annie, stop. Shush. I'm trying to listen. Everyone be quiet."

"Frank's the one that pushed me. It's not my fault."

"Okay, Annie. Be quiet, please."

"So, you say three men entered your home last night? Did you recognize any of them? Have any of them ever worked for you in the past?

"I didn't recognize them, but they seemed to be familiar with our house. They somehow knew we keep the door unlocked and they found the money fairly quick. As if they knew where it was."

"Can you describe them? Can you describe the car?"

"They were black men. Two of them were big and the other one was smaller. They were wearing overalls and long sleeve flannel shirts and each one had a handkerchief covering his mouth. The tall ones had bushy hair and the short one was bald. I don't know what kind of car it was. It was big and tan. That's all I remember."

Thomas scribbles on his notepad, flipping pages, then continuing to write. "Mrs. Puchalski, you said they stole money from you?" How much was it, again?"

"They stole six-hundred dollars out of the cookie jar in the kitchen. George had just sold some properties. He owns a lot of properties and he decided to sell two of them recently. He must have hidden the money there, because I didn't even know it was there."

"I see. Okay. So, six-hundred. If you didn't know it was in there, how do you know it was six-hundred dollars?"

"Uh, because I heard them count it."

"Before they ran out the door? Did you hear the gunshot that killed your husband?"

"Yes … and yes. It was a loud pop, but it didn't wake any of the children."

"Do you recall what time you heard the gunshot?"

"About fifteen minutes after they burst into our house. Around twelve-thirty I'd say. They came in, they threatened me and tied me up, then they shot George. They searched the house, emptied the cookie jar and found the money. That's when they left."

"What time did you wake your son?"

"Around six o'clock. Then I sent him to you."

"Well, you're fortunate I went to work early this morning, Ma'am. I'm usually not in the office until after eight.

The screen door opens and Deputy Moser reenters the house. "Sheriff, I found these items in the woods, just off the property." Moser sets an empty milk bottle, a jug and some torn paper from a cigarette pack on the table. He sniffs the jug. "Smells like hooch, boss. Also, I found some tracks nearby. Only two sets of tracks though. Not three."

The bums. The bums must have left those things in the woods after Mama fed them. Why doesn't she tell him?

"Nice job, Deputy. Can you take a drive and ask Coroner Henshaw to come by and pick up the body of Mr. Puchalski as soon as possible? And while you're out can you talk to the neighbors? See if they saw or heard anything unusual? Maybe get a make on the car or the men."

"Will do, Sheriff."

"Mrs. Puchalski, can I have a chat with Stanley here in the kitchen, while you wait in the living room with your other children?"

"Of course, Sheriff."

Stanley takes a seat at the kitchen table. "How are you doing, son?"

"I'm doing okay ... I think."

"Did you notice anything strange around midnight to say, one in the morning last night? Any talking? A gunshot? Anything at all?"

"Not much of anything, sir. Oh, I did hear a loud crack in the middle of the night. It sounded like fireworks. But I thought I was dreaming and I went back to sleep."

"Interesting. What time did your mother wake you up?"

"I don't know. It was still dark. Probably around five or six in the morning."

"Did you notice anything strange or out of place around the farm in the last few days? Strangers walking around? Strange automobiles driving by? Odd conversations you might have overheard?"

Should I tell him? Mama didn't. Maybe she forgot. "Well, I did see two men yesterday walk up to my Mama. They were bums. She gave them some bread and milk and some other stuff, then sent them away into the woods. I could swear one of them looked like my uncle Syski."

Thomas sits up in his chair. "The men were white? Not black?"

"Yes sir."

"And you say one of them looked like your Uncle Syski?

"Yeah. I mean, at least I think so. I was kind of faraway working in the cornfield, so I'm not sure."

"Where does he live? Your uncle. Does he visit often?"

"He lives in Lisbon with my Aunt Mary. I've never seen him here on our farm before."

"How is your mother related to your uncle?"

"Aunt Mary is Mama's younger sister. Uncle Syski is her husband."

"And your sister Sophie is staying with your Aunt Mary right now, right?"

"Yes sir. Mama sent her to Aunt Mary's on Friday after Papa hurt them both pretty bad."

"Did your Papa hurt them often? Did he hurt you too?"

"Papa mostly hurt Mama and Sophie. Sometimes me. The next day he beat Mama so bad, she lost her baby. He beat her because he found out she took Sophie to Lisbon."

Thomas frowns and scratches the back of his head. "I'm very sorry to hear that. Thank you, Stanley. You've been a tremendous help, son. I am truly sorry about your father."

Stanley looks towards the front door. "Someone's at the door."

The deputy is back. That must be the coroner with him.

"Mrs. Puchalski, can you bring your children into the kitchen to stay with Stanley for a bit, while Mr. Henshaw does his job?"

"Of course." Frank, Annie and Billy walk to the kitchen and sit at the table. Mama slices four pieces of apple pie and serves everyone. "Eat this for now. I'll make more food later."

What's that? A stretcher? Two men enter the bedroom and load Papa's body onto a gurney. They cover him with a white sheet. They hurry to remove the body from the house and load it into the ambulance. *I can't believe that was Papa under that sheet. Who did this? Why is this happening?*

Deputy Moser reenters the house. "Sheriff. Can I have a word with you outside, please?" Thomas follows Moser onto the porch.

Stanley places his dish in the sink and walks over to the sofa to eavesdrop on the conversation. Mama gathers the plates off the table and places the scraps in a bucket.

"Sheriff, I spoke with several of the neighbors. Three of them said that two white men in their mid-twenties knocked on their doors Saturday night. One night before the murder. They told me the men were asking where the Puchalski farm was. Said they were looking for work. A little odd to be looking for a job on a Saturday night."

Thomas crosses his arms. "This story is getting fishier by the minute. Things aren't adding up. The boy said he saw two white men approach the mother on Sunday. He said she gave them milk and food, which might explain the milk jar and jug you found. He swore one of the men looked like his uncle. She never mentioned it. Okay, check around the woods some more. See if anything else turns up. I'm going to pay this Uncle Syski a visit in Lisbon."

Deputy Moser walks the property a second time looking for anything unusual or out of place. Thomas walks inside.

"Mrs. Puchalski, can you provide me with the address of your sister Mary in Lisbon? I'd like to chat with Sophie and your brother-in-law for a bit."

"Here, let me write it down for you, Sheriff."

"I'll be checking in over the next few days, Ma'am. Please stay close to home in case something turns up or I have more questions."

"I'll be here Sheriff. If I do go anywhere it'll be to pick up my daughter in Lisbon."

"Very good. Lisbon is where I'm headed now. Thank you for all your cooperation. You have my deepest sympathies. Oh, one more question. Do you own any firearms? Have you ever used a firearm? I guess that was two questions."

"George has a shotgun and a rifle he uses for hunting. I mean, used for hunting. I've never fired either one."

"Thank you, ma'am. No handguns? Small caliber revolver?"

"None that I'm aware of."

"Okay. I only ask because the bullet wound in your husband's temple was small. Like from a .22 or .25 caliber weapon. Good day, ma'am."

Finally. He's gone. Stanley holds his hand to his stomach. "Mama, can we please have lunch now?"

"Yes, son. I'm so sorry. I know you all are very hungry. Let me see what I can whip up."

Stanley slides open the kitchen drawer where he saw the .25 caliber revolver the night his father came home drunk and slept on the sofa. He lifts the towels. No revolver.

CHAPTER FIVE

WEDNESDAY, SEPTEMBER 15, 1920 – The morning sky is clear and the air is cool in Southington—the morning of Papa's funeral. Mama tailored one of Papa's old suits to fit me. I've never worn black—never been to a funeral—and I've never had a pair of trousers ride up my butt crack quite like this.

Mama borrowed a gray pinstriped suit for Frank from the Johnson's youngest son. Frank's stocky thighs are stressing the seams of the trousers. Billy got off easy with a pair of black nickers held up by suspenders, a white dress shirt and black bow tie.

Sophie helps Annie fit into a white silky dress Mama made for her. Annie's thick chestnut curls are too darn cute. Never knew she had so much hair. There's something different about the way Sophie looks this morning. Her black cotton dress, stockings and black beret make her look almost grown up. She isn't slouching and her clothes actually fit.

And Mama ... well Mama looks beautiful. Her black wool dress and jacket make her look regal. I'm not keen on the bucket hat, but it matches her purse and gloves. It's nice to see her dressed up.

Stanley's ears perk at the sound of tires crunching gravel and rolling to a stop in their driveway. "Mama, Aunt Mary and Uncle Syski are here. Should we all get in their automobile?"

"Yes. It's time to go. The service starts at nine."

Warren is only a few miles away. Saint Mary's Church is where the funeral is being held and where they'll bury Papa. The drive is quiet and quick. A lot of folks from the community and neighboring farms showed up. Papa was very well liked.

Papa's corpse is on display in a shiny black casket, lying peacefully on pearl-colored silk bedding. The casket sits near the altar at the front of the church. He's dressed in a tan suit and maroon tie, hands folded across his chest. The mortician did a swell enough job covering his head wounds.

I guess you get the front row when the dead fella's your Papa. *I swear that was Uncle Syski I saw the other day. Look at him sitting there. He has the same brown-curly hair. And there ain't no way two people could have that same beak for a nose.* Stanley catches Aunt Mary's eyes. She smiles.

Mama stands. She motions for us all to follow her. She carries little Billy in her arms and walks past Papa. She whispers. "I'm sorry this happened." Her eyes well and she sniffles as she returns to the pew with Billy on her hip.

Annie walks past Papa, barely glancing at him. Her arms are crossed. She fidgets and frowns then hurries to catch up to Mama. Frank is next. He touches Papa's arm. He stands in silence for a moment, then joins Mama.

Stanley is motionless staring at the lifeless body. Tears flow freely down his cheeks. His knees tremble. "I love you Papa. I'm so sorry." *At least Mama and Sophie are free now.* He wipes his eyes with the sleeve of his jacket and returns to his seat.

Sophie is the last to pass by Papa. She vacantly stares at the man who beat, and tormented her. The man who kept her in constant fear for her life. Now he lies still and rigid–unable to lay a violent hand on her or Mama or anyone ever again.

She breaks the silence of the room. "Good for him." The other people in the church are confused by what she means by the remark. She whispers. "You're free now Papa. Free from the liquor. Free from the women. And I'm free from you." She turns and rejoins her family.

Mary and Syski walk past the casket to pay their respects. Syski kisses the corpse on the forehead. "Rest in peace, George." Mary pats the corpse on the shoulder and whispers. "Rest in Hell you bastard."

At ten o'clock the Priest concludes Mass. The body is carried to the gravesite by Papa's four brothers who arrived from Steubenville the night before. George Puchalski is lowered into his final resting place in Saint Mary's Cemetery in Warren, Ohio where he'll spend eternity.

After the funeral, Detective P.J. Gillem and Deputy Sheriff Moser approach Syski.

"Mr. Olesyski?"

"Yes, what can I do for you gentlemen?"

"Mr. Olesyski, you are under arrest on suspicion of the murder of George Puchalski. Turn around. I'm going to cuff you and take you into custody."

"What? What for? I was nowhere near Southington the night Puchalski was murdered. He was murdered by negroes. Do I look like a negro to you? Are you joking?"

"We have witnesses that say you *were* in the area. We also have a witness that says you did it. Let's go. Turn around."

Aunt Mary confronts Moser and Gillem. Her voice quivers with panic. "Where are you taking my husband? Let him go. What did he do?"

"Ma'am, please step back. Your husband is being charged with the murder of Mr. Puchalski."

"What? But he didn't do it. Stella? What's going on? They arrested my husband. Tell them he didn't do it."

Mama blankly stares. She doesn't blink. She covers her mouth with her hands, then slowly lowers them. "I don't know Mary. I don't know. Stanley get the children. We need to go home."

Mary whimpers. "You know something, Stella. I know you do. What did you do? Tell me. Please tell me what's going on."

"I don't know anything. I don't know why they arrested him. We have to go now. I'm sorry. We'll find a ride home."

A detective stops Mama as she leaves the cemetery. "Mrs. Puchalski, I'm Detective William Younger. I'm sorry to bother you today, but I have some questions I need to ask your daughter Sophie and your son Stanley."

Younger turns to Sophie and smiles. "Sophie I'm Detective Younger. I know this is a very difficult day for you and your family. But would you and your brother mind riding with me to the precinct and answer a few quick questions? It won't take long, I promise. You're not in any trouble. Your mother will be right outside the door."

Sophie looks at Mama. Mama nods. "It'll be okay sweetie."

"Mrs. Puchalski, can you all please follow me? I'll drive you."

"Can I bring my younger children? I don't have anyone to watch them at the moment."

"Sure. That won't be a problem. We have a lounge and I'll assign an officer to care for them during the questioning." They climb into Detective Younger's automobile and drive away. Mama rubs her face and wrings her hands. It's obvious she's very upset.

***

"Mrs. Puchalski, you can wait here outside the room. You can watch from this window. Your younger children are in good hands. Sophie? Stanley? Follow me please." Younger closes the door to the witness room.

Mama watches through the window. She can't hear anything, but at least she can watch.

"Please have a seat on the sofa. This shouldn't take too long. Be comfortable."

Sophie sits and folds her hands in her lap. "Thank you, sir."

Is she admiring the detective? Maybe, it's his strong jawline and thick slicked-back brown hair. Maybe it's his bright green eyes that seem to twinkle each time he looks at her. The fella's handsome, no doubt. *Oh my God, I think she's in love with him. Never seen her look at anyone like that before. It's embarrassing.*

"Sophie, please call me William."

"Okay. William."

Oh geez. She's blushing. He's ten years older than you, Soph.

Younger pulls up a chair, spins it around and sits with the back of the chair facing them. He rests his arms on the top of the chair. He's friendly and charming, that's for sure.

"Do either of you know if your Uncle Syski may have been at your farm the night your father was killed? Have you heard any talk or rumors about it?"

Sophie twirls a strand of hair with her finger, glancing at the floor. "William. I do know something. But I'm afraid to tell you."

Yeah. I'm afraid William, cuz I have a crush on you.

"Sophie, you are perfectly safe here. I can protect you. If you know something, you need to tell me what it is. Okay?"

"Okay. Um … William. Monday, when I was eating breakfast at my Aunt Mary's in Lisbon, Uncle Syski sat at the table with me. Aunt Mary was outside feeding the dog. Uncle Syski told me he murdered Papa. He said if I ever told anyone, he'd murder me too. I don't want him to kill me."

Holy shit. It was him that day at the farm. Why is Mama hiding it?

"It's okay, Sophie. Your Uncle is in custody. He's locked up in a jail cell. He won't be getting out anytime soon. You're safe. Thank you for telling me."

"Stanley, you told Sheriff Thomas you think you might have seen your Uncle Syski and another man at your farm last Sunday. Is that right? Did you see him there?"

Mama is intently watching through the window. She looks concerned by the frown on her face.

"I really think I did. It looked a lot like him. I'm not sure though. I was kind of far off."

"You also said the men talked to your mother. Surely, she would recognize him, right?"

"I asked her about it and she said they were both drifters. She gave them some food and milk and sent them away."

Younger scratches his head. "Do either of you know of anyone who might know that your father hid money in the house?"

Sophie glances at the ceiling fidgeting with her necklace. "Well, I guess my mother would know."

"Anyone besides your mother or siblings? Any of the farmhands? Any friends or business acquaintances? Anyone he possibly owed money to?"

Sophie raises her eyebrows as she adjusts her dress. "No, no one I can think of."

"Me either. Papa never spoke of it."

Younger leans in close. He speaks in a gentle tone. "Sophie. Stanley. Do you ever remember seeing any negroes around your farm recently? Did your father ever hire any negroes to do work for him?"

Stanley nods. "Yes. We had a black farm hand that Papa fired recently for talking back to him and trying to protect Mama."

"Do you know his name?"

"No. I don't really know the farm hands that well. I think he goes by Horace. I don't know his last name. He stood up to Papa, so Papa fired him."

"I see. Stanley you were the one that went to the Sheriff and reported the crime, correct?

"Yes."

"Sophie, you were staying at your Aunt Mary's, correct?"

"Yes, William. Mama took me to Aunt Mary's last Wednesday."

Why does she love saying his name like that? Snap out of it, Sophie.

"And what was the reason for the visit? You stayed for several days, correct?"

"Yes. Papa beat Mama very badly that day. I tried to help her, so he beat me too. He hurt us both very bad ... and Stanley as well. Mama thought it would be best for me to get away for a few days until I felt better ... and to keep me safe from him."

"I'm sorry to hear that. You're a beautiful young lady and no one deserves that. Did your father beat you or your mother often?"

Tears well in Sophie eyes. "Thank you, William. Yes. Papa was very cruel. He beat me often. He beat Mama often. He usually didn't hurt the younger children. But he was cruel to Stanley too." Stanley takes Sophie's hand and squeezes it softly. Her tears bring tears to his eyes. He glances at Mama. She's fidgeting in her seat. Her eyes wide with concern.

"I know this is hard for you both. I'm very sorry. Bear with me. We're almost done. Stanley, did you hear anything out of the ordinary the night your father was killed?"

"I thought I did. I woke up in the middle of the night. I thought I heard a loud clap or popping sound. Like fireworks going off. I just thought I dreamt it, so I went back to sleep."

"I see. Sophie, can you tell me when your father first started hurting you? And are you able to tell me about the things he did to you?"

Sophie stares at the floor. She bites her lower lip, then raises her head and gazes at Younger. Her chin trembles. She rolls her shoulders back and places her hands in her lap.

"He was always mean to me. But he didn't start beating me until I was around twelve or thirteen. He held me upside down once and beat me non-stop. I bit my tongue and was bleeding from my mouth, but that didn't stop him. I don't even know what I did that day to deserve it.

"Another time he chased me with his belt. I ran outside and climbed a tree to hide from him. I woke up the next morning in the tree. I couldn't remember how I got there. I was so confused."

"Last year I ran away. I went to the children's home and asked them to take me in. But they just called the police and the police took me home. Papa beat me for hours. He kicked me and punched me and whipped me with his belt. He yelled awful things at me and called me names I shouldn't repeat." Sophie sobs and whimpers.

Stanley places his arm around her. "It's okay Sophie. He's gone now. He can't hurt you anymore. I got you now. I'll keep you safe."

Mama pounds on the door. "That's enough. I want my children back. They have nothing else to say."

Younger looks toward the door, then glances at Stanley and Sophie. "We're finished here, for now. Thank you both for speaking to me. It was very helpful. I'm very sorry you have to go through this. I truly am." Younger opens the door allowing Mama to enter. Sophie rushes into her arms.

"It's okay my sweet girl. It's over now. You don't have to answer any more questions. And nobody is going to hurt you ever again." Mama glares at Younger. "Can we go now? Please."

"Yes, Ma'am. I have a car ready to take you all home."

"Officer Wilkins, can you drive the Puchalski family back to their farm in Southington?"

"I can do that. Please follow me. We'll pick up your younger children first. Then I have an automobile out front, ready to take you all home."

***

Stanley peers out the screen door from the living room. "Mama. We have company. Sheriff Thomas and Deputy Moser are here. There's another automobile with some men getting out and looking around the farm for something. Here comes Sheriff Thomas. Should I let him in?"

"I'll get the door. You go to the kitchen."

Sheriff Thomas knocks, rattling the screen door on its hinges. "Can I help you Sheriff?"

Mrs. Puchalski, can you step outside for a moment. Away from the children. I have some information I need to share with you?"

Mama opens the door and steps onto the porch. "What information? Did you find them? The real killers?"

I'm sorry, Mama, but I have to know what's going on. Stanley tiptoes to the sofa and sits near the screen door allowing him to eavesdrop.

"Please sit on the porch swing." Thomas sits on the rocker facing Mama. He waves to Deputy Moser. Moser opens the rear door of the patrol car and helps a young man in shackles to step out. He escorts the man to the porch. The young man stares at the floor.

"Mrs. Puchalski, this is Vincenzo Georgevich. I believe you two have met."

The blood seems to leave Mama's face. Her palms sweat. Her breathing becomes shallow.

"Mrs. Puchalski, do you know if your brother-in-law Frank Olesyski was in Southington the night before the murder or the night of the murder of your husband?"

"No. I don't know. How would I know that?"

"It's just a question, ma'am. I have to tell you we have three neighbors who told us they saw two young white men in the local area the night before the murder. All three stated they asked about the location of your farm."

She's light-headed and begins to sway. Her temples throb. Her skin grows cold and clammy.

"Are you okay, Mrs. Puchalski? Do you need some water?"

"Yes … no, I'm okay. I'm just not feeling well."

An officer approaches the porch. "Sheriff. We located the revolver in the woods, exactly where Georgevich said it was. We'll take it in for ballistics testing along with the slug Deputy Moser recovered from the bedroom wall—see if we have a match."

"Thank you, Hansen. Please bring the weapon over here, so we can show it to Mr. Georgevich and Mrs. Puchalski.

Thomas glares at Mama and points to Georgevich. "Did this man murder your husband?"

"No-o-o-o." Tears stream down her face.

Thomas places his hand on her shoulder.

"Mrs. Puchalski, please calm down. It's okay. Just tell us what happened. We're here to help you. Take a deep breath. Relax. Now tell us what happened."

She's only able to take shorts breaths. Her heart races. Her palms are moist.

"George was cruel. He beat me. He beat my children. I lost six babies because of his cruelty. My Sophie, my poor, poor Sophie. George beat her up so bad. I don't care what he did to me, but not to my Sophie. Not to my baby. I hate him so much." Her body shakes. She grips the arm of the porch swing with both hands.

"It's alright, Mrs. Puchalski. I understand. Your husband beat you and your daughter. He was a bad man. But who killed your husband? Stella, who killed George?" Thomas' voice echoes then fades. Stella's mind drifts back to that dreadful night.

She is suffocating from the weight of George on top of her. He's drunk and belligerent. Her scalp is on fire as he violently yanks her head back. Stella fights to endure the pain and humiliation—praying for the moment he is done with her. He brutally rapes her.

When it is over, she slithers out of bed finding the courage and strength to escape him. Slipping into a house dress she walks into the kitchen. She opens a kitchen drawer removing a flashlight and her pistol, placing one in each pocket of her dress. She shuffles out onto the porch, wincing as she sits. She waits, peering into the darkness. Waving the flashlight in the air, flicking it on and off like a light house signaling a distressed ship in the harbor. She is interrupted by Stanley momentarily. She sends him to bed.

From the woods emerge Georgevich and Syski. Sensing Syski's nervousness and smelling the moonshine on his breath, she shoves the pistol into his hand.

"Here. Take this." She points to the hallway. "He's in there. Be very quiet. Don't wake him."

Syski trembles from a mixture of adrenaline and liquor. "Are you sure you want to go through with this, Stella?"

She grabs his hand and slaps a fat money roll into his palm. "Yes. Just do it."

"Okay, okay. Wait here." His trembling increases and spreads throughout his body. He glances at her, then enters the hallway.

She grows impatient and shoos him along. Each step he takes causes his pistol hand to shake more violently. She grows angry. A realization comes over her, she will have to force the issue. She pushes Syski into the room with George.

The pair hover like two wraiths in the night over the sleeping body of George Puchalski. Syski leans over the bed and places the nose of the pistol near George's right temple. His hand trembles uncontrollably causing George to stir. Stella grasps his trembling arm and steadies his hand. The instant George relaxes, she guides Syski's hand and points the revolver barrel at George's right temple. She places her finger over his and together they gently squeeze the trigger. A crack rings out in unison with a scatter of fiery-red sparks lighting up the dark.

George's body convulses then lays still in the darkness. Syski panics and flees the room. "Run Vinnie."

The two men rush out the front door leaving it wide open, disappearing into the woods. Stella runs from the room slamming the bedroom door behind her. She rushes into the living room and collapses onto the sofa. She curls into a ball, sobbing and shaking.

Thomas' echoey voice returns and becomes clearer. "Mrs. Puchalski, who murdered George?"

Stella's face contorts and her eyes grow wild. "He would have killed my Sophie if I didn't do something to stop him. He was cruel."

"Mrs. Puchalski, who murdered your husband?" Pointing to Georgevich, "Was it this man?"

She shakes her head. "No. This man was there but he didn't kill George. I paid Syski to kill George."

Thomas' eyes widen and his brow raises. "Syski? Your brother-in-law?

Stella nods her head. "Yes. Frank Olesyski. I paid him the six-hundred dollars I stole from George to shoot him. I did it to save my Sophie. To save my children from his cruelty."

"Mrs. Puchalski, please tell me what happened that night."

Her voice calms. A sense of relief overcomes her. The truth is finally revealed. "I offered six-hundred dollars to Syski to kill George. He took the money. I don't know this man, Georgevich. I only met him once. He was there with Syski, but had nothing to do with the shooting. They were supposed to arrive on Saturday but they got lost in the woods. They found our farm Sunday morning. I fed them and had them wait in the woods until dark, when George fell asleep.

I signaled them with my flashlight. Syski shot George with my pistol. I made up the story about the three black men to account for the time it took to send Stanley to fetch you."

"Hansen, can you show the revolver you found in the woods to Mr. Georgevich?"

"Yes sir." Hansen displays the revolver.

Mr. Georgevich, is that the weapon used in the murder of George Puchalski?

Georgevich nods and meekly responds. "It looks like the weapon."

"Can you show the revolver to Mrs. Puchalski?"

Hansen shows Stella the revolver.

"Mrs. Puchalski, is this your .25 caliber revolver?"

She covers her face with her hands. Then places her hands in her lap. She calmly states, "Yes. It's mine."

"Is this the weapon used to murder your husband?"

"Yes."

"Thank you, Officer Hansen. Place the revolver into evidence and have it tested against the slug we located in the victim's room."

"Deputy Moser, please take Georgevich back to his cell. I think we're finished here." Moser nods and escorts Georgevich back to the patrol car and drives away.

"Mrs. Puchalski, I'm sorry ma'am, but I have to place you under arrest. I'll make arrangements for your children and ensure they are safe and taken care of." She sobs, cradling her face with her hands. "Mrs. Puchalski, please come with me." She willingly follows Thomas to his automobile.

Stanley bursts out the front door. "Mama! Where are you taking her?" Stella turns and locks eyes with him. Her lips mouth, "I'm sorry. I love you."

"No, come back. Mama come back." Stanley falls to his knees. As the automobile drives off, he falls face-first into the thick grass of the yard. He violently cries, grasping handfuls of grass and pounding the ground with clenched fists. His world has been shattered into a million tiny fragments. First Papa, now Mama. What will they do? What will become of them all?

Sophie, rushes outside and falls on the ground next to him. She lays over him, sobbing. "It'll be okay. We have each other. We have each other. Mama will be back."

Frank, Annie and Billy stand on the porch watching as Mama is driven away. Annie rushes down the porch steps and chases after the patrol car. "Mama! Mama!" Frank stands on the porch not saying a word. Tears stream down his cheeks. Billy sits on the steps quietly watching. He waves at the automobile in his innocence, oblivious of the tragedy surrounding him.

A female officer approaches Stanley and Sophie. "Gather your siblings and your things, please and come with me."

***

Sophie holds Billy's hand and grasps her small valise with her other hand. Frank holds Annie's hand. Both Frank and Annie carry a small bag. Stanley blankly stares straight ahead, gripping a banged-up leather suitcase. The old mansion is an ominous and overwhelming sight. The County Children's Home. An orphanage.

There was a boy who once lived here. He had a lot of accidents, until one day he had an accident so bad, they had to take him to the hospital. Nobody ever saw that boy again.

I wonder if anyone will ever see us again?

"Are you ready children? Follow me, please."

Stanley glances at Sophie. "I guess we're orphans now."

PART II - CHAPTER SIX

FRIDAY, SEPTEMBER 17, 1920 – The Victorian mansion stands three stories. Green shutters decorate its many windows. The exterior is covered in white clapboard. Three red-brick chimneys rise over the black rooftop billowing white puffs of smoke into the gray Ohio sky. Enormous trees cover the property providing ample shade to the grounds.

Stanley glances at Sophie and frowns. "Benny Thompson told me little kids get bullied here by the bigger kids and the nuns and orderlies are all mean."

Sophie shakes her head and rolls her eyes. "We don't know if that's true. Benny Thompson tells stories. He just repeats everything he hears."

"All I'm saying, Soph, is we gotta be careful here … look out for each other."

The officer stops walking and turns and faces them. "Quiet please. No talking."

The siblings climb three steps to a long narrow porch. The officer knocks on a pair of tall wooden chestnut doors. Minutes later, one of the doors swings open and a Catholic nun emerges.

"Good day. And who do we have here?"

"This is the Puchalski family, Sister. This is Sophie, Stanley, Frank, Annie and little William."

Little William? You mean Billy?

"Well, it's very nice to meet you all. My name is Sister Agnes. I'm going to be your guide today. I'll help you through the process of settling into your new home."

"Have a great day, Sister." The officer steps off the porch and leaves the children in the hands of Sister Agnes.

"Follow me please children."

Sister Agnes leads them through a foyer and into the living room of the old mansion. *Never seen floors so clean.* The patterns on the rugs look strange. Golds, maroons, elephants. They have to be expensive. *Wonder where that stairway leads? Cherrywood?* Someone very rich must own this place. There isn't a speck of dust on anything. Everything smells like wood and polish.

Sister Agnes points. "Please take a seat." They sit squished together on a small Parisian leather sofa. Sophie pats Stanley's thigh. "It'll be okay. I promise." He nods and wipes a small tear before it can run down his cheek. They lean on each other and try and make themselves as comfortable as they can.

***

Stanley sighs. "Seems like we've been sitting here for over an hour. What's taking so long?"

Sophie places her arm around him. "I don't know. It does seem like we've been here an awful long while. I don't know how much longer *Little William* can sit still." She giggles.

Sister Agnes returns to the living room accompanied by a female staff member. "This is Miss Harriet. Girls, you will go with Miss Harriet for a quick shower and physical exam. Boys you will wait here."

Sophie rises from her seat and takes Annie by the hand. Billy jumps off the sofa. "Stay here with Stanley, Billy. We'll be right back."

He frowns and plops back on the sofa, arms folded and his lower lip puffed out. "I wanna come. No fair."

The boys sit. They wait. They wait some more. Billy falls asleep in Stanley's lap. Frank lays his head on Stanley's shoulder and closes his eyes.

Sister Agnes returns. "Boys, this is Mr. Kelley. He is going to administer your examinations."

Stanley whispers, "Billy. Wake up."

Who the hell is this fella? He has a block head and a beer gut. Why's his hair so greasy? He has no chin. Is that lipstick, or are his lips really that red? Makes him look like a fish.

Kelley checks their ears and looks at their hands. "Get up boys. Follow me." They follow the orderly down the hallway and out the back door to a patio in the back yard. Other children are playing in the yard. But everything stops when the boys reach the patio.

Stanley squints and pans across the yard. "Okay, this is weird. Frank, everyone's staring at us."

"Alright boys, take off all your clothes and put them on that bench." Frank's eyes widen.

"There are kids over there watching." Kelley walks up to Stanley and grabs him by the shirt. "I don't give a shit. Strip down, now."

Frank's face is ashen. Stanley helps Billy remove his clothes. "Ah. Everyone's gonna see my butt."

"It's okay Billy. Nobody's looking at your butt. Just close your eyes. If you can't see them, they can't see you. Okay? Frank, just do it."

Frank removes his clothes, covering himself with his hands. Tears well and his eyes rapidly blink. He lowers his head and frowns. Stanley removes his clothes joining his brothers in complete nudity and humiliation.

"Turn and face the wall."

An icy blast steals Stanley's breath and stings every inch of his body. The shock of the blast turns to shivers. Billy screams and runs away, but Kelley grabs him by the hair and shoves him against the wall.

Stanley takes Billy's hand. "He's just a little kid, asshole."

Kelley grins and pulls a thick wooden rod out of his back pocket. He whacks Stanley across the buttocks. The numbness of his skin from the cold barely registers the sting from the whack.

Gasps and snickers resonate. His jaw tightens. His teeth chatter. "Just hang on fellas. It'll be over soon."

Five minutes seems like five hours. Kelley shuts off the water and throws each boy a towel.

"Now sit on that bench."

The bench is weathered and splintery. Kelley runs a fine-tooth metal comb across the scalp of Billy, then Frank. Stanley feels the cold metal comb dig into his scalp. He bites his lip. Tolerating the pain. *Is this what it's going to be like?*

Kelley hands each boy a stack of clothes. "Get dressed. And throw your dirty clothes in this laundry bag. You'll get 'em back after they've been sanitized and inspected for lice and fleas."

He escorts the boys back to the lobby. Sister Agnes scowls, then sneers at Kelley. "Mr. Kelley. What happened to this boy's head?"

"He wouldn't hold still." Kelley smirks and strolls away, whistling some moronic tune he surely composed himself.

Billy looks up at Stanley. "Why's your hair pink?"

"Billy. Sh."

Sister Agnes pats Stanley's hand. She examines his scalp. Her eyes are wide. Her mouth frowns and crinkles at the corners. "Grab your luggage boys. I'll show you to your room."

The dorms are housed in a two-story red-brick building behind the main house. Clean bricks. Must be a newer construction than the mansion.

Billy points. "Swing. I wanna swing ... I wanna swing."

"Maybe later, Billy. I'll take you and Frank in a little while."

They cross a wide patio and enter the dorm building. "This is the reception room. This is where your family may come and visit you. This is also where you will visit with your sisters every Wednesday and Sunday after breakfast. Now follow me and I'll show you the dining hall and pantry."

The boys follow along.

"This is where you will dine. Breakfast is served at seven in the morning, lunch at noon and dinner at six p.m. You will need to line up with the other boys for meals each day. Now, let's go take a look at your quarters. Your room is on the second floor. Your sister's room will be on the first floor with the other girls."

She escorts them up a flight of stairs. "This is where I leave you. You each have a sheet, a blanket and a pillow folded on your bed. You *will* make your bed before you leave this room. Understood? Welcome, to your new home." She smiles and eases the door shut.

Frank rolls his eyes. "Finally, we're alone."

The room is small. A set of bunkbeds sit against the far wall. A cot sits against an adjacent wall. There is a single dresser and a small closet door. The floors are wooden and the walls are painted mint green. A single window provides a view looking out over the patio roof with the playground in full view. The air smells sanitized. Like medicine.

Stanley places his hands on his hips. "Okay, fellas. Let's make our beds. Frank, take the upper bunk. Billy can have the lower one. I'll take the cot." He helps Frank and Billy place their sheets and blankets neatly on their beds. The linen smells fresh and crisp.

"Okay ... play now? I wanna swing."

"Okay, Billy boy. Let's go see the playground."

There are picnic tables in the yard, a swing set, a teeter-totter and a tire swing hanging from a large tree, next to a sandbox. Thick trees and brush surround the property. The yard is mostly green grass and clover with a few random dirt patches.

"Let's go see the sandbox, Billy."

Frank and Billy build forts and dig holes in the sand, momentarily forgetting their circumstances.

Hm. That's our window over the porch roof. The rain gutter might be a good way to climb up and down. I think Sophie and Annie are on the first floor somewhere. Gotta find out where they are.

A young boy is sitting and playing by himself in the sandbox next to Frank and Billy. He glances up at Stanley, squinting. "Who are you fellas?"

"I'm Stanley and these are my brothers Frank and Billy. What's your name? How long you been here?"

"I'm Eddie. I'm eight. Been here almost two years. My momma and pop didn't want me around anymore, I guess. So, they left me here. I hardly ever see them. When I'm older, I'm running away from this place."

Stanley sits in the sand next to Eddie. "Why's that Ed? Why do you want to leave?"

Eddie frowns. He stares at the sand without blinking. The tone in his voice softens. "Because, it ain't safe here. That man? Mr. Kelley? The one that hit you today? He likes hurting kids. You fellas need to stay away from him. He beat a kid so bad, they had to take him to the doc. We never saw that kid again."

So, the story's true. Shit.

Eddie points to two teen-age boys across the yard. "See those brothers?"

Stanley nods. "Sure. What about 'em?"

Eddie's eyes water. He squints. "They do bad things to little boys ... like me."

"What kind of things?"

Eddie hangs his head. He draws in the sand. "Bad things. They pull your trousers down and do bad things to you." At that moment the two boys approach the sandbox. Eddie springs to his feet in a panic and sprints toward the dorms.

"These your brothers?"

Stanley remains seated on the ground. He glances up. "Yeah, they're my brothers. Why?"

"I'm Marco. This is my little brother Angelo. We own this playground. Anyone who wants to play here has to ask our permission."

Stanley rises facing Marco. Marco tightens the gap between them. Angelo moves to Stanley's right side. Marco is slightly taller than Stanley. Angelo is a runt.

Marco mockingly stares. He doesn't blink. "You got something to say, punk?"

Just stare him in the eyes. Let him know you're not afraid. That's what Papa would say.

Stanley keeps tabs on Angelo in his peripheral view. Marco grins. "Cat got your tongue? Nothing to say? I'll let you and your brothers slide just this once. But don't let me catch you on my playground without my permission ever again. You got that?" He kicks sand on Frank and Billy. The brothers walk away laughing.

I know I can take him. "Keep laughing assholes."

Stanley, brushes sand off of Billy and walks both his brothers back to the dorm room. "Take care of Billy for a little bit. I'll be right back, okay?"

"Where you going Stanley? We didn't even hardly get to play."

"Don't worry about it. Just take care of Billy and stay here in the room, okay?"

Stanley returns to the playground. He spots the brothers sitting at a picnic table across the yard. He palms a smooth flat stone and takes a seat on the swings.

Marco stares at Angelo and shakes his head. "Can you believe this punk? He just don't wanna listen." The brothers approach.

"Hey punk. What did I tell you earlier? Angelo chimes in. "You really are a stupid shit, kid."

As soon as they're within ten feet, Stanley hurls the stone at Angelo's head.

WHAM!

The stone bounces off Angelo's forehead collapsing him in a heap. He cries out. Blood gushes.

With Marco distracted, Stanley charges and tackles him. Before Marco can react, he delivers a series of blows to Marco's face, bloodying the bully's nose and busting his lower lip.

Marco, fights back and tries to push Stanley away. Angelo, leaps from the ground screaming and sprints to the back door of the main house. Marco manages to wrestle Stanley off of him. The boys stand and circle each other.

Stay in a good fighting stance. Stay balanced.

Stanley swings a swift left hook but misses. A debilitating ache hits his crotch like a sledgehammer and shoots up through his groin and into his stomach. Stanley falls on his back. *Deep breaths, deep breaths.* Marco pounces on top of him. All he can do is try and block the punches. Stanley grabs hold of Marco's thigh and bites. Marco squeals and rolls away holding his leg. "You bit me! You little piker."

Get up. Don't quit. Stanley charges. The boys exchange punches. Stanley ducks a right cross then grabs Marco by the balls and squeezes as hard as he can. Marco yelps, unable to fight back. Stanley grips harder on Marco's crotch and pulls him in close. "This is my playground now. Don't you ever come around me or my brothers again. You understand?"

"Alright. Alright. Okay. Let go. Please."

John Kelley rushes out the door. Stanley squeezes tighter. "Let go, please let go. You win, okay?" Marco squeals and whimpers.

"Let go Dammit, I said let go. That's enough." Kelley grabs Stanley by the collar and swings him to the ground.

"Are you okay Marco?" He whines and babbles cradling his balls.

"Yes sir. I'm okay."

Kelley points at the dorms. "Go to your room. Go now."

Marco, avoids eye contact with Stanley and bumbles away blubbering, hands on his crotch.

Great. Face to face with block head and his ruby-red fish lips.

"We don't tolerate this kind of shit here, you little bastard." Kelley pushes Stanley backwards. "Follow me, Puchalski." Stanley dusts himself off and complies.

"Now you're in my office. Not a good place to be as you'll soon learn ya little shit. Sit down."

Stanley sits in front of Kelley's small wooden desk. The office is tiny. Almost like a broom closet. He must really be important. An old autographed photo of James Walter Braddock hangs on the wall behind him.

"You think you're a boxer, huh?" Kelley points to his photo of Braddock. "*This* was a boxer. They called him the *Cinderella Man*. An Irish boy."

Kelley folds his arms and scowls. "So, what the hell went on out there?"

Stanley shrugs. "I was just defending myself and my brothers."

"From what? I didn't see your brothers anywhere. Who started the fight? Angelo said you hit him with a rock. He needs stitches."

"They started it ... I finished it."

Kelley stands. "Okay, smartass. You finished it. Did you hit Angelo with a rock?"

Stanley throws his hands up. "There was two of them ... I"

"So, you did hit him with a rock. Kelley pulls a sawed-off canoe paddle from his desk. He slaps his free palm with the paddle. Stand up, turn around and grab your ankles.

Stanley complies. It wouldn't have mattered what the answer was. It seems the paddle was coming out either way.

He must get a real thrill out of this shit. Sick son of a bitch.

Man, this floor is dirty. What's he waiting for?

SMACK! A bolt of lightning strikes his buttocks. He flinches. He bites his lip and gasps for a breath.

Holy shit that hurt! I ain't ready for the next one.

"What? Not crying yet? I must be losing my touch."

The next one lands. A fire rages across his backside. His knees nearly buckle.

Crap! How many more? My ass is numb. I don't know if I can take any more this.

"Oh, you're a tough kid alright. I have one more especially for you, tough guy."

Excruciating pain rips like a thousand knives. But this time on the back of his thighs. His knees buckle. He kneels on all fours on Kelly's filthy floor, eyes closed, gasping and fighting back sobs.

"Now get the hell back to your room and remember this lesson. We do not tolerate fighting here. Just remember, I let you off easy this time. Next time it won't be so much fun."

I have to get up. I have to get out of here. He shuffles his way out of Kelley's office. Burning numbness tingles like electricity down his legs and backside. *The dorm seems so far. Just get to the stairs. One step at a time.*

Stanley opens the door to his room and collapses in his cot.

Frank gawks. "What happened?"

"Nothing. We'll go play on the playground again tomorrow, okay fellas?"

Frank nods. "Okay."

Billy frowns. "No fair."

The boys remain in their room the rest of the day, playing games and playing with toys to pass the time. The day's events fade, but the sting on Stanley's thighs and buttocks remains as a painful reminder of life in the orphanage.

Frank and Billy snuggle into their bunk beds, while Stanley sits on the cot.

"When do we get to go home, Stanley?"

Stanley removes his shoes and socks and tosses his dirty socks at Frank. "We don't. We're stuck here. Mama's in jail and we don't have any money. Go to sleep." Stanley lies back on his cot and closes his eyes, trying not to focus on the pain on his backside.

***

The boys are startled by a pounding on the door. "Wake up. Line up for breakfast." The boys quickly dress and head downstairs.

Frank and Stanley stand in line and fill their plates with food. Billy is led by one of the nuns to an area designated for toddlers and placed in a highchair.

Stanley points. "There's an empty table. Let's sit here and eat."

Frank sets his tray on the table. "Okay. Hey, there's Sophie and Annie."

They all wave at each other. Billy twists and squirms in his highchair to stay in eye contact with his brothers.

"Whoa. Who kicked my chair?"

"Eat your breakfast, boy. Do not wave at the girls. Don't even make eye contact."

"I was just waving at my sisters."

Oh great. A close up of blockhead's ugly face again. Wash your hair and wipe that lipstick off. Ever heard of a toothbrush? Ug.

"I don't give a shit you little turd. Do not look over there. How's your ass feeling today Puchalski?"

Stanley mumbles, "Better than your face looks."

"What? What was that?"

Stanley lowers his head and picks up his fork.

"Yeah, I thought so. I'm watching you Puchalski. Eat your meal."

Kelley smirks and mockingly eyeballs Stanley as he moves away. He resumes his stroll around the hall whistling his annoying tune. It sounds like a combination of a marching hymn and horror music from Dracula.

Frank grabs his arm. "Stanley. What's going on over there?"

A young boy is arguing with one of the nuns and refusing to eat. She grabs his hair and shoves his face into his plate, splattering food all over the boy and the table. "Lick it up. You *will* eat your food before you leave this table, young man."

He cries out and shakes his head violently. She yanks him by the hair again and shoves food in his mouth until he gags. "Swallow it." The boy spews vomit all over his plate. The nun shoves his face into the vomit. "Now you eat that."

Stanley stares at Frank. Frank's eyes are wide. "Don't worry. I won't let that happen to you. Promise. Just … don't watch. Frank. Don't watch."

The nun continues to force-feed the boy. He chokes and convulses.

"Okay, is anyone going to do something here?" *Kelley is just grinning over there. He's enjoying this. Sick bastard.*

The little boy vomits all over himself. The nun grabs him by the ear and marches him out of the dining hall.

Stanley whispers. "Is it just me? Why doesn't anyone else notice that? They're all oblivious to it. This place is a nut house."

Stanley feels a tap on his shoulder. "Boys. Come with me. You're allowed to visit with your sisters today. Isn't that exciting?"

The nun holds Billy's hand as she escorts the boys to the recreation room.

Billy jumps into Sophie's lap on the sofa. Annie runs straight into Stanley's arms.

"Pick me up. Pick me up."

Frank squeezes in, next to Sophie. She hugs him. Stanley sits on a chair across from Sophie, Frank and Billy, holding Annie on his lap.

Sophie smiles and wrinkles her nose. "How are you and the boys doing? Staying out of trouble, I hope?"

Stanley glances around the room then leans into Sophie and whispers. "We have to get out of here, Soph. I'll find a job and save some money. We can live by ourselves."

"What? How are you going to do that? Where are you going to go? Frank and Billy need you here. So, do we. Please don't leave us." Sophie's eyes glisten. "We have food. A place to sleep. And we're together. When Mama gets out, she'll come and take us home."

"Mama ain't getting out anytime soon. She went to jail for murder, remember? Yeah, Papa probably deserved it, but we lost Mama too. And it's her fault we're even in this mad house to begin with."

"But how are you going to leave? They watch us day and night. And where are you going to find a job?"

"I'm sure I can get out the window and climb down the rain gutter. Then I'll just run away and go back home. I'll get our stash from the cornfield. And I think I know where Mama hid some money in the house."

"That's not going to be enough. We'll need a lot more than that. We'd have to find a house to stay in. We'd need food. How's that going work? Wait. What about Aunt Mary?"

"I'm sure Aunt Mary is so angry at Mama for getting her husband sent to the big house, we can forget that idea. We're on our own, Sophie. We have to figure this out ourselves."

Frank's eyes widen. He raises his brows. "You're going to leave us?"

"Just for a little while. I'll be back to get you. I promise."

Sophie hugs Frank. "He'll come back. Don't worry."

"Just give me a little time to figure this all out. Everything will be alright. I won't be gone long. Let's talk more next time we meet."

Two loud claps. "Time is up. You can see each other again on Wednesday. Time to go back to your rooms now and receive your chores for the day, children. Then you will all attend Mass."

Billy plays on the floor with some old toy cars. Frank colors on a piece of paper. Stanley stretches out on his cot and closes his eyes. The door swings open and an older boy steps in. "Get up. You all have work to do. Did you think this was some kind of vacation club? Follow me."

Mops, towels and cleaning supplies. Another fun day in the orphanage.

"Mop this hallway and then clean the toilets in the latrine. Get on it. When you're done put your mop and supplies back in that utility closet over there."

"What about my little brother Billy?"

"I'm taking him to the playground while you two idiots finish your work."

Billy whimpers. He turns his head as they walk away, trying to keep his brothers in sight.

"No wonder this place is so damn clean. All this child labor. C'mon Frank, swing that mop back and forth like this. Dance with the mop. Pretend it's your girlfriend."

"I don't have a girlfriend."

"And you won't anytime soon if we don't get the hell out of here."

Hours later the boys place their mops and supplies into the utility closet. It was a lot of work, but nothing compared to farm work.

"You promised we could play on the playground again."

"Okay, okay. Let's go find Billy."

The playground is filled with mostly younger children today. No Marco or Angelo. Frank scopes out the grounds. "Hey Billy."

Billy's eyes light up. He leaves the sandbox and runs to Frank hugging his big brother's legs. Stanley relaxes on one of the benches. Frank and Billy run around the yard playing—forgetting why they're here for the moment.

Wish I could be watching them running around our old farm instead of this shithole.

The rest of the day is quiet and uneventful. They return from Mass as another night looms in the orphanage.

***

Bang, bang, bang. "Line up for breakfast in five minutes."

"Frank, help Billy get his shoes on. Let's go. We don't want to miss breakfast." The boys scurry down the stairs and slide into the meal line.

Frank grimaces. "What's that? It looks like rotten mush."

"I think it's porridge. Nasty looking. Just put a lot of sugar on it. Let's sit here."

Frank nudges Stanley. A few tables over sit Marco and Angelo. Angelo has a large bandage across his head and Marco has a bandage on his nose and is sporting a black eye. They glance at Stanley.

Hold the stare. Stanley lowers his brows and glares at them. He doesn't blink. Angelo immediately looks away. Marco holds the stare, then looks away.

After breakfast the boys walk to the dorm. Back to cleaning toilets and mopping floors. "Looks like the girls are headed to the laundry room. Why's that fat ass, Kelley hanging around them?"

***

Wednesday. It's visiting day. Sophie and Annie sit on the sofa. Billy leaps into Sophie's lap. Annie kisses her little brother all over his face and neck. Billy giggles. Frank plops down next to Annie placing his arm around her. Stanley tickles Annie. She squirms and wriggles to get away from the teasing. Stanley sits on an easy chair. He scoots the chair next to Sophie.

Sophie's eyes are wide and doe-like. They only flutter when she's scared. Like when Papa was around.

"What's wrong Soph?"

She leans in close to Stanley. "We do need to get out of this awful place."

"Did something happen to you or Annie?"

She looks away for a moment. Her eyes flutter again.

"That man. The whistler? He walked into the laundry room yesterday where Annie and I were folding linen. He asked if we were your sisters. Then started saying how Polish girls have the best … you know, backsides. He got close to me. I could feel his hot nasty breath on my neck. I moved away from him. Then he pulled the top of my dress … and, he tried touching me."

"That son of a bitch. Stay away from him, Soph. I'm going to kill that fish-lipped asshole."

Sophie takes Stanley by both hands. "Shh. It's okay. Little Annie kicked him right in the shin and saved us. We ran to our room. We're okay. I don't want you to worry about that. We'll be more careful next time."

"I don't know how you can always be so calm, Soph. I'm going to leave tonight. I'll be back for you all soon. I promise. I'm gonna get us all out of here when I return."

Sophie hugs his neck and whispers. "I know you will. Just be careful out there and don't stay away too long. We'll be waiting for you. I'll pray for you every night."

Sister Agnes walks into the reception room and claps her hands twice. "Alright children. Visitation is over for today. On to your chores now." She takes Billy to play in the yard. Sophie and Annie walk towards the laundry room. Stanley and Frank walk to the dorm.

"Here's your girlfriend. Get ready to dance. Hey what's that metal box up there? A toolbox. Swell."

I'll just borrow this panhead and put this right back up there. Nobody will even know the difference.

"What are you doing? What was in the box? Hey, don't push me."

"Don't worry about it. Just do your damn job and dance with that mop. Hey, I gotta a better idea." Stanley tosses a bar of soap onto the floor. He slides the bar to Frank using his mop.

Frank catches the bar with his mop. He grins.

"Score! It's three to zip. C'mon. Try to score on me. Shoot it Frank."

***

Eight o'clock in the evening is always lights out.

Billy's asleep.

"Frank. You awake?"

"Yep. I can't sleep."

"Let me climb in here for a minute. I need you to listen to me little brother. I need you to be strong. I have to leave here for a while and get some money saved up, okay? Then I'm coming back to get you out of here."

Frank sniffles. "You're leaving, now? But, when will you be back? What about Marco?"

"I'll be back soon. Promise me you'll be strong. Strong for Billy. Strong for Sophie and Annie." Frank lowers his head and barely nods. "I promise."

"Marco won't bother you anymore. I took care of that."

Stanley embraces him, then shoves him face-first into the bedding. "Finger daggers." Stab, stab, stab … Frank kicks him in the face. A bloody nose, just like Papa's boxing sessions.

"Okay, I think we're done here Frank." Stanley squeezes his nose with a sock to stop the bleeding. "Ya got me good. Now get some sleep."

Frank peeks over the edge of his bunk smirking. "Ha-ha. That's what you get. You don't want to fight me. I'm too tough for you."

Stanley laughs. "Yes, you are. You're a tough little booger. Now get some shuteye."

Frank's soft sobs turn to deep sighs and an occasional snort. It's time to go.

Flannel shirt. Overalls. Boots. Cap.

The window is stuck. Probably from the old paint. Let me scrape some of this shit off first. Oh, and I guess unlocking the latch might help.

"Shimmy this part. Pry the bottom. Push. C'mon … damn it's cold."

Stanley whispers. "Goodbye Frank. Bye Billy. I'll be back. I love you fellas."

There's a nervous twinge inside his stomach as he steps out onto the patio roof. The yard is eerily quiet. Most the lights are off in the main house. *Hope you're all sleeping.*

Laying on his stomach he dangles his feet over the side of the roof. He slides down the rain gutter and jumps to the ground. Not a soul around to stop him. Stanley disappears into the darkness of the trees and brush on his way to being far from the orphanage.

CHAPTER SEVEN

Early October is chilly. Too chilly for a flannel shirt and overalls. He folds his arms as he walks along a dirt road trying to trap as much body heat as he can. He inhales the frosty air and puffs out breaths of steam. A hint of smoke from a fireplace reaches his nostrils. The thought of sitting in front of a warm hearth causes his body to shiver.

He's free. For the first time in his life. Right now, at this very moment, he only answers to himself. He knows Market Street to Parkman Road is the way home back to Southington. Back to the farm. Follow it until the scenery begins to look familiar.

The sun peeks over the crest of the horizon behind him. *An automobile. Get off the road. They'll be looking for me. Got to be careful and keep moving. Try to blend in and not draw attention.*

The long stretch of road looks identical for miles. Areas of dense woods and tall grasses line unfamiliar farm fields and rolling hills. Hours pass.

"Hey. I know this area. The Winfield's live over there. And that way is old man Johnson's farm." *There's the old dirt road I've walked a million times. I'm close now.*

His stomach knots and his heart sinks as the old farmhouse comes into view. "Home." The farm is empty. The horses, cattle, pigs and farm tools are gone. The farmhouse is gloomy and haunting. Boards cover its windows like a coffin hiding the secrets of its tragic past. Eerie silence looms in the air.

How, can a place I once called home, now seem so odd and lifeless? I belonged here once. Had a life here. Now it's a strange land. A place where the familiar and the unfamiliar meld together as one.

"I think this is the edge of the corn field. But where's the stone?" He carefully steps along the edge of the field scouring the ground for anything familiar that would lead to the location of the sandstone. The dirt has been overturned and it's hard to know exactly where the corn field begins or ends.

He sighs. "Maybe it's not here. Maybe somebody found it." His foot catches a dirt clod causing him to stumble to his knees. Beneath the dirt he can see the edge of a round stone. "Here you are." He sweeps the dirt off the sandstone with his hand and flips it over. The old leather pouch lies at the bottom of the hole. "It's all still in here. Thank you, God."

He places the pouch of coins in his pocket and wanders over to the farmhouse. *How do I get in? The cellar window? Maybe it's still broke.* Placing both hands on the hopper window he pushes it open. He slides in, feet first. *Don't get stuck.* "Damnit. How'd I rip my sleeve? Shit."

The cellar is mostly empty. The air is musky and dank. Mostly empty shelves and scattered trash remain. A few dusty old jars and can goods. No sign of the old still except for the empty barrel.

"An empty whiskey bottle? No doubt it was Papa's. Hm. Smells like dust. Might make a good water bottle.

"Hey, a burlap sack. I can use that. A can of baked beans. Canned peaches. A jar of Mama's jam. Pickled eggs? Are they still good? In the bag you go."

A brown bone-handle gunstock pocket knife lies on an old workbench. "Papa's pocket knife. I can't believe nobody took this. It's mine now."

He approaches the steps leading up to the kitchen. His stomach tightens. "Please be unlocked." The air seems to warm with each step as he moves closer to the door. He holds the knob. His breathing labors causing his heartbeat to rise as he eases the door open. The air is heavy. Almost suffocating. The deafening silence creates a faint ringing in his ears as he moves through the kitchen into the living room.

"The furniture is still here."

He eases the door open to Mama's room. Heart racing now. There's a stench of death still lingering here. Very faint, but evident. The old mattress sits on its frame stripped of all its bedding. Stains of old dry blood penetrate the fibers where Papa laid his head. Faded blood spatters speckle the wall. "Papa. Oh, Papa."

He slides his hands across the wooden floor. "Where is it?" Here. This one's loose. He pulls a small board from the floor revealing a small nook beneath. A small cedarwood box, hand-carved with patterns of flowers in an art nouveau style lies hidden beneath the floor.

He removes the box from the nook. *It feels heavy. I hear coins.* He opens the clasp and lifts the lid revealing a stash of quarters and a folded piece of paper. "Thank you, Mama." He unfolds the note.

Dear Son,

If you are reading this note, then I know you found the money I've hidden here. I also know you are here, to keep your promise. Take care of your brothers and sisters. I'm so sorry you have to bear this burden my son. I hope someday you'll understand and forgive me for all you have to go through. Before you leave the farm, check the barn. In the loft under the hay, there is a small ceramic jug. Papa used to hide money in it. Go find it. Hopefully it's still there. God bless you and protect you, my precious boy.

Love,

Mama

There are 102 quarters in all. $25.50. Stanley chuckles. *Thank you, Mama.* He knows 102 is a lucky number in Poland. He places the quarters in his leather pouch and pockets the note. He walks out of the room and closes the door behind him.

He plops on the old sofa, stirring up a cloud of dust. Shimmering motes swirl quietly, dancing on beams of light being cast across the room through slits in the covered windows.

He closes his eyes trying to recapture the past in his mind's eye. Mama and Sophie in the kitchen making breakfast. Little Billy in his high chair making a mess. Frank and Annie banging their forks on the table demanding to eat.

Droplets roll off his cheeks onto the sofa in tiny pitter-patters. This used to be home. Now it's an empty room full of phantoms and echoes of the past. Whistling breezes penetrate the walls in quiet whispers.

A piece of Mama's tatting pokes out from one of the sofa cushions. He grasps it in his hand. She never finished it. He smells it and brushes it along his cheek. His body slides sideways onto the sofa falling like a felled tree. He breaks into uncontrollable tears, clutching the tatting. His body shakes from deep sobs, eventually turning into soft sighs and deep yawns. Exhaustion overtakes him.

***

Voices outside. Rattling at the door. The sound of a key. Wake up!

"How long have I been asleep?" *I got to get out of here. Fast.*

Stanley leaps to his feet and runs across the living room to the kitchen as the front door opens. The familiar old squeak of the screen door echoes through the walls. Stanley opens the cellar door and dashes down the steps almost in a single bound.

"Hey, is someone there? I could swear someone just ran into the kitchen."

Stanley tosses his burlap sack out the window and climbs out. He lifts the sack and is face-to-face with a fat old man. Looks to be in his fifties. A farmer, but nobody from around here. He flicks a toothpick around in his mouth revealing a few missing teeth. *What the hell is he doing here?*

"Where you headed, son? What were you doing in that house? Stealing?"

"No, I … I just needed a place to sleep for a while. I'm trying to get back home."

"You look like you're running away from home to me. Where do you live? I can give you a ride."

"Nice of you to offer, but I really don't need a ride. I need to be on my way now."

"Wait. What's in the sack? Let me see." The old man snatches the sack.

Stanley kicks him in the shin and yanks the sack out of the old man's hand. *Run to the barn.*

"Phil! There's a boy out here. He stole something from the house. I think he's headed to the barn."

Stanley scales the ladder to the loft and pulls the ladder up behind him. He hides behind a stack of haybales, sucking in air, while his heart races. *Deep breaths. Slow it down now. Slow it down.*

"I think he came in here. Check over there."

"I don't see anyone, Pa. Why do we care about this kid? Let's just get the furniture and leave."

"No, he's got something in that sack. I wanna know what it is."

Stanley stays quiet. He peers out the window behind him. It's about a twelve-foot drop. He moves slowly towards the window and kicks something with his foot. The jug. It rolls along the wooden floor of the loft. *Damnit.*

"He's up in the loft, Pa. Looks like he pulled the ladder up with him. Let's just go."

"Come down here, boy. Phil, bring me that bench. I'll boost you up there."

Stanley tosses the jug into the sack and sits on the window sill. Okay. One, two, three … He leaps from the window and rolls as he hits the ground. He sprints towards the apple orchard. "Don't look back. Don't look back. Just run."

"Do you see anything?"

"He ain't up here. He must have jumped out that window and ran off. He's gone, Pa. Can't we just get the furniture and leave?"

"There he goes. Through that orchard. Get after him, boy."

Stanley darts through the trees in the apple orchard. He turns to see if the men are following him. He stops for a moment and picks a couple ripe apples. He places one in his sack and chomps a bite out of the other.

"Ha. There's no way that old fart and his fat son are going to catch me. They can barely run."

Stanley disappears into the woods and makes his way towards the railroad tracks. The B & O runs through Southington every day. A train is sure to come along within the hour. They always do.

Stanley walks along the tracks. "Those old hogs must have gave up." A whistle shrills in the distance. Puffs of white smoke rise above the tree line. He steps into the cover of some brush and waits.

The train slows on a curve of the track. As it passes, he grabs a rung of a steel ladder and hops into an empty railcar. He plops against a dirty wooden wall. His stomach churns and gurgles. "Let's see what we got in here. Hm. Pickled eggs for lunch? Why not?"

Papa's blade was always sharp. *Mm. Rubbery eggs never tasted so good.*

His stomach satisfied, he bunches the burlap sack into a ball and stretches out. The droning hum of the tracks numbs his mind into deep relaxation. *I promise Mama. I'll get them out of there. I'll take care of them ...*

Stanley finds himself in the middle of a golden wheat field. Grains of wheat flow in perfect rhythm with the gentle breeze. He hears Sophie screaming. He runs through the fields searching but can't find her. He yells for her, but the screams continue. When he finds her, the skies boil with black clouds. He sees the silhouette of his father holding her upside-down and beating her mercilessly. Blood runs from her mouth. She wails and begs for mercy. He rushes to help her, but he can't reach her. Billowing black clouds engulf him and he is pulled into a black void.

***

A whistle blasts. He jumps. "What? Ouch." The back of his head throbs after slamming into the wooden wall behind him. The train seems to be slowing. The air is frigid. Much colder than when he hopped the train. *How long have I been asleep? It's like an icebox in here.*

He pushes off of the wall to help himself stand. His left knee buckles. Prickly pins shoot through his wobbly leg. "C'mon, blood. Get back in there."

He grabs his burlap sack and drags his limp leg to the open car door. His feet dangle out the door as he attempts to gather any clues to help him learn of his whereabouts. "Looks like a freight yard of some sort."

What's that say?" *86th Street and Burley. Patches of snow on the ground. Swell. Going to be even colder here. Where the hell am I?*

He jumps off, nearly collapsing from underestimating the condition of his shaky leg. A blast of chilly wind blows through his body. He shivers and his teeth chatter. Icy gusts continue to assault his exposed skin and face. "Not dressed for this kind of weather. I gotta get out of this damn cold. Holy shit."

"What's that over there? Smoke? Where there's smoke there's got to be some heat, right?"

Just follow the smoke. He hunkers down in an alley near an old building and opens a can of peaches. He devours the fruit making sure he drinks every last drop of the sweet juice. He tosses the empty can down the alley.

Shivering turns to shaking. Gotta get warm somewhere.

He continues along the alley toward smoke stacks in the distance. He peeks inside some rusted-out trash barrels along the way looking for anything useful. An old blanket, maybe? A tarp? Something or someone yanks him by the collar.

"Whoa." He drops his sack and is face to face with a dirty bum dressed in rags and a heavy pea coat. He's being choked by a stinky ragged glove. His back is pushed against the wall. *Do something.*

"Whatcha got in the bag you little shit?" The combination of alcohol and rotten teeth cause Stanley to gag.

Papa always said to attack first. I've had enough of this bullshit.

Rage, caused by years of taking beatings from Papa catches fire in his heart. *No more. Nobody is going to do that shit to me anymore. Nobody.*

Stanley lands a swift kick to the man's groin. The old bum recoils. He grabs a handful of greasy hair and smashes the heel of his hand into the bum's face just like Papa taught him. The bum falls backwards onto the gravel, blood pouring out his shattered nose.

"I need that coat." He pounces and drives both knees into the old bum's chest. Stanley beats the man's face with swift blows until the bum is out cold. Years of boxing lessons and beatings have taught him well. He's a street fighter now.

Stanley rips the heavy overcoat off the bum's grungy body. The warmth from the coat calms his shivering almost instantly. He searches the man's pockets and finds an old silver pocket watch and thirteen cents in change. *It works. Looks expensive. Probably stolen.*

The semi-conscious old man lies moaning on the ground bleeding from the nose and mouth. Several bloody teeth lay on the gravel next to him as tiny witnesses. Stanley leaves him there and makes his way out of the alley.

Smokestacks sit atop several huge buildings. It's a mill. A steel mill. A large sign hangs over a dirt road leading into the mill. It reads *United States Steel – USS – South Works, Chicago, Illinois.*

He gasps. "Chicago? What?" Stanley, follows the road past a chain-link fence and walks into a small wooden office building to get out of the weather. A burly Polish man flips around in his chair. He wrinkles his brow, cocks his head and stares.

"Are you lost boy?"

"Is there anything I can do around here to earn some money, or some food, sir?"

The man belts out a loud guffaw. "Well, what can you do?"

"I can do anything you need me to do, sir. I'm good with my hands. I've worked on a farm all my life."

The man, crosses his thick burly arms and glares. He's thinking. A stoic face turns into a big grin.

"How old are you boy?"

Stanley lies. "Sixteen."

The man chuckles. "Sixteen? Come back in morning. Six o'clock."

The man points to the door. "Now, get da hell out of here. I'm busy. Oh, and boy. Don't be late."

Stanley wanders around the local area and finds a saloon. Hot tea and a warm dinner and a room for the night. What else could a nearly thirteen-year old boy on the lam from Southington, Ohio ask for?

Dear Lord, please bless this meal and this place where I rest my head tonight. Thanks for watching over me and helping me win that fight. Please protect Sophie, Frank, Annie and Billy. And please keep Mama safe. Amen.

CHAPTER EIGHT

One minute till six. The office is empty. "Hello? Hello? Anyone here?" *Damn. Hope I'm not too late.*

"You're late. Come with me boy ... and leave bag on table." Stanley follows the Polish man he met yesterday into the heart of the steel mill.

"My name Sebastian Kozlowski. Call me *Koz*, boy. What's your name?"

I can't tell him my real name. "Stanley. Stanley ... um ... Miller"

Koz scoffs. "Stanley Miller. And you want to work in mill, Miller? Is dat your real name? Uh. Who cares? Okay, Miller. I take you to see blast furnace. Then show you what you be doing today. Okay? You work for me. Understand? I pay you ninety-seven cents per hour. Eight-hour days, six-day week."

"Yes sir. I understand." Stanley's stomach gurgles.

"Boy, you eat anything this morning? You hungry?"

"Uh ... no sir. I didn't eat."

"I see. You have place to stay? Where you sleep last night?"

"I-I, uh, found a room up the street ... at a saloon."

Koz stops walking. He reaches in his pocket and pulls out a green apple. He polishes the fruit on his jacket and hands it to Stanley.

Stanley humbly accepts the fruit. "Thanks, Koz."

"I have extra room in house. I think you ... maybe living in street. You stay with me, maybe help around house." Koz smacks him on the back. Stanley stumbles a couple steps forward. *This guy doesn't know his own strength.*

"That's okay, Koz. I'm fine. I can find a place to live and take care of myself."

"Ah, you proud boy. Pride not put food in belly nor roof over head. You want job, you stay with me. Agreed?"

Stanley lowers his head then slowly nods. "Yes sir. Agreed."

"You Polish, Miller? Wife makes damn good kielbasa. You like kielbasa?"

"Yes sir. I ate a lot of kielbasa and eggs back home."

When Koz grins, his cheeks puff out, his eyes squint and his face and the top of his bald head turn cherry. He's as wide as he is tall and solid as a tree stump.

"Ah, then you *are* Polish." He slaps Stanley on the shoulder, knocking him sideways. "I like you Miller. I think you do just fine here. But … we'll see."

"This is blast furnace. Very hot." Koz hands him a broom and a shovel. "Today you clean this area. Tomorrow we shall see. I'm short one bar catcher. Let's see how you do. You prove yourself first. I be back at end of day. Any questions? Ah, don't ask."

Where to start. There's a ton of shit on this floor. Damn.

"Holy shit, it's hot in here." Beads of sweat are already forming on Stanley's brow and he hasn't even begun to work yet. He shovels piles of dirt, soot and debris into several rusted fifty-five-gallon metal drums. Scraping, shoveling, emptying. Over and over until the floor reveals itself. Sweep shit into small piles. Scrape, shovel, empty. Over, and over.

"I'm drenched." He runs his finger up his forearm. "Where'd this ashy grease come from?" His stomach rumbles. Grit burns his throat. "I'm going to finish cleaning up this crap if it kills me." He pauses for a moment, pulls the apple Koz gave him from his pocket and devours it. He tosses the core into one of the barrels.

***

Koz returns at the end of the shift. He stands arms crossed and scowls as he stares at the empty floor. He checks the barrels and glares at Stanley.

Say something. I busted my ass all day. Why does he look angry?

"Miller. No way did I expect you to finish all 'dis. You must be crazy boy. Very nice job. Very nice."

"Thank you, sir. Could I get a drink of water? I've swallowed a ton of this junk all day."

"Of course. Of course. I forget to show you where water is. Follow me."

Warm water never tasted so good. A splash of water runs over his hair pushing dirt and soot into his eyes. "This crap is all over everything. I can't see."

"Ha-ha. Here Miller. Use hanky to wipe eyes."

"Thanks." Stanley chugs another cup of water.

"Slow down, boy. You get tummy ache. Okay. Time to take you home and clean you up. You meet wife."

Koz walks Stanley to his automobile. "Hop in, boy."

"Steel mill been good to me. Been foreman ... twelve years. Wife and I immigrate from Poland ... um, 1903. Mill provides home for us as benefit. We have plenty room. You take extra bedroom. Deal?"

"I appreciate that very much. You have any children, Koz?"

"No. No children. We try, but no work out. Wife thirty-five now. Too old."

Koz's home is a modest one. Two-stories, blue shingles and a small porch. "Here's my home. Now your home."

Koz's wife greets them with a large pitcher of ice tea. She's a tall, slender woman with short blonde hair, bright green eyes and near-perfect facial features.

Wow, she's really pretty. What's she doing with Koz? Ha.

"Hello. I'm Frances. Would you like some tea?"

"Nice to meet you ma'am. I'm Stanley." He empties the glass in a single gulp.

Frances' eyes widen. "Wow. I'm flattered. Koz didn't you give this poor boy anything to drink today?"

"Yes, yes. Boy just work hard. Very hard worker."

"Come along gentlemen, wash up, please. I have supper waiting for you inside." A familiar scent of kielbasa and Sauer Kraut fills the air. A painful reminder of the home he no longer has.

"I haven't had a real dinner like this in weeks. Thank you, ma'am."

"Stanley, would you like a szarlotka for dessert?"

"What is that exactly?"

"It's a Polish dessert. Sort of a cake made with apples. Taste it. Tell me what you think. And please call me Frances."

"That's damn good ... uh, I mean ... that's delicious."

"Glad you enjoy it. Here. It's much better with a tall glass of cold milk."

Tastes like apple pie, but cakier with a crunch on top. "The scor … lada was delicious. Thank you again."

Frances giggles. "It's szarlotka. Sar-Lot-Ka. Let me show you where you can bathe and where you'll be sleeping." Stanley follows Frances up a set of carpeted stairs. The home has a pleasant scent to it. An aroma of spice or a combination of spices. It's hard to identify which ones. Sort of a cinnamon and vanilla scent and something else. Frances also keeps a very neat and tidy home. Everything seems to be in its place.

"I appreciate this. Thank you both so much for taking me into your home."

"You're welcome." Frances crosses her arms and eyeballs Stanley from head to toe. She puckers her lips and slightly squints. "Koz said you were sixteen. How old are you *really*?"

"I'm sixteen. I swear."

"When's your birthday?"

"November fourteenth."

"So, you'll be seventeen soon?"

"Oh no, I'm almost sixteen … I meant."

Frances nods her head. She raises a discerning eyebrow. "Uh-hu. Goodnight, Stanley."

It's amazing how hot running water can easily remove grease and grime. A luxury the farm never had. The heat penetrates and relaxes tired muscle fiber and eases a weary mind.

***

"Miller. Wake up boy. Time to go."

"What the hell? I just closed my eyes."

Koz drives Stanley to the entrance of the steel mill just before ten in the evening. A young Irishman meets them at the gate.

"Boy, that's Brian Fitzpatrick. Go with him. He'll teach you what you need to know."

"Brian. Here is new man. Stanley Miller. Very hard worker."

Dang, this fella's tall. Red handlebar mustache. Are those scars on his forearms?

"I hear yer our new Catcher, lad?"

"What's a Catcher?"

Brian jerks his head. "Well if ya don't know, yer about to find out, lad. I hope you can stand the heat. I'm yer partner. I'm called a Rougher. You lad, are the *Bar Catcher*. We work together as partners rolling the steel. I roll it through the roller, and you catch it on the other side. Am I making sense? Well, by the look on yer face, I'm not so sure."

The sweltering heat of the bar mill is suffocating. It sucks the air out of your lungs and the steals the moisture from your throat. Your skin is on fire and your eyes dry out like a sandy arid desert. You're left with an unquenchable thirst and a pounding head.

"Here ya go, boy. These are yer tongs. And here are yer gloves. To protect yer hands, ya know. Try not to touch the metal. It'll melt the skin right off yer bones."

The first pair of cherry-red bar steel slides out of the furnace. The Heater passes it to Brian. Brian pushes the bars through the rollers to Stanley.

"Yer working like an old pro, lad. Keep it up."

The work isn't much harder than farm work. The difference is, farm work doesn't require a person to work in front of a raging inferno. It wears a body down quick. Keeping up with the crew for hours is an extreme challenge for anyone working near the gates of hell, let alone a twelve-year-old boy.

"This will be the last set before we take a short break over a pint."

On the final return, Stanley catches his left forearm on the hot metal. "Son of a bitch." *Nobody saw that. Good.*

Bottles clanking and ice rustling signal the sounds of breaktime.

"Here lad. You've earned it." Stanley reaches for his first beer. "Lad. I warned ya to be careful. What happened to yer arm?" Brian removes a wooden box from a metal tool shed. "Here, let me wipe some salve on that wound. Ya earned yer first stripe like a man. Makes ya official."

"Let's go boys. Breaktime is over."

The fire from the furnace steals a person's energy like a wraith from hades. The pace is grueling. The heat unbearable. Relaxing for even a second can have dire consequences.

"Lad, ya look a wee bit pale. Here. Take this bucket and walk over there. Spew what's ailing ya. You'll feel better. Then get back to work. We'll wait fer ya."

Stanley hurls every ounce of fluid and solids from the bottom of his gut into the pail. It sucks the last of his energy from his young body, but also provides relief from the nausea. He finishes the last set of hot metal.

Koz appears at the end of the shift. "Brian. How did boy do?"

"He was a bit wonky at first, but he caught on fast."

"Let's go Miller. Time to go home."

Ninety-seven cents per hour working six eight-hour shifts is forty-six dollars and fifty-six cents per week. Minus tax, leaves around forty dollars. Assuming I can keep all my earnings, it's going to take almost a year to save the two-thousand dollars I figure we need. That's too long and I might be dead by then.

***

SUNDAY, NOVEMBER 14, 1920 - Stanley's thirteenth birthday. No work today. His first month at South Works passed quickly. Birthdays aren't often celebrated in Polish tradition, so Stanley doesn't mention it.

"Good morning, Frances. Something smells good."

"Scrambled eggs, potato pancakes and kielbasa. Have a seat."

Stanley glances around the room. "Where's Koz?"

"He's out back chopping fire wood. We ate already while you slept. So, go ahead. Enjoy your breakfast."

The backdoor swings open. Koz is red in the face and out of breath. He looks like a bald Saint Nick. "I'm too old for 'dis crap. Miller, you chop wood. Make Koz's life easier."

"Ha-ha, Koz. I think you need the exercise more than me, by the size of your belly."

"Funny. You funny boy. Put coat on. Join me outside for hot tea." Koz pours two cups of tea and walks out the backdoor.

"Thank you for breakfast, Frances. I'm really full." He wipes his mouth with his sleeve and follows Koz. They sit on an old wooden bench. Steam boils over the cups of tea into the chilly air.

"Miller, I never ask you. Where you from boy?"

"Ohio. Southington. It's near Warren."

Koz nods and sips. "You very long way from home. Why come to Chicago? Where family? Parents?"

Stanley sips and swallows. He sighs a little. "Papa is dead and Mama sits in a prison cell." He takes a long sip. "My brothers and sisters and I were sent to an orphanage in Warren. I ran away and hopped a train. I had no idea where it was headed. It brought me here. I want to get back to Warren and rescue them from that hellhole. They're my responsibility now." Moisture wells in his eyes and a tear runs down his cheek. He wipes the tear and turns his face away from Koz.

Koz nods and pats him on the shoulder. "You good boy, Miller. No, you good man. That takes big balls and very, very much love. Nothing more important than family." Koz strokes his chin. "Let me help you and family."

"You and Mrs. Kozlowski have already done so much to help me. I couldn't let you do that."

Koz sips. He takes a deep breath and places a burly hand on Stanley's knee. "Boy, what you know about hooch?"

Stanley grins. "Papa used to cook a home brew in our cellar on the farm. He'd sell it in the Polish neighborhoods. He'd never drink it himself. Vodka and whiskey. Those were his drinks."

Koz points a meaty finger at Stanley. "Now dats interesting. What if I tell you, I want to give you … second job? I need good man I can trust. You make twice in one day, what you make in one week at steel mill. You keep job at steel mill but maybe be driver for me. What you think of dat?"

Stanley shrugs his shoulders. "I don't know how to drive, Koz."

"Ahh, dats no problem. I teach you. I teach you to drive. Sound good? By look on face, I think is good deal."

"Koz, you're crushing my hand."

"When you save enough money, you go back and save family. I understand. You come back anytime. You always have job here with me."

"I … I don't know what to say."

"Say *yes*. Now let's go back inside, Huh? I'm freezing my balls off out here."

"Honey Bunny, boy and I going for drive. Be back in few hours."

Frances glares and places her hands on her hips. "I'll have lunch for you boys when you return. Stay out of trouble. And come home hungry."

Koz, nods. "Ya, ya, no worries my love. See you in a while."

"Okay, sit in driver's seat. Ever drive tractor?"

"A few times."

"Okay good. Dis similar but not same. See pedals? Brake on right, reverse in middle, clutch on left. Okay? Use left hand for dis switch. Down to go, up to slow. Use right hand for throttle. Down open, up close. Easy, right? All you need is fancy footwork and good hands. This lever is handbrake. Up for neutral, forward for go."

"Okay, right pedal is brake, middle reverse and this one is clutch. This is the throttle and this one fires the engine. How do we start it?"

"I demonstrate. Let me get out first. See. Pull choke, turn crank quarter turn, clockwise. Do slowly. Dis primes engine. Okay, turn key to *battery*. Push left switch up, pull throttle down a little bit. Put lever in neutral."

"Got it. Now what?"

"Now I crank like dis."

The rumble of the engine stirs a nervous energy in his being. His heart thumps with excitement. *Okay, I got this ... I hope.*

"Okay, Miller let's go. Put into gear. When speed reach twenty miles per hour, double-shift into second. Go, go, go ..."

Stanley, drives along the dirt road jerking and jumping all over the place until the engine stalls. "Try again boy. Relax. You got dis."

They start the engine a second time. He double-shifts. Metal grinds on metal making an awful screech.

"Easy now. Shift faster boy. Okay, you doing great. Stay calm." Koz looks out his window and rolls his eyes.

Holy shit, I'm driving. I can't describe it. The wind blowing in my face. The vibration of the engine and the bumps from the road below. All the pedals and levers and switches. It's like trying to dance and rig a fishing line all at the same time.

"On days for delivery, we go to docks. There is vegetable truck parked full of whiskey, beer, gin and other liquor in hidden bottom. I drop you off. You drive truck to place of business. Understand?"

"What kind of place is it?"

"You know what *speakeasy* is? Called speakeasy cuz we don't speak about in public. Also called *blind pig* or *blind tiger*. Don't ask me why. Maybe cuz someone goes blind. Prohibition, you know. Park around back and leave truck. Knock on door and say, *delivery*. Walk back to road, where I pick you up. When I get paid, you get paid. Easy enough, right?"

"Where's the speakeasy?"

"No worry, Miller. First time, you follow me. Okay? Now let's go home. Wife will have big lunch waiting for us. Hope you hungry, boy."

***

Two-forty-five early Monday morning. "Come on lad, keep up. You're sluggish tonight. We need ya to concentrate man."

Sluggish. Grime, sweat and sweltering heat will do that to you. Not to mention the thought of rum running. Making a lot more money, just driving an automobile full of illegal liquor around town in the cool air. *What the hell is Koz doing here this late?*

"Are you ready for first run, Miller?"

Stanley wipes his brow with his sleeve and removes his gloves. *Finally. Something fun to do.*

"Yeah, I'm ready. Let's go."

***

They arrive at the docks of Lake Michigan. "Miller, that's your truck. The keys are under floorboard. Follow me to delivery location."

The streets are quiet. Yet, the night is alive with renewed energy. The sounds of his boots sloshing beneath him are a reminder of the bitter wet cold. Strange how the air doesn't feel so cold when you just stepped out of a blazing furnace. The opposite sensations are an invigorating slap to one's senses.

Under the floorboard? I ain't seeing 'em. Shit. Oh, there. Okay. "Alright. I got this."

The rumbling of the engine and both hands on the wheel provides a rush of power and control to his spirit. Double-clutch into second. There you go. Damn, this truck is noisy. Delivering vegetables at three in the morning isn't crazy, right?

Driving on empty streets in the middle of the night makes the engine sound a hundred times louder. "He's stopping. That must be it." *The Old Chicago Inn.*

Okay. Down the alley. Looks like as good a spot as any to park. Leave the keys on the floorboard.

The small black rear door to the Old Chicago Inn is hard to make out in a dark alley surrounded by dirty brick walls. It's also a nice place to get mugged and your ass kicked.

Knock, knock, knock. *Anyone in there? Seems deserted. Do I knock again?*

Knock, knock.

A slot in the door slides open. "What do want, punk?"

"Delivery."

A short pause. "Where's the key?"

"I left it in the truck."

"Well go get it, dumbass. Bring it to me."

He runs to the truck and grabs the key and takes it back to the voice behind the door. He slips it through the slot into a gnarly hand. The hand grabs the key and slams the slot closed.

"I guess that's it. Shit. That was easy."

He jogs to Koz's automobile.

"Everything good Miller?"

He nods. "Too easy, Koz."

Koz peels out into the darkness headed back to South Works. He leaves Stanley at the entrance so he can finish his shift.

***

His bed never looked so inviting as it does this morning. No time for a bath. Just sleep.

"An envelope?" *Something from Frances, maybe?*

"What the hell? All Twenties." *One, two ... eighty dollars?*

"Holy shit."

He stuffs the bills into a sock and slides it under the mattress. He lays on the bed, hands folded behind his head. Fast, easy cabbage. An answer to a prayer.

The sock grows fat. Another sock is added. Months pass. Two fat socks are full of twenty-dollar bills and change. It's time to go back to Warren.

CHAPTER NINE

WEDNESDAY, MARCH 9, 1921 - HOMECOMING – Over five months have passed since escaping the orphanage. Stanley shuts the door and empties the contents of the money socks onto the bed. "Two-thousand, eight-hundred and fifty-five dollars. What?"

He rolls the bills into tight wads and tucks them neatly back into the socks. He drops the socks into the burlap sack along with the rest of his belongings. He checks his timepiece. 8:17 a.m.

Living with Koz and Frances the past several months has been more than just a blessing and a safe haven. It's been a place to hide from memories that torture and torment his mind and spirit. A place to build inner strength by reflecting on the past. And maybe … just maybe, come to terms with the reality that his life has changed. Changed forever. It's time to go home.

He descends the stairs with the sack over his shoulder and his peacoat under his arm. He walks into the kitchen where Koz and Frances are eating breakfast.

Frances smiles. "You want some breakfast, honey? Wait. Are you going somewhere?"

Koz stops eating. He places his fork on the table. He stares for a moment in silence, then nods and rises from his seat. "Time to rescue family?"

A well of tears blurs Stanley's vision. A small cramp sits at the base of his throat making it hard to swallow. "I'd love some breakfast. Then I have to go."

Koz grasps Stanley's shoulders and looks him directly in the eyes. He scowls, then grins. "I understand, son." Koz hugs him, squeezing the air out of him. He pats him on the back and fights back tears of his own.

Frances steps in front of Koz. Her embrace gives Stanley's heart the permission he needed to be able to leave in good spirits.

"I'm going to miss you both. You've been so good to me and I can never repay either of you for everything you've done for me. I will come back someday soon to visit you both. I promise."

"Sit Miller. Eat breakfast. Can't leave on empty stomach. After breakfast, I take you to railway station. You ride train home in style, not hop train like bum."

Frances' kielbasa and scrambled eggs with bacon bits never tasted so good. Freshly baked buns still steam beneath the napkin of a wicker basket. And fresh-brewed tea to wash it all down.

Leaving both of them behind is bittersweet. But, the journey back to the orphanage can't wait. There's one goal. One focus. Sophie, Frank, Annie and Billy. He's had to put them out of his mind these past months to keep from going insane with anxiety. But now they are all he thinks about.

Stanley places his fork and napkin on his empty plate. He grabs his old burlap sack and slings it over his shoulder. "Thank you for breakfast. I'm going to miss you, Frances."

Frances' lower lip trembles. "Wait. I have something for you." She reaches into a closet by the front door and hands him a brown leather valise. "Here. Put your things in this instead of that dreadful bag. My gift to you."

Stanley chuckles. "Thank you." He shoves the burlap sack into the valise and kisses Frances on the cheek.

"Let's go Miller."

Frances sits tall on the porch waving. She dabs the right corner of her eye with a kerchief as they drive away.

"I can't thank you enough for taking me in and giving me a job, Koz. I'll never forget you or Frances."

"Okay, Miller. Try not to make old man cry. Leave me some dignity. You good boy and I wish you all da best for family. And don't be stranger. Come visit. Anytime. You always welcome in my home. You family too."

The clock tower and pink granite of the Dearborn terminal is a magnificent sight as they pull into the station. "This your stop. Here's five bucks ... to pay for ride home."

"I can't take that. I have money. I can buy my own ticket."

"You hurt Koz's feelings. Take money. You have telephone number and address. Write sometime. Let me know if you ever need anything. Anything at all."

"You're crushing my hand again, Koz."

Koz's eyes glisten. He nods and winks. "Now get the hell out of here."

***

"One-way ticket to Warren, Ohio please."

Sitting on a seat and looking out the window is a much different view than lying in a dirty railcar. The beautiful scenery flies by in a blur. The hours pass like minutes.

As Warren comes into view, he sets his valise in his lap in anticipation of the stop. His foot taps the floor in a rapid steady rhythm as he stares out the window at the familiar sites and the Ohio countryside.

He deboards the train and sets his valise on the ground long enough to slip into his peacoat. It's a brisk forty-something degrees. He notices a group of taxi cabs parked along the sidewalk waiting for potential fares to approach.

I have to see the farmhouse. Figure everything out from there.

"Taxi. Can you take me to Southington?"

"Any address in particular?"

"The edge of town will do."

"You got it son. Hop in."

The drive is quiet and quick. He hands the cabbie a couple greenbacks and exits the vehicle.

Southington, Ohio. He closes his eyes breathing in the country air. He walks along the railroad tracks towards the old farmhouse. There is nothing in the world that can compare to the smell of home. Feeling the rich dirt beneath your feet. Seeing familiar sights and hearing familiar sounds touches the spirit with a comforting warmth like no other. Yet, at the same time they stir up troubling memories and powerful emotions from the past.

"Hey, the old market store."

A peach, bread, milk ... um, candy sticks and a newspaper.

"Thank you, sir."

"Hey, don't I know you, kid?"

"No sir. I don't believe so. I'm from Chicago."

***

The old farm sits void of the life that once thrived here. The buzz of a few insects can be heard. Wispy soft winds blow over dirt fields. Fields no longer full of crops. The wind chills his nose and cheeks with its kiss. The sky is white and gray with swirling clouds and there's a soft peaceful rumble in the distance promising rain.

The old barn. Beams of light shine through gaps in its weathered boards, bathing the floors and walls with soft illumination. He climbs into the loft and sets his valise on a mound of old hay. He sits on its creaky floorboards and closes his eyes.

Waves of emotion flood through his inner being. Tears well then stream. Cold wetness rolling down his cheeks. He lies against the floor and curls into a ball. His chest is numb. His breathing is ragged. He cries and laments. Moaning and bawling. Allowing all the hurt, fear and torment in his broken heart to be unchained and freed from their prison.

Papa. Why did this have to happen? Oh Mama. Why? If only I could go back in time. I would have stopped you. I would have begged you not to.

Trembling sighs turn to deep yawns. The damn broke. It needed to break. Soft pitter-patters ping off the tin roof. Thunder rumbles in the distance. The strong earthy smell of rain permeates the air.

He wipes his eyes and face. The smooth coolness of milk soothes the rawness in his throat. He removes a T-shirt from his valise and balls it into a pillow. A storm approaches. Strange how the majestic violence of thunder and lightning purifies the heart like the voice of God calling to your spirit. The droning rumble carries the mind into the deepest and most relaxing of slumbers.

***

A loud crack echoes in the middle of the night.

A bullet hole oozes blood down the side of his father's head. He stares at Stanley with empty sorrowful eyes, then slowly turns and fades into the darkness.

Stanley gasps for air sitting upright. He listens to the steady rain coming down outside the barn. *Was I dreaming?* A dark shadowy figure stands beside him. A paralyzing chill grips his being. He can't move. He whispers. "Papa?"

His father stares at him with dark empty eyes. Thunder crashes and a bright flash lights up the barn. He keeps his eyes closed tightly. *God, please make him go away.* He peeks through a slit in one eye, then exhales. Nobody there. Burying his head beneath his heavy coat he inhales then slowly exhales, calming his frazzled nerves.

***

The early morning sun bathes the loft with its warmth. Soft beams of light peek through gaps and cracks in the walls and ceiling of the old barn. The air is damp with the scent of wet hay. The rafters come into focus. *Did that really happen last night? Or did I dream that?*

He descends the loft and walks towards the farmhouse. The old well pump still works. Ice cold. He fills his empty milk bottle and guzzles the pure clean water to quench his rabid thirst. He wanders over to the front of the farmhouse.

Seems like forever since I sat on these steps. Wonder who took the old rocker? That old piece of crap was ready to fall apart.

"What's in the news? Hm. Need to find an automobile and a house."

Damn this peach is juicy. "What? You again? You're lucky I never ate you for breakfast, ya varmint. Here you go. You like peaches? Oh, you just wanted the pit. Well at least *you* still have a home here. Yeah, go back and hide in your tree. I never liked you either. Beggar."

Stanley scours the newspaper ads section. Two ads catch his eye.

FOR SALE: 1915 Chevy 490 Touring in excellent condition. $275 cash. Call WA-4437 and ask for Jack.

FOR RENT: 4-bedroom 2-bath colonial home fully furnished in nice neighborhood. $25 per month. Gray Avenue, Youngstown. Deposit required. Call YT-2278 and ask for Mr. Williams.

The newspaper fits neatly in his back pocket. *Alright. Three-hour walk back to Warren.* The air is pure and fresh after last night's rainstorm. It's a beautiful day in spite of the forty-nine-degree temperature. He walks along the driveway and onto the old country road, he and Sophie used to walk, delivering milk or exploring the countryside.

"I can't wait to see you all again."

***

Stanley walks into a local market in Warren. "May I use your telephone?"

The clerk points. "It's five cents per call."

A nickel drops into the slot. He picks up the phone and dials.

"Yes, I'm interested in your Touring. Is it still for sale? I have the cash."

"Sure. It's still for sale. What's your name?"

"Stanley Miller. I'm at Johnson's Market. Can you meet me here?"

"Sure. I know where that is. See you in twenty."

A second nickel drops into the slot.

"Koz. This is Stanley."

"Miller! How are you boy? Miss us already, huh?"

"I'm doing good. I need your help."

"Anything. Just ask."

"I need a house to rent … for when I get my family out of that orphanage. I found one in Youngstown I can afford."

"You have telephone number? I make call for you. I have friends in Youngstown. Well, more like acquaintances."

"The number is YT-2278. Ask for Mr. Williams. The place is on Gray avenue."

"Okay. Let me make call. Call me back in one hour."

"Thanks, Koz. I really appreciate it."

A roadmap. Might come in handy.

"That'll be fifty-cents."

Map in hand, he walks outside and relaxes on an old wrought-iron garden chair. *Youngstown. Looks like I take Market Street most the way.*

About a half-hour later a black Chevy Touring drives up to the store. A heavyset man steps out. "Stanley? Stanley Miller?"

"That's me. I'm Stanley, sir. We spoke on the telephone."

The man folds his arms and frowns. "I'm Jack. How old are you son?"

"I'm eighteen, sir. Can I take it for a spin?"

"You don't look eighteen. More like thirteen or fourteen. You even know how to drive?"

"How many thirteen-year-olds have scars on their arms from working in a steel mill? Hand me the key and we'll find out if I can drive."

Jack pauses then bursts into laughter, tossing him the key. "I hope you have the two-seventy-five kid. Give it a spin."

The engine fires. Stanley lifts the hood. "Runs smooth. Looks clean."

"It's in perfect condition, son. Go ahead. Take it around the block."

Stanley drives up the road and around the block and returns, parking near the front of the market.

"Would you take two-twenty-five?"

Jack grimaces and rubs his bristly chin. "Two-sixty is the lowest I'll go, kid. I have other people interested."

Stanley sighs and hands him the cash. Jack shoves the bills into his pocket. The two shake hands and Jack walks into the market store.

Stanley returns to the metal chair. Time drags, when you're waiting and impatient.

He glances at his timepiece. "Okay. That's about an hour. Sir, can I use your telephone again?"

"You don't have to ask, young man. It's a pay phone."

"Hey, Koz ..."

"I spoke to Mr. Williams. He has house waiting for you. Just meet him there, give him money. You good to go. No questions asked."

"Thank you so much. I owe you."

"Ba-ha. Yes, you do, Miller. You be careful now. You hear me?"

"I will. Thanks again. Tell Frances I said, 'Hi'."

He fires up the engine, shifts into gear and drives off.

"Youngstown, here I come. Thank you, Koz."

***

Mr. Williams is waiting on the porch steps when he arrives. "Nice car. Are you Mr. Miller?"

"Yes, sir. Here's the twenty-five dollars for the rent."

Mr. Williams squints and scratches his head. "Well ... there is a deposit required. Another twenty-five. Your friend said you were eighteen. Look a tad young to me."

"I understand. Here's fifty. And I just turned eighteen."

Mr. Williams pockets the cash and pulls a rolled-up document from his back pocket. "Your friend vouched for you. This is a copy of the lease agreement. Read it and keep it in a safe place. Mr. Kozlowski has agreed to sign the lease and take responsibility. I'll make those arrangements with him. You have my number if you need anything, Mr. Miller. You'll find the place is fully furnished. Welcome to your new home."

The housekey in his hand doesn't seem real. *How is this possible? I can never repay all the kindness and generosity Koz has shown.* Angels appear in our lives from the most peculiar places and sometimes in the most unlikely of people. Koz isn't a saint by any means, but he's everything a father should be.

***

Dawn peeks through the sheer curtains in his new home. The tic-toc of the clock he fell asleep to last night becomes clear and in focus again. Everything is falling into place so easily. Too easily. It rattles the nerves a bit. Today is Friday. The time to rescue his family has arrived.

Back on Market Street. *My first automobile. Sophie and Frank are going to shit beans when they see this. Just got to figure a way to get them all out of there.*

The orphanage sits shaded and quiet. A calmness masking the sadness behind its walls. A nauseous feeling churns in his gut. Five months have felt like five years.

"There's my window." *I hope you're both still in there.* He parks his automobile around the block. He cases the grounds. *I'll just stick around till dark.*

CHAPTER TEN

The click of opening and closing a pocket watch is gratifying in an odd sort of way. 9:42. It's plenty dark enough. The grounds appear deserted.

Stanley walks along Market Street. He buttons his coat and pulls a stocking cap over his ears. He stealthily moves from shadow to shadow along the walls of the orphanage and thick trees. Lights out was at eight o'clock. A single light glows in the reception room of the dorms. He scampers across the lawn toward the brick wall of the dorms and makes his way near the rain gutter.

The rain gutter rattles as he pulls his body upward toward the patio roof. The metal bites his fingers. Reach. *Just grab the roof. Pull yourself up. C'mon ... shit.*

He mumbles. "I gotta rest for a minute. Holy crap. Going up that thing is way harder than going down."

He tip-toes across the roof, staying close to the left wall until he reaches the window. It's hard to keep from shivering. "It's locked. Shit."

He peers inside. The darkness of the room reveals shadowy figures lying on the beds. He removes his beanie and gently taps on the window pane.

Come on Frank. I'm not the boogeyman. Wake up. He continues tapping. No movement.

A light outside the bedroom door flips on, shining light beneath the space under the door and into the room. He hides against the wall next to the window. He carefully peeks. The light emanating from the hallway dimly illuminates the room. He sighs. *Is that Frank? Looks like him.*

The light goes out. He gently taps on the window pane. Frank stirs and lifts his head, and glances towards the window. He jumps. He sits frozen. Stanley motions to him to be quiet and open the window. Frank presses his face against the window pane and screams. It isn't Frank! Hallway lights go on. No time to climb down. Jump. Just like the loft window. It's about the same height.

He jumps. He feels a sickening crunch and a debilitating ache in his left ankle. His foot landed in a hole. Crawl. Hop. Get out of here!

Lights flip on outside in the yard. Voices hollering. Flashlights everywhere. He manages to stand on one leg and hops into the trees off the property, then rolls into a ditch covered in brush.

Voices approach. "Check the yard, then check the trees and bushes."

Footsteps stomp all around him. Beams of light flash overhead. Stay quiet. His heart pounds. He sucks in the icy air. Someone's coming. Hold your breath. Something slithers over his legs. Don't move, stay still.

"Don't see anyone over here. All clear." Voices mumble and begin to fade.

Slithering continues up his legs towards his torso. A black snake. One shot at this. "Get off me." He swats and kicks the reptile and scrambles out of the brush. Flashlight beams crisscross in the night. He raises himself onto one foot. His right thigh burns and cramps, carrying all his weight. He hops one step at a time towards his escape.

The engine fires. He disappears quickly into the night. Far away from the orphanage. Complete and total failure. His throbbing ankle makes it difficult to drive adding to his sense of defeat.

"Where'd they go? How the hell am I going to find 'em now? Call it a night. Just have to figure something else out tomorrow."

The ankle is purple and swelling fast. Turn it left, turn it right, point, lift. "Doesn't seem to be broken. Here goes. Oh, shit that's cold." He plunges his bare foot into a bucket of cold ice water.

***

"Hello operator. Can you connect me to the children's home in Warren, please?"

"Yes, sir. Just one moment."

Stanley rehearses. "Ahem. This is … this is her uncle …"

"Sir, I can connect you now. Go ahead."

"Um, thank you. Hello?"

"Yes, this is Sister Agnes. May I help you?"

Oh shit. Alright, alright, best man voice. "Ah, yes ma'am. This is Sophie Puchalski's uncle from Chicago. Would it be possible for me to speak with her?"

A long pause. "Sir, I can arrange for her to call you. Can I have your telephone number?"

"Well, I'm calling from a pay telephone. I don't have a telephone at home. Is there a better time I can call to speak with her?"

"I see. Is there anything I can help you with?"

"No, no. I just want to check on her and see how she and her brothers and sister are doing. I'd just like to visit with her for a bit, if that's okay."

"You mean you also want to know how your other niece and nephews are doing? If you are in town, visiting hours are Wednesday and Sunday from nine a.m. to ten a.m. Just come in and sign in."

"I'm not actually in town, ma'am. Would it just be possible to call at nine tomorrow morning and visit with her on the telephone?"

"I understand. I can arrange that. Please call back tomorrow at nine and ask for me. Sister Agnes. Oh, and does Sophie's uncle have a name?"

"Thank you, ma'am. Um, yes. It's … uh … William Younger. U-Uncle William."

"Damnit, I hope that worked. Crap."

***

"Good morning operator. Can you connect me to the Warren children's home?"

"One moment, please. Go ahead, sir."

"Hello?'

"This is Sister Agnes. May I help you?"

"Yes Sister, this is Uncle William. May I speak to Sophie Puchalski?"

"Let me retrieve her, please. You may have fifteen minutes to speak with her. Hold on."

"Hello. This is Sophie."

"Soph. It's me."

"Stanley? Where, in tarnation have you been?"

"Shh ... can anyone hear you? Call me Uncle William."

"No. I'm alone ... Uncle William. I knew it was you. We've been worried sick. We thought you weren't coming back."

"Sophie, listen. I only have fifteen minutes. I've been in Chicago. I saved a bunch of cash. I have an automobile and a place to stay. No time to explain all that. It's time to get you all out of there."

"Really? Oh, my goodness. I have so much I want to tell you."

"That'll have to wait for now. I tried to get into Frank and Billy's room last night, but another kid was in there. Where did they move the boys to?"

"What? That was you? I heard you had everyone running around looking for a burglar. They put thumbscrew locks on all our windows. Oh, and they moved Frank and Billy next door. Frank said four brothers took over their room a week after you left. So, they moved the boys into a smaller room right next to your old room."

"Smaller? Smaller than the one we were in? Okay. Before your visit is over, tell Frank I'm going to come to his window tonight after lights out. I'll tap three times. He knows where there's a tool box. Tell him to go into the hall closet and get a pair of pliers from it. He'll know what I mean. Tell him to loosen the lock on his window. Then on your Wednesday visit, Frank will slip you the pliers to unlock your window. Hide them in your room. Wednesday night I'm getting you all out of there. Understand? I'll get you and Annie first. Then Frank and Billy."

"Okay. Got it. They're telling me our time is up. Gotta go. I love you, Stanley."

***

Walking with a limp isn't the fastest way to get things done. But at least the ankle is feeling somewhat better and the swelling has gone down some. The ripped linen made a decent wrap to stabilize the ankle. It's lights out, but there's more activity than last night. The orphanage must be on high intruder alert. It's going to be risky. Stanley crouches and darts from tree to tree until he reaches the rain gutter. He pulls himself onto the roof.

Tap, tap, tap. Stanley crawls along the roof, staying hidden in the shadows. Frank grins. He removes the thumb lock. They both wiggle and shimmy the window frame just enough to allow Stanley to crawl through.

Frank cries. His body shakes. He clings to his older brother. "Stanley. I missed you. I didn't think you were coming back."

"I've missed you too little brother. We're getting out of here. I told you I'd be back."

Frank sits on the edge of the bunkbed and puts his shoes on.

"You can't come yet nitwit. Okay, here's the plan. Take the pliers and give them to Sophie when you see her on the Wednesday visit. Make sure nobody sees you. Wednesday night, I'm going to get Sophie and Annie out first. Then I'll come and get you and Billy."

Billy opens his eyes and cries.

"It's okay Billy. Shh. It's just me, Stanley."

Billy crawls out of bed and rushes into his arms. His warm little body and the familiar smell of his oily hair reminds him how much he's missed the little fart.

"Ah, Billy. I've missed, you, ya little bird turd." Stanley hugs him. "Be a good boy, okay? I'll come back for you in a couple days. I promise."

He carries Billy to his bed and tosses him onto the mattress. "Okay, go to sleep. And don't tell anyone I was here, okay? It's our little secret."

"Kay, fat hog. Hahaha."

"Ha-ha. Lay back down, now. Close your peepers, or the fat hog will eat your toes."

Stanley holds Frank's face in his hands. *Bruises. A black eye.* "Frank, who did this to you? When did this happen?"

Frank lowers his eyes. "Marco. He wanted me to touch him … in the privates … and I said no. So, he started punching me. I told you. You said Marco wouldn't bother me. He's a queer."

Stanley's jaws clench. His senses heighten. "That bastard. Is he still in the same room with Angelo?"

"Yeah. Eddie was right. He loves to hurt kids."

"Let me borrow this baseball. Give me a sock. Stay here. I'll be right back."

Stanley eases the door open and peers down the hallway. He sneaks along the wall to Marco's room. He slips inside the door and gently closes it behind him.

Marco is asleep on a bottom bunk. He checks the top. Angelo is facing the wall, snoring. He gently shakes Marco and pulls him up by the collar of his pajamas. Marco groggily moans and peers through one eye. Stanley swings the homemade club and whacks Marco in the temple. He goes limp.

Stanley grabs him under the armpits and drags him onto the floor. He strips him down to his skivvies. Angelo continues to snore. He peers out the door and down the hallway, then drags Marco out of his room.

He leaves him lying next to the stairs. Then he yanks Marco's shorts off leaving him naked. He balls up Marco's skivvies and tosses them down the flight of stairs. Marco moans and writhes. Stanley pops him again knocking him out.

He walks back to the boy's room and hugs Frank. "Don't tell anyone but Sophie that I was here. Understand?" Frank nods and grins.

Stanley opens the window. "Leave that open for a minute, okay? I have an idea." He slips back out into the hallway and tiptoes to the edge of the stairs. Marco groans. He's regaining consciousness.

Stanley peers down the stairwell. "Hey! There's a naked kid up here! Help!"

He darts into the room and closes the door. "Let's listen."

Heavy footsteps clomp up the stairs.

"Stay right there, boy. Do not move."

"I don't ... I don't know how this happened. Someone took my clothes. They left me out here in the hall. Please. Please. No."

Smack! "Get your naked ass back in that room, you little pansy." Smack! Marco screams.

Frank punches the air and whispers. "Whoopee." He crawls back into bed grinning from ear to ear.

"Gotta go now fellas. Stay in the room, okay? Let me know what happens to Marco."

He slips out the window, scales the gutter and limps back to his automobile. He bursts into laughter. "You had that coming, Marco. I hope they whipped your ass good."

***

It's Wednesday. He parks the automobile a few hundred feet up Market street. The night is chilly. His cheeks are numb from the caress of the icy breeze.

Okay, blankets in the back seat. Pipe in my pocket in case there's trouble. Rope. Sheep sling. Hope this works. God please let this work.

It's eerily quiet. Almost too quiet. The grounds are dark. A perfect night to move unnoticed like a phantom across the yard. He taps on Sophie's window and waits. There's movement in the curtains and Sophie's eyes peek through the glass. Together they slide the window open. Annie pops out first. She hugs Stanley's neck and buries her face in his chest as he carries her to safety in the woods.

"Stay here, Annie. I'll be right back. Stay quiet and don't move." Her wide round eyes stare back at him with fright. Her tiny lips pucker.

He grabs a valise and a small handbag. He helps Sophie through the window, then slides it closed without a sound. Holding hands, they scurry to where Annie is hiding.

"Take Annie to that automobile. Both of you hide under the blankets in the back seat. I'm going to get Frank and Billy. I'll be right back."

Sophie points. Her eyes blink rapidly. "That one right there?"

"Yes. Hurry. Stay in the trees. And be quiet."

He carries a rope around his right shoulder and slides his arm through the sheep sling. He slides the pipe into the back of his pants and scales the gutter onto the roof. Frank already has the window open.

"Sh. Come on fellas. Time to go." The brothers climb out onto the roof. Stanley taps Frank on the shoulder and points to the Chevy parked up the road. Frank climbs down the gutter and jumps to the ground.

"Lay down on the sling, Billy." *That's a good knot. Papa did teach me to tie a respectable knot.*

Billy giggles. "Shush. Be quiet Billy." Stanley ties the other end of the rope around his own waist.

"Frank, get ready to catch Billy." He hoists him over the side of the roof. But Billy panics. His arms flail. He screams.

"Billy shut up." The quick release of the rope burns like hot coals in Stanley's palms. The porch light turns on in the rear of the main house.

"Frank. Grab Billy. Run." Frank scoops up Billy, and disappears into the darkness.

Stuck on the roof. His heart pounds. An orderly steps onto the lawn and shines a flashlight around the perimeter. "Anybody there?" On his way back to the porch, he stops. He picks up the rope.

He shines his flashlight towards the roof. "Get your ass down off of that roof right now. Now!"

Stanley slides down the gutter. It's John Kelley. Old fish lips himself.

"Hey. I know you, you little bastard. Puchalski."

Stanley wheezes struggling to breathe with Kelly's hand squeezing his throat tighter by the second. Stanley clutches Kelley's wrist with his left hand and reaches for the pipe with his other. He swings the pipe with a quick powerful stroke desperate to break free.

Kelley's grip is broken when the pipe cracks his wrist. He squeals, grasping his arm.

"I'm going to kick your little ass, shitball."

Stanley's heart races. He wriggles free, but only for a moment. *Get to the automobile.* His hair is yanked pulling him onto his back. The weight of Kelley sitting on his chest crushes his ribs in suffocating agony. Trapped. *Where's the pipe?*

Flashes of electricity rip through his head with throbbing pain. Warm blood runs all over his face, as Kelley holds one hand on Stanley's throat and punches him in the face with the other. "This is where you die you little shit." Stanley can't breathe. He gasps, struggling to fill his lungs with precious air.

Is this really it? All this way, only to die here at the hands of this sadistic fat bastard?

Kelley's mocking voice echoes and fades. His ugly face blurs and blends into the darkness. Silence envelops him. Golden fields of wheat blow across the old farmhouse in Southington. He sits under an old oak tree with Sophie. Mama calls them into supper.

A surge of air fills his lungs. Shadows return to focus. Kelley is on the ground. *What? He ain't moving.* Sophie hovers over Kelley's limp body. She glances at Stanley and drops the pipe.

"Come on. Grab my hand. Get up." He struggles to his feet. They cling to each other and rush to the automobile. "Get in Soph."

He turns the key but the engine stalls. Again, and again, but it continues to stall.

"What's the matter Stanley? Go! Go!"

"I'm trying. The engine won't turn over."

Shouting and commotion stirs at the orphanage like an angry hill of fire ants scrambling to locate their attackers. Orderlies spread out to cover the area. Flashlights shine beams in every direction.

"Please, Hurry."

He climbs out of the vehicle and lifts the hood. Loose battery cable. There. That should do it.

Sophie cries. "They're coming this way. Hurry, hurry." Stanley leaps into the front seat. A humming vibration under the seat brings needed hope to a dire situation. "Drive. Drive away. They're coming." He slams the Chevy into gear peeling out and slinging a rooster tail of dirt and rocks at the crowd chasing after them.

They stare at each other, eyes wide and mouths agape. Annie and Frank stay hidden under the blankets holding on to one another as the Chevy speeds towards freedom into the chilly Ohio night. Billy sits on top of the blanket giggling and waving at the crowd.

**

Six o'clock in the morning. The Puchalski family is awake and stirring. An old familiar smell of breakfast fills his nostrils. The farmhouse in Southington. Those were the best breakfasts in the world. Sophie has Mama's touch for making a great meal. *Is this all real? Did we really escape? Or is this all simply a wonderful dream?*

"Hold hands everyone. You too Stanley. We need to say a special prayer and ask for the blessing of our first meal together." Sophie's eyes are wide and moist and rapidly blink. Her voice cracks with emotion.

After the prayer, Stanley taps his fork on the table. "We have to make a pact. They'll be looking for us. We have to change our name. We aren't the Puchalski family anymore. Starting today, we are the *Miller* family. Everyone swear on it. Swear it, and never talk about any of this to anyone for the rest of your life. It all has to remain our secret. We all take it to our graves and never speak of it again."

Sophie locks eyes with Stanley. "I swear."

Frank sits up in his chair. "I swear Stanley."

Annie crosses her heart. "I cross my heart and hope to die."

Billy copies Annie, crossing his heart several times. "I sway too. But, I no want you to die, Annie."

Our family name died that day. We buried it. Never to be spoken again. Not to each other, not to our children or our grandchildren. The secrets and scandals of a family are to be guarded and respected. Protected from the judgmental eyes of the outside world. We embraced a new legacy that morning to carry us and our family into the future.

CHAPTER ELEVEN

FRIDAY, MAY 18, 1923 – TWO YEARS LATER – CANTON, OHIO - The Miller family has been living in a small rental home on McKinley Avenue SW the past year and a half after leaving Youngstown far behind.

Sophie received a letter in the mail today. A letter from Mama.

Dear Sophie,

I was so happy to see you last month when you visited me. You've grown up so fast. I'm so proud of you and Stanley for taking care of Frank, Billy and Annie. I know it has been so hard. I know your brother Stanley doesn't understand why I had to do what I did. I hope someday he can forgive me. I did it for you my sweet Sophie. I couldn't bear to watch your father continue to hurt you and rob you of your spirit and your life. I was so afraid he was going to take you away from me. I couldn't live with knowing I did nothing about it. I loved your father, Sophie. I loved him so much. But he was so cruel to us and I love you more. I'd do anything for you. Anything to keep you safe.

I have some wonderful news my sweet, sweet girl. I have been released from prison early. I am staying in Lisbon with your Aunt Mary who has found it in her heart to forgive me for what I involved her husband in. Please visit as soon as you can. I can't wait to see you all. I'll be here waiting.

All my love,

Mama

***

It's half past eight in the morning. Stanley and Sophie load the children into the automobile along with all their luggage. It's been three long years. How will it feel to see Mama again? Will Billy even remember her?

At 10:21 a.m. the 1915 Chevy rolls to a stop in front of Aunt Mary's home. Aunt Mary sits on the porch drinking lemonade and tatting.

Sophie steps out of the automobile and helps Annie and Billy exit. Mary slowly stands. She places both hands over her mouth and cries out. "Oh my God. Stella. Stella, come here. Quickly. Oh, my dear ..."

The Miller family gathers in the front yard. Mama appears behind the screen door. She eases the door open and walks onto the porch almost in a trance. A mother's love cradles her children in her arms only for a brief time, but holds their hearts inside hers for eternity.

She makes her way down the porch stairs, weeping uncontrollably, her arms trembling and outstretched enough to engulf all her children at once.

Annie cries out. "Mama!" She dashes along the walkway into Mama's arms. Frank and Billy follow close behind.

"My babies, my babies. Let me look at you. Oh, you've all grown up so much. Mama's here now. I'll never leave you again my sweet children." She pinches Billy's cheeks until they're pink.

Sophie and Stanley stand back and watch as Mama kisses their siblings and sends them up the porch stairs to Aunt Mary. She turns to Sophie with open arms. Sophie rushes into Mama's bosom, laughing and crying at the same time. Mama squeezes her and clings to her, rocking her back and forth. She cradles Sophies face and whispers, "Nobody will ever hurt you again my precious child. Go and hug your Aunt Mary."

The moment is here. That moment where you don't know how to feel, or how to react. Don't know what you're supposed to think, or do. She's gaunt and haggard. Her eyes are sunken deep into an ashen face. Her hair has grayed. She's looks frail.

She trembles, standing there vulnerable and afraid. It saddens the heart to see someone you love wasting away, gripped with age and worn down by worry and anxiety. A sadness resonates deep in the windows of her eyes reflecting the pain of three long years lost.

Their eyes lock in a solemn stare. She betrayed us for what she did to Papa. She forced us into a life of survival and hardship. All the pain of the orphanage. Years on the run. Here she stands. But the years have been hard on her too.

Yet even in all their sorrow, her eyes reflect an unconditional love and adoration for him. She hesitantly extends her arms. He lowers his eyes staring at the ground. He can hardly breathe. His chest aches with tension. He wipes a single tear from his cheek and sucks in a deep breath trying to calm his nerves.

His heart is filled with compassion and forgiveness for her. He has missed her so much. He pauses, then rushes up the walkway and embraces her. Her trembling body breaks into sorrowful tears and sobs. Her feeble arms cling to him. Nothing on earth can compare to the loving embrace of a mother. It fixes everything that's broken. It mends every hurt. It soothes the heart and restores the soul. It's finding yourself back in the arms of home.

Stella stares at her son. He's grown tall. His shoulders have broadened and his arms are etched with muscle. He bears a scar on his left forearm. His blonde hair has darkened and his jaw has squared. He's handsome. Like his father. Tears stream down his cheeks. Light scintillates off fiery sapphire eyes that pierce her very soul with their intensity.

"Please forgive me, my son. I love you so much. I'm so sorry … I'm so sorry. You should have never had to bear all this burden. Please, please forgive me."

He holds her tightly to his chest, kissing her on the head. Taking in the scent of her hair. "I love you Mama. And I do forgive you. I kept my promise and took care of Sophie and Annie and the boys while you were gone. I understand now what you were trying to tell me years ago in the barn. I know why you did what you did. You had to protect Sophie." He places his arm around her and escorts her to the porch and inside Aunt Mary's home.

Mama, Mary and Sophie work together in the kitchen putting together a grand homecoming meal of pork, potatoes, carrots, cabbage and freshly baked egg bread. A reunion at the dinner table. Eating. Laughing. Crying. So much to catch up on. So much time to make up for.

***

The aroma of frying sausage wakes him. Sophie is singing in the bath. Kids are still asleep. He walks downstairs and sits at the kitchen table. Mama sets the table and prepares a large breakfast of kielbasa, eggs, bread, quark cheese and coffee.

"Mama, do you want me to wake up the kids for breakfast?"

"No son. Let them sleep for a while. You go ahead and enjoy your breakfast."

"I have to go back to Canton. I have a house and a job there." Mama stops what she is doing and glances at him. She wipes her hands with her apron and folds her arms, giving him her full attention.

"Sophie is in nursing school in Canton. She met a boy. Nice fella. I think she's gonna marry him." Mama listens, not saying a word.

"Frank, Billy and Annie should stay here with you. They need you more than me or Sophie. I've got a good job and a life in Canton."

Mama breaks her silence. "I understand son. I'll take care of the little ones now. It's not your burden anymore. I'm happy for you both. Sophie needs a good man in her life. And you need to be free to live your own life. Go find your happiness sweet boy. Just promise me you'll visit often."

He takes her hand. "I promise Mama. I will."

Sophie joins him at the table with a bath towel in her hand, dabbing her wet hair. "What's for breakfast? Oh, that looks so, good." She sticks her tongue out at him.

Mama places a plate of food in front of her. A piece of kielbasa bounces off of Sophie's forehead. "Perfect shot. Stick that tongue out again, ha-ha."

A wet towel engulfs his face. Sophie and Mama burst into laughter. Stanley rips the towel off his face and wraps it into a ball. "Very funny. You're such a comic."

Mama places a pair of cheaters on her nose and peers at Sophie. "So. Who is this boyfriend?"

Sophie glares at Stanley. "What? You told her? Really?"

Stanley scoffs. "Hey, it's true, right? He *is* your boyfriend."

Sophie ignores him and turns towards Mama. "He's nice. He's handsome, and he's good to me."

Mama squints, adjusting her cheaters. "So, where did you meet this handsome, nice boy? And what's his name?"

"Well, his name is Michael. We met in school. We were just friends until he asked me to a dance. We fell in love. He wants me to meet his parents in Pennsylvania."

Mama crosses her arms. "I see. Well, you should finish your nursing school before you think about getting married and being in love, Sophie."

Sophie's eyes widen. "What? Who said anything about getting married? Stanley!"

"Uh … I need to load the automobile and check the oil. I'll be right back. Ha-ha."

"Get back here." Sophie looks to Mama for support. The women sit in silence for a moment, then burst into laughter.

"Come on Soph. We gotta get going. Get dressed. I'll wait for you in the automobile. Gimme a hug, Mama. We'll come visit you in a few weeks, okay? Promise. Come on Soph."

Sophie gives Mama a huge hug and a kiss on the cheek. "Bye. Be back soon." Mama grabs Sophie by the wrist and pulls her back into her arms. She hugs her tight. "Be safe my sweet child. God go with you."

Aunt Mary walks into the kitchen. She throws her arms up. "Where are they going?"

"Stanley has a job and an automobile now and Sophie wants to get married to some boy named Michael. They grow up. They don't need you anymore."

***

Sophie sings as they drive through the green rolling hills of the Ohio countryside. She sings louder and more boisterous as they go along.

Though April showers may come your way,
They bring the flowers that bloom in, May,
So, if it's raining have no regrets,
Because it isn't raining rain you know, it's raining violets…

Stanley reaches over and puts his hand over his sister's mouth as she continues to try and sing.

"Soph, I am so happy for you and Mikey. I think you should marry him and have ten kids and live a beautiful life in Pennsylvania or wherever you two decide. You deserve that."

"But what about you, Stanley? Will you be okay?"

"Please don't think I'm crazy, but I still see Papa. He shows up at night by my bed sometimes. He looks so sad and tormented."

Sophie sits quiet for a moment, then turns her body towards his. "I don't think you're crazy. I felt Papa following me around for years. One day when I felt him there, I told him I forgive him for everything he did to me. I told him I want him to be at peace. After that, I never felt him around anymore. Maybe you should do the same. Now keep your eyes on the road. You truly are a terrible driver, geez."

Who could ask for a sweeter more loving sister than her? She'll never know how much she's adored. She also doesn't need to know all the seedy connections in Canton Stanley has made. *Little Chicago* they call it. They say Al Capone once hid there to avoid the Feds. Setting tile is a good living, but bootlegging is where the money is. And that's where Stanley is headed.

PART III - CHAPTER TWELVE

SATURDAY, JULY 11, 1925 – CANTON, OHIO - It's been nearly five years since Papa's murder. Mama has been out of prison for the past two years raising Billy, Annie and Frank, and living in Lisbon with Aunt Mary. Sophie moved on with her life and married Michael Chestnut. They moved to Pennsylvania to start a new life and a family. And me? I've been working as a tile setter during the day and running rum at night. Any extra cabbage I make, finds its way to Mama to help support her and the family.

Bellamy's. A local speakeasy on the seedy side of Canton known as *Little Chicago*. Stanley blends in with the seedy neighborhood known for its brothels, speakeasies, gambling dens and gangsters. A sketchy side of town. But Bellamy's provides him with a lot of greenbacks from its bootlegging operation. Working with gangsters is one thing. Becoming a gangster is another. Never allow them to do you a favor. Stay out of their debt. Just do the work offered and accept the chowder. It isn't a family you want to be a member of. And that family usually ends up burying members, killed by their own hand.

Tonight, however, isn't about business. It's about relaxing and enjoying the music, the crowd and cold Cascade beer.

"Hey, Miller. How's that burger?" He slips Stanley a hefty envelope full of cash.

"The burger is good, Max. Thanks pal."

"Maxie. Send me another beer. Put it on my tab" Stanley spins around on his barstool scanning the room. "Nice crowd tonight."

Max slides a foamy brew down the bar. "You don't have a tab, Miller. When you going to learn that?"

Max started his job at Bellamy's three years ago when he was sixteen. He's been a regular bartender the past two. Sometimes you make a friend in this world and you feel like you've known that person your entire life. Max is that friend. He comes from a big Italian family in Cleveland. He has a gift for making people laugh. Folks naturally relax in his presence. Probably why he snagged the bartending gig.

His thick raven hair is slicked straight back and shaved neatly around his ears. He's always grinning. And why not? The mug has near perfect teeth, set in a solid jaw covered in light scruff. He's tall and stocky with a bit of a beer belly and there's always a sparkle of boyish charm behind his playful coppery eyes. He carries a scar across his left brow, splitting one of his bushy eyebrows. He swears he earned it in a bar fight. Just more of his bullshit.

A speakeasy is a rugged, harrowing business to be around. I look out for Max and Max always has my back.

Wow, who's that dame? Her movements are so graceful. She wears that gray skirt, maroon cloche hat and light gold blouse so ... nice. Wavy brown curls fall in velvety layers around her shoulders. Full glossy-red lips. Couldn't miss those even in the dim light of this smoky bar. Rosy cheeks on satin-white skin. Laughing eyes as green as the Irish countryside adorned with long thick black eyelashes that flutter when she smiles.

A nervous twinge accompanies a curious desire to observe her. *I got to meet this girl.*

Holy shit, she just looked at me. Why's she turning her back to me? Now her friend is looking at me. Am I that obvious?

"Hey Max send over a round of whatever that table is drinking and put it on my tab."

"You don't have a tab, Miller."

"Okay, here's five bucks. Just do it."

Max shakes his head and laughs as he mixes up a concoction of gin, honey, orange juice and a squirt of lemon juice.

Stanley watches intently. "What the fuck is that, Max?"

"They're called Bee's Knees, dumbass. Just drink your beer. This is too much class for a bum like you."

Stanley chuckles. "Who's the dame in the maroon hat?"

"I think that's one of the Flagg girls. Her name is Emily, or Emilia or something like that. Wait. Her name is Emma, I think. She's too good for the likes of you Miller. Forget about it. She comes from a big Irish family. She ain't gonna give a dirtball like you the time of day. Fat chance, buddy. Ha-ha."

"Put your kisser right on my ass, Max. Just send over the drinks. And tell them where they came from asshole."

"You got it boss." Max delivers the drinks and points at Stanley.

Stanley mumbles to himself. "Why are you laughing Max? You, jackass. Just give 'em the drinks."

"Cheers ladies." Stanley raises his beer glass. Both women accept the drinks then return to conversing. Ignored. Not a good start.

The juke box kicks on with a new Gene Austin song…

Five foot two, eyes of blue
But oh, what those five foot could do
Has anybody seen my girl?
Turned up nose, turned down hose
Never had no other beaus
Has anybody seen my girl?…

The crowd grows as the night moves on. Where do all these people come from? Businessmen, lovers, blue-collar workers, flappers hustling potential marks, veterans from The Great War, a drunk couple attempting to do the Charleston, and Miss Flagg over there flashing a cold shoulder.

EmmaMae stands and walks towards the lady's lounge. She flashes a glance his way. He raises his glass. "Cheers." *Swell. She hates me.*

Moments later she returns from the lounge. *Here she comes again.* He winks. She rolls her eyes and struts past him mildly shaking her head.

"Wait. What? Ha-ha. What's that hanging off her shoe? Is that …?"

"Max, watch my beer. I'll be right back."

He steps on a two-foot piece of toilet paper and scoops it up.

"Excuse me? Miss?"

"Yes. May I help you?"

The urge to burst into laughter is almost unbearable. He can feel his face smirking. He extends his hand with a ball of tissue. "I think this belongs to you."

"Oh my gosh. Did I bring that with me from the lounge?"

"It sort of followed you."

"Well, thank you for saving me from further embarrassment."

His heart is pounding and moisture starts to bead on his brow.

"You're welcome." He shoves the ball of tissue into his pocket.

She crinkles her nose and glares. "Aren't you ... going to throw that away?"

"Uh ... yeah. I'll get rid of it for ya. Can I buy you and your friend another drink?" She pauses, looking him up and down then frowns. "I don't think so. But thank you."

"Okay. Uh ... I'm just going to go get rid of this, now."

She raises her eyebrows. "Wonderful. Thank you again."

Back to the bar where it's safe. A fresh brew waiting.

Max bursts into laughter. "Looks like you got the icy mitt. This one's on me, buddy."

"Yeah, tell it to Sweeney." Stanley tosses the wad of tissue at him. "Can you get rid of that for me?" Max shakes his head leaving the tissue on the floor. He walks away chuckling. "Ah, Miller. She hates you. Give it up."

Gangsters are a frequent sight in any speakeasy. Bellamy's is no exception. This guy is almost advertising himself as a thug the way he's dressed and the way he just strolled into the bar. Black fedora, gray chalk striped pants and matching vest, two-tone shoes. And what's with the walking stick? The thug sits at a table with two of his pals. The table right next to EmmaMae's.

"Max. Who's this guy?"

"Who? That mug? He's just a low-level thug. Works for Jumbo Crowley. Name is Jimmy I think."

The three thugs shoot bourbon. Their laughter grows more obnoxious by the minute. Jimmy approaches EmmaMae's table. "Can I buy you two dolls a drink?"

EmmaMae scowls. "No thank you. Can you please leave us alone?"

His pals laugh. Jimmy grabs EmmaMae by the arm. "How's about a dance, doll?"

She jerks her arm away. "Gets your filthy hands off of me, brute. Go chase yourself."

Bullies. No tolerance for bullies. Especially ones who bother ladies or kids. Stanley rises and sets his beer on the bar. He feels a hand on his shoulder. Max frowns and shakes his head.

Jimmy slams his stick on EmmaMae's table spilling their drinks. He turns to Max and hollers, "Bring these two beautiful dolls another drink on me." Jimmy approaches the bar, attempting to put some swag in his step, but it only makes him appear more of an idiot.

Max mixes two fresh drinks and sets them on the bar top, ready for pick-up. When the thug reaches the bar, Stanley places his hand next to the drinks. "Why don't you leave the dames alone?"

Jimmy glares, unblinking. He lowers his brow. "Who the hell are you? Mind your own damn business and scram, you ugly fuck."

A jab in the chest with the walking stick was the trigger Stanley needed. No thinking about it. Just an instinctive reaction and the excuse he needed to act.

Stanley grabs the stick from the thug's hand and cracks him across the head, knocking off his hat and sending him spiraling into a backwards balancing act. He grabs Jimmy by the throat and rocks him with a left hook to the jaw. Jimmy crumples to the floor like a pile of dirty clothes. Blood drools from his lips.

The other two thugs rush to their pal's aid. One grabs Stanley from behind and holds him, while the other sends a series of punches into Stanley's ribs. He wheezes, gasping to catch his breath. Fighting to break free.

The sound of a shotgun being cocked silences the crowd and the disturbance.

"That's enough! Let him go. Take your friend and get the hell out of here."

The two thugs drop Stanley to the floor and help Jimmy to his feet.

Jimmy eyeballs Stanley. "You're a dead man." Stanley picks up the walking stick and tosses it to him. He watches as the men leave the joint.

Max waves at the crowd. "Nothing to see here. Let's get back to having fun." He helps Stanley to his feet and escorts him back to his barstool.

Stanley sits at the bar sipping his beer. "Thanks Maxie. I owe ya one, pal."

Max shakes his head and places both palms on the bar top. "I told you to not get involved Miller. Those are bad fellas. If I were you, I'd hit the road and get the hell out a here. Lay low for a couple days."

A soft hand caresses his shoulder. He spins around on his barstool. EmmaMae stands before him, extending her hand and looking like a movie star who just stepped off the Silver Screen.

"Thank you. Thank you for having the guts to do something that no other man in this joint was willing to do. I'm EmmaMae. EmmaMae Flagg."

Her hand is soft and petite. Fits perfectly inside his. "You're welcome. It's the second time tonight I've had to save you though. It's kind of becoming a habit. My name's Stanley Miller. Nice to finally meet you ... officially that is."

Her coy smile sets his heart on fire. "My friend Hazel and I are going to leave now. It is a real pleasure to meet you, Stanley Miller."

Leave? Panic races through his body like flames across a dry grassy field. *What if I never see her again? Do something.*

"Uh ... same here. Can I walk you two to your car?"

She nods and folds her arms. "Yes Stanley. Yes, you can."

He slides his empty beer mug towards Max and raises an eyebrow. He escorts the two women out the rear door. Max stares in amazement then returns to drying beer mugs, chuckling to himself.

"We're parked over here."

"Hey, um ... EmmaMae, can I buy you dinner sometime?"

She hesitates. *Why would she hesitate? To tease? To play coy? Maybe she was just being polite all along?* She, places an analyzing finger on her cheek and smirks. "Hm."

Say yes. Please say yes.

"I think maybe ... you've earned that chance, Mister Miller." She scribbles her telephone number on a piece of paper and hands it to him. "That's my number. You can call me when you're ready to take me to dinner. But don't get any ideas, buster. It's just dinner. My way of thanking you."

He opens the door for EmmaMae, then for Hazel. He's mesmerized by the red taillights as they fade into the night.

It was worth the beating. He shoves the paper with the telephone number into his pocket, spins around on one heel and struts in the direction of his Chevy. The wet sidewalk glistens from the reflections of dim streetlights. Did she really just now, agree to go to dinner? Never felt so smitten or had feelings like this about anybody. The image of her smile, her full red lips, the way she bats her eyes … those eyes, green as a virgin forest. It isn't just her beauty or her smile though. It's her confidence, the way she carries herself. She's fearless. Poised. Different than other dames. How long do I wait to call her? I want to call her now. When I get home, I'm calling her.

Blissful paradise abruptly disappears. Violent hands grab and pull at him, ripping his clothes. He didn't notice the dark alley he was passing. His skull explodes in agony. Blows pound his ribcage knocking every ounce of air from his lungs. He swings and kicks at the dark to no avail. Cold, wet gravel clings and digs into his face. Boots pummel his body from every direction. Three shadowy figures move away from him blending into the darkness. Everything is out of focus, fading, muffled voices … buzzing … blackness.

CHAPTER THIRTEEN

Sunlight breaks over the horizon casting a soft morning glow over the dank and dirty alley. Stanley drags himself to a grungy brick wall and struggles to prop his body upright. His head throbs. An annoying ring resonates in his ears. He peers out a slit in his puffy left eye attempting to regain his bearings. His right eye is swollen shut. Gravel mixed with dry blood is stuck to his cheeks. He can barely breath. Every breath he attempts sends an agonizing jolt through his torso.

He reaches into his pocket. The cash is gone.

He shoves his hand into every other pocket that isn't already ripped to shreds. *Her number. It's gone.*

Using the brick wall to balance himself, he manages to stand. He sways and stumbles his way from the alley to his automobile. He struggles to find the key under the floor mat, then collapses into the driver's seat. He cranks the engine. The roads are quiet and clear, affording him to drive cautious and slowly. He hits every curb with each turn he makes.

Arriving home, he parks sideways in the driveway and stumbles up the porch steps and into his living room. Wheezing and coughing he collapses on the sofa and closes his eyes. *Home. Made it home.* Everything goes black.

***

The afternoon sun casts shadows through the curtains that dance along the walls. Each rattling breath he manages inflicts excruciating pain, like broken glass scraping his ribs. How long have I been asleep? He gingerly removes his shirt. Everything around him moves in slow motion.

The cool running water of the kitchen faucet temporarily relieves the burn in his swollen eyes and cheeks. Soap dissolves the grime. Pebbles of gravel create tiny pings as they fall off his face into the sink.

A roll of masking tape from his toolbox is all he has to wrap his ribcage and stabilize broken bone. A cold flank steak from the icebox brings the swelling in his face somewhat under control for the moment.

What's this? A gash. It's deep. Using a mirror, a carpet needle and thread, he cross-stitches edges of flesh, pulling them tight until the wound on his scalp is fully closed. He washes and bandages dozens of minor flesh wounds, scrapes and gouges.

Four aspirins later, he uses the banister to pull his battered body up the stairwell, one step at a time, never realizing how many steps there were till now. Dragging himself into his bedroom, he collapses in a heap on his bed. He positions his body the best he can to allow himself to breathe and find whatever comfort he can. He closes his eyes trying not to focus on the pain. Wondering if he's going to die.

***

The early morning urge to piss and nagging hunger pangs gurgling in his stomach are motivation enough to leave the confines of his bed. Every movement sends stabbing pain rippling across his ribcage. Each breath batters his chest like the swat of a baseball bat. Bone rubs against bone. He can hear it. He can feel it.

He steadies himself trying to focus. The walls swirl around him. He shuffles to the toilet and fills the porcelain bowl with a steady stream of pink urine. "Well, that can't be good."

Tapping on the front door echoes from downstairs. He shuffles towards his bed and pulls a pistol from the nightstand. He tucks it into the rear of his pants. Making his way downstairs, clinging to the banister he squints, trying to recognize the shadow standing at his front door. Halfway down the stairs the door creaks open. He places his hand on the pistol.

"Hello? Anybody home? Stanley?" The sound of Sophie's voice resounds through the walls of his home like a choir of angels. She sets a bag of groceries on the floor and dashes up the stairs. "Oh my God. Stanley? What happened to you? Are you okay?"

He raises his thumbs. "I'm okay Soph. The other guys … not so good." He laughs, then winces.

"Here, let me help you to the sofa. Let's take a look at you. I know a little something about nursing."

"Really, Soph. I'll be okay. I'm fine."

She shakes her head. "Take off your shirt. Let me see." She helps him slide his arms out of the sleeves of his shirt. "What on earth did you do here? We have to take this tape off. Hold still. It's stuck on there, pretty good. This might sting a little."

"This might sting a little? Did they teach you that in nursing school? Shit! That hurts. Are you crazy? Just … just rip it off quickly. You're torturing me."

"You have a broken rib. Maybe two. The bruises are bad but they'll heal. We have to keep a tight wrap on these ribs though. Let's put something cold on your chest to help the swelling. And you have to take deep breaths. The last thing you need is a case of pneumonia."

He grunts. "It hurts too much to breathe."

She pats his hand. "You have to take deep breaths. *Every day.* It's very important."

He nods and coughs. "Okay, Soph. I'll do my best to breathe. But it's not easy, I'm telling ya."

She places a wet towel and ice over his ribs. "Oh man. Ah shit, that's cold. Are you out of your mind?"

She smirks. "Don't be such a crybaby. I'm going to call Michael and let him know I'm going to stay with you for a few days till you feel better. So, don't worry. I'm here now. At least I can make use of the little bit of nursing school I had."

He cringes from the cold ice. "You didn't finish nursing school? Why? I can't think of anyone who would make a better nurse than you."

She frowns and tilts her head. "Michael wanted me to quit nursing school after we married. I didn't want to, but he insisted. Maybe I can go back someday … and finish."

"Promise me you'll go back. That was your dream."

She removes the ice, then tightly bandages his ribs. "I will. You just try and get some rest. I'm going to whip us up some dinner."

I can't honestly say I'm not happy to see Sophie. The bandages and Sophie's loving touch almost make the pain bearable. Just having her around is a pleasant distraction. And hell, I'm starving.

***

FRIDAY AUGUST 21, 1925 - SIX WEEKS LATER The ribs have healed, the cuts and bruises are nearly all gone. There's just a hint of swelling in his right eye. He's short on cash. Time to get back to work and join the world again.

Bellamy's. This old joint has never looked so nice. Never thought I'd ever think Max's ugly face would be a pleasant sight to embrace.

"Great to see you back, Miller. You are one crazy son of a bitch."

Stanley waves him off. "Ah baloney."

"No really. You need your head examined. By the way, those thugs that jumped you? I have their names. I talked to Mr. Crowley a couple days ago. He asked about you. Said he wants you to do a tile job for him. I told him you're the best."

Stanley's ears perk. "What's their names, Max?"

He hands Stanley a piece of paper and leans across the bar. "I shouldn't give this to you. You be careful out there. Let that shit go."

Stanley, holds up the piece of paper. "Sure Max. I'll do just that." He heads for the door. "Oh, and Miller. That Irish girl you took the ass kicking for? Weeks ago, she asked me where you were. I told her you were dead. You should call her."

He pauses at the bar. "Yeah, thanks for that Max. But I lost her number. And I don't know if she'll ever even speak to me again. It's been so long."

"Yeah, well I figured if she was asking for ya, you either never got her number, or you lost it, ya dope. He slides a napkin across the bar.

"How can I ever thank you, man?"

Max laughs. "You can start by paying for your own fucking drinks from now on, ya cheap bastard. Your ass squeaks when you walk. Now go chase yourself. Scram."

***

"Operator, can you connect me to CT7721, please?" A nervous pit squeezes his insides as the telephone rings.

A soft voice answers. "Hello. May I help you?"

"Uh … Hi. EmmaMae?"

"This is she. Who's this?"

"It's Stanley … you know … your rescuer."

Silence. "Stanley? Where have you been? You never called me. I thought you got lost. So, what's going on in your life?"

"Well I sort of had to take care of some business with my new friends the night we met, and well … it's a long story. Listen, I was calling to see if I could take you to dinner tonight. I know it's short notice, but are you free?"

"I don't think so. I already gave you that chance and you stood me up. I don't give second chances."

"EmmaMae, please. I really want to see you. I would have called you sooner, but I had some problems I had to work through before I could. I can tell you more about it at dinner. Please EmmaMae." He holds his breath.

"Wow, you really sound desperate. But, no thanks. Good luck to you, though." Click.

***

It's half past eight in the evening at Bellamy's. EmmaMae is having a cocktail with her girlfriend Hazel and enjoying jazz music blaring from the jukebox. Hazel asks, "Whatever happened to that hard-boiled guy you gave your number to?"

EmmaMae shakes her head and scoffs. "He never called me. Well, he did finally call me. But six weeks later. Can you believe that? What a boob."

Hazel frowns. "Are you kidding? Who does he think he is? What did you tell him when he finally called?"

She leans in towards Hazel, bobbing her head side to side. "I told him he wasn't getting a second chance. And to blow."

Hazel giggles. "You're so mean. How did he take it?"

EmmaMae rolls her eyes. "He didn't take it well at all. He begged and pleaded … and I hung up the phone."

Hazel's jaw drops. "Oh my God. You *are* mean."

"I'm not mean. I'm just not one to allow any man to treat me badly. He deserved every bit of that."

Max is tending bar tonight when he notices EmmaMae sitting with her girlfriend across the bar. "Ooh. You're going to owe me bigtime, buddy." Max prepares two cocktails and walks the drinks to their table.

"These are on the house, ladies." Max places the drinks on the table in front of them. EmmaMae glances at him. "Thank you, but I don't accept drinks from strange bartenders." Max waves his hands in the air. "No, no. These aren't from a stranger. These are actually on the house. My treat."

"Okay, Max. What do you want?"

Max feigns a surprised look. "What? I don't want anything. Just being friendly, that's all." She glares at Max. "I'm not buying it. What do you want?"

Max grabs a chair and flips it around and straddles it. "Okay. You're on to me. I want to talk to you about my buddy, Stanley. I saw him for the first time in weeks today and I gave him your phone number. Did he call you?"

She sighs. "Max, I gave your buddy my phone number six weeks ago when we first met. He never called me. He had the gall to call me earlier today. After all this time. What a moron. I gave you my number to pass on to him so he'd call me and I could have the pleasure of hanging up on him."

Max places his hand over his face and shakes his head. "EmmaMae. I gotta tell you something about that night you met Stanley." She rolls her eyes and crosses her arms. "Stop. There's nothing you can tell me that will change a thing. But you know what? Go ahead. I'm sure this will be entertaining. Right Hazel?"

Hazel giggles. "Yeah, go ahead Max. Tell us."

He glances at EmmaMae for a moment, then places his hand on the table in front of her. "After Stanley walked you and Hazel to your automobile, he was jumped by those three thugs that were bothering you two all night. They all three beat him senseless and left him in an alley to die. He suffered two broken ribs, a broken eye socket and a whole lot of cuts and bruises. He looked like shit. Couldn't get out of bed for weeks. His sister nursed him back to health. Now, he probably didn't tell you that, cuz that's the kind of dumb mug he is."

EmmaMae is visibly shaken by the news, but pretends to be unaffected. "Okay. Go on."

"You gotta give Stanley one more chance. He took a terrible beating for you. He at least deserves a second shot, doesn't he?"

She meekly responds, "Well, I-I had no idea. That's horrible. Why didn't he just come out and say that?"

Max throws up his hands. "That's just Stanley. He won't complain. He won't just come out and say it. He's not like that. He has his pride."

Her walls of defense lower. "Max, please ask Stanley to call me again."

Max beams and nods. He flips the chair around and returns it to its original spot. "Enjoy the drinks, ladies. I'll tell him." He winks at Hazel. She bats her eyes and blushes.

***

Early Sunday morning Max knocks on Stanley's door.

"What the hell are you doing here, Max? Why aren't you in church confessing all your sins?"

Max belts out a guffaw. "I should be there confessing all of your sins you filthy bastard. Let me in."

"Wanna beer?"

Max shakes his head. "Not this early ya drunk. I'll take a Coca Cola though."

"Okay the suspense is killing me. Why the surprise visit? You get kicked out of your place, Maxie? You can have my sofa."

Max stares at him and grins. He maintains the stare and continues to grin.

"What the hell you grinning at? You're creeping me out."

Max rubs his chin. "You owe me buddy. You owe me big time."

"What are you talking about? What the hell did you do now?"

Max places his hand on Stanley's shoulder. "Buddy, I had a talk with EmmaMae last night. She asked me to have you call her again."

"You saw her last night? What the hell did you tell her?"

Max raises his palms to Stanley. "Don't worry man. I didn't tell her much. Just enough to get her to understand that you deserved a second shot, damnit. Just take the shot and call her, okay? Today. Right after I leave. Got it?"

Stanley lowers his head. "You're right. Thank you for whatever you did, pal. I'll try calling her again. I'd do anything for another chance."

Max leaps up from the table. "Well ya dumb mug, you have one. So, take it and run with it. And let me know how it goes. I gotta go now. Come by later and see me."

"Operator. Where can I connect your call?"

"Uh … yes ma'am. Please connect me to CT7721."

CHAPTER FOURTEEN

"Hello? May I help you?"

"EmmaMae?"

"Yes."

"It's uh … me again. Stanley. Please don't hang up."

A few static crackles break up the dead silence on the line.

"I … I won't hang up. How are you?"

"I have to be honest here. I called because I really want to see you. I really want to buy you that dinner I owe you. Can you maybe consider giving me another chance?"

She giggles. "You don't owe me dinner, Stanley. But I do owe you something."

"What could you possibly owe me?"

She whispers. "I owe you a second chance. Ask me again to go to dinner with you."

He sighs. "EmmaMae. May I *please* buy you dinner?"

She pauses. "Pick me up at seven tonight."

He exhales. "Alright. Great. Uh … where can I pick you up?"

"Oh, right. My address is 1803 18th Street Southwest. See you then. Don't be late. And you better show up, buster."

An anonymous voice breaks into the line. "Hey, can we use the line now?"

Stanley ignores the voice. "I promise. See you tonight."

"Okay, see you tonight, Stanley."

"Hang up already."

"Shut up, moron"

EmmaMae is shocked. "What?"

"Not you EmmaMae, the asshole on the line."

"Oh …"

"Get off the line already ya bums."

EmmaMae's sweet voice turns into a growl. "Shut your face … bastard"

Stanley bursts into laughter. That was unexpected. This gal is full of surprises.

***

EmmaMae answers the door in a navy-blue day dress and a light blue sweater. He hasn't seen her since the first night they met in the smoky dim light of Bellamy's. Seeing her for the first time in the light of day reveals so much more of her beauty. Beauty that went unnoticed. The manner in which she stands and presents herself. So proud and confident. There's a friendliness in her green Irish eyes, almost an orneriness that wasn't evident the night they met. She holds your stare with no fear or shyness. Like she's waiting for your next word, so she can pounce on it with her wit and make a fool of you.

The light reveals no flaws in her satiny milky-white skin. Her chestnut hair burns with fiery auburn highlights where the sun touches it.

How can I be so lucky?

"Wow, Stanley. You clean up real nice, fella. Where are you taking me this evening? Uh ... Stanley? Are you there?"

"Um ...Thank you. Wow, you're even more beautiful than I remembered."

"Awe. That's very sweet. I love flattery, so feel free. Flatter me."

He removes his fedora and wipes a sweaty brow with the back of his hand. "I'd like to take you to dinner at Bellamy's, where we met. If that's okay with you, of course. Afterward, I thought maybe we could go to the nickelodeon ... to see *Phantom of the Opera*. Ya know ... Lon Chaney ... hang'n from a chandelier ... in a mask ... chasing Mary Philbin around the sewers trying to kidnap her. Have you seen it?"

She smiles a coy smile and wrinkles her nose. "Uh, no, I haven't seen the film. I ... read the book. I don't recall the plot going quite like that, but ... dinner at Bellamy's ... and ... the nickelodeon. Sounds like a perfect night to me."

***

Max is serving drinks and polishing the bar when they arrive at Bellamy's. He roars with laughter when they walk in. "Miller. You are in way over your head, buddy. Here. This is for you." He hands Stanley a fat envelope.

"Thanks, Maxie. Now dry up and get back to work, ya bum."

"This is the table where you sat when I first saw you. Mind if we sit here?" He pulls out her chair.

"Such a gentleman. I am so impressed."

Max approaches their table and winks at Stanley. "So, what will it be for the fine couple, tonight?" Stanley eagerly waits for her to order.

"May I have the roast duck with a side of white rice and the cranberry walnut salad? And can I have that with a glass of Chardonnay, please?"

Max nods. "Of course, you may, Miss. And just so you know, Stanley here is full of crap." Max turns to Stanley. "And what will the big ugly lug have?"

Stanley shakes his head. Tonight, is not the night for Max to be at the top of his annoyance game. "Give me the grilled salmon and a baked potato and mixed vegetables. And add a Cascade brew to that."

Max smiles. "You got it boss." He winks as he walks away.

"Stanley, what happened to you? Why didn't you call me?" She knows why after talking to Max, but she wants to hear it in his own words.

"They have a great parfait here for dessert. The apple pie ain't bad either."

She raises an eyebrow and lowers her tone. "Stanley. What happened to you? Why didn't I hear from you?"

Max approaches and serves their drinks. "Here you go Miss. And here you go Casanova." He winks at Stanley.

"Damnit, Max, will you stop winking at me? It's creepy."

Stanley wipes his face with his hands, then pushes his hair backward. He stares at EmmaMae for a moment, collecting his thoughts. "You know the three thugs that were here the night I met you?"

She leans in towards him, her eyes wide and unblinking, giving him her full attention.

"Well, let's just say they waited for me. Outside. Right after you left. They jumped me. Kinda caught me by surprise. It took a little while to heal up. Like … six weeks."

She places her hand over her mouth. "Oh, my goodness, I am so sorry. I had no idea." She reaches across the table and softly strokes a faint bruised area over his right eye with the tips of her fingers. "I feel like it's my fault this happened."

"No, no, no. That was my choice. I hate bullies. I couldn't sit and watch that punk harass you and do nothing about it. I should have been more careful when I left. I guess you just had me a little distracted, is all."

"Thank you again for what you did. You're very brave. You just weren't very smooth with your approach on trying to get my attention. You'll have to work on that."

Max delivers the couple's meal. Stanley points at Max, daring him to wink.

Max throws his hands in the air and smirks. "What? I'm going, I'm going."

The couple enjoy a nice dinner and pleasant conversation. Stanley checks the time. "We should get going to the nickelodeon." He escorts EmmaMae to the backdoor.

"Maxie, put this on my tab." Stanley winks.

Max tosses his washcloth on the bar. "You don't have a tab Miller. How many times do I have to remind you? I'm not paying for this."

The bright flickering lights of the nickelodeon brings a smile to her face. He pulls to the curb and parks. Her face quickly turns from happy to fearful.

"What's the matter, doll?"

She glances at him with widened eyes. She doesn't speak. She points. In line is one of the thugs from the night they met at Bellamy's. A night Stanley won't forget anytime soon.

"Keep the car running. I'll be right back."

"But … where are you going? Stanley?"

He exits the automobile. "Stay in the car. I'll be right back. Don't worry." He purchases a ticket and enters the nickelodeon. He follows the thug and his girlfriend up the stairs into the balcony, staying in the shadows and observing where they sit.

The couple walk along the aisle and find seats towards the middle of the front row. They laugh and talk as the lights dim. The thug places his arm around his lady friend.

Stanley approaches and taps him on the shoulder. The thug turns toward Stanley, still laughing from his conversation. A realization comes over his face. More like a recognition and panic. His brow raises and his eyes widen.

"Remember me, cheese head?" Stanley grabs him by the throat and stands him up. The thug attempts a feeble swing but misses. Stanley smacks him in the face with an open palm. Then he grabs the thug by the jacket and the seat of his pants and launches him over the balcony onto the carpeted floor below. Screams echo throughout the theater creating chatter and confusion.

Stanley sprints out of the theater to his automobile where a nervous EmmaMae awaits. He slams the automobile into gear and speeds off into the night. "I think Phantom is a bit overrated anyway. I'm sure the book was probably better."

She stares at him, astonished. The corner of her mouth twitches as she smiles. "Well, you promised me ice cream."

"That's true. I did. Taggart's on Fulton."

***

The couple sit at a quiet table in the rear of the parlor. She gently runs her spoon across the top layer of her chocolate sundae. She holds the spoon in front of her mouth. "What did you do to that fella at the nickelodeon? Did you conk him on the head or something?"

He fidgets, analyzing the question. He points his spoon at her. "Well let's just say I converted him with a little leap of faith. I brought some reality to the show. Gave him a starring role."

She points at his timepiece. "May I see that?" He reaches into his pocket, undoes the clasp and hands it to her.

"Oh my gosh. This is beautiful. Wherever did you get this?"

"I found it. Or maybe it found me. It's a long story."

His eyes meet hers. They share a silent moment.

"Time is too slow for those who wait, too swift for those who fear, too long for those who grieve, too short for those who rejoice, but for those who love, time is eternity."

The words quiet her heart. She stares into his eyes, barely a blink. Her lips slightly parted. Her eyes sparkle and crinkle at the corners. "Is that Shakespeare?"

"It's a quote from an American minister named Henry Van Dyke. A lot of people mistake it for Shakespeare."

She hands him the timepiece. "You've taken such good care of it."

He returns it to his pocket. "This timepiece tracks the seconds of my life. I think the day it stops ticking, is the day I die."

"Speaking of time, it's getting late Mister Miller, and I have to work tomorrow."

He caresses her forearm with the tips of his fingers. "Can I ask you what you do for a living?"

"Of course. I'm an operator. I may have even connected a number for you once or twice ... or maybe listened to one of your private conversations."

"Ha. If you were only so lucky. Let me get you home."

***

He walks her to her front door. They bump arms attempting a clumsy hug. Awkward and frozen they stare at each other for a moment.

He cradles her face in his hands and moves his lips towards hers. She steps back holding her arms out. Her eyes dart in every direction but his. She blushes.

"I'm so sorry EmmaMae. I was just ..." He takes her by the hands. "Good night. When can I see you again?"

"Soon." She bats her eyes and smiles as she slips through the door. Click.

Why do I feel half drunk? His head spins, his heart aches. He turns to walk down the porch steps and trips on the last step, ripping his pant leg and falling face-first into the front yard. "Holy shit. God, I hope she didn't see that."

He hears a knock on the window. She points at him, laughing hysterically. He feels a rush of tingling heat surge into his face. He forces a smile and waves.

"Damnit. You Idiot." He picks himself off the ground and drives away.

CHAPTER FIFTEEN

It's early Saturday morning. Stanley parks in front of Jumbo Crowley's home. Crowley is a notorious crime boss in the Canton area and Stanley is laying a floor of Spanish tile for him today.

He's never met Jumbo. No doubt that's him standing in the open doorway. He's a beast of a man. Over six-foot. Dressed in plaid shorts, a wife-beater tee shirt, and a brown fedora sitting sideways on his large round head. A mammoth-size beaked nose splits a ruddy complexion on his face. He puffs on a fat stogie and grins as he watches Stanley approach.

"Mr. Miller." He extends a meaty hand adorned with gold rings and a thick gold fishbone bracelet.

The floor is already ripped up and stacks of red Spanish tile are waiting to be set. Stanley sets his tools on the floor, laying out a strategy in his mind on how to set the tiles.

"I'm going to leave you to your work, son. I have some business to tend to. If you need anything, holler for my assistant, Louie. He'll get you what you need." Stanley nods.

"And Miller. When you're finished with the floor, I want to discuss a little matter with you."

A small twinge surges through his chest. *What the hell could he possibly want to discuss?*

"Yes, sir."

***

Stanley completes the tile job in just under three hours. *Looks damn good.*

"Hey Louie. I'm finished for the day. Jumbo said he wanted to talk to me before I left. Can you let him know?"

Jumbo returns to the kitchen. He stands with his hands on his hips puffing on another fat stogie. He grunts as he bends over to examine one of the tiles.

"This one is chipped. Replace it. Other than that, I'm very pleased with your work, son. Very pleased. Let's step outside here for a few minutes and sit by the pool."

"Can I call you Stanley?"

"Of course. Yes sir."

Jumbo's stern grimace creates a sense of uneasiness in his gut. "I heard about what happened at Bellamy's. I want to apologize to you for how some of my boys behaved. They had no right to act in such a manner."

"Um ... well thank you, Mr. Crowley."

Jumbo snuffs out his cigar in an ashtray that rests on a small table next to him. "Stanley, I also heard that one of those boys found themselves flying over a balcony like Peter Pan."

Beads of sweat form over Stanley's temples and brow. A combination of humidity and his uncertainty as to where this conversation is headed. Jumbo reaches inside a small wooden box. "Cigar?"

Stanley leans forward and takes the cigar and slides it into his shirt pocket. Crowley isn't a person you want to offend.

"I respect you, young man. I understand why you might be a little angry. I would've done the same thing if I were in your shoes. I hate bullies. Women are to be treated with respect. Except my wife of course. She's the bitch from hell."

Stanley sighs and chuckles. "Thank you, sir."

Jumbo leans back in his chair and lights up another stogie. He takes a deep puff and blows the sweet-smelling smoke towards Stanley. "That's why I'm going to look the other way, son. I wanted you to know that.

"I'll see you in the morning. When you finish the grout, I'll have Louie pay you for your time. You know your way out."

This is almost too good to be true. Let's see if Jimmy Russo is home. Maybe shove that walking stick right up his ass.

Stanley parks his automobile a block away from Russo's home. He throws on a long-sleeved shirt and places an old fedora on his head.

Hm. Looks deserted. Let's check the backdoor. The knob turns and the door eases open. The kitchen is quiet. Voices upstairs. He sneaks into the front room.

Well looky there. The walking stick.

He shuffles through an old desk drawer and finds a revolver. Stanley puts the revolver in the rear of his pants. He grabs the walking stick and tiptoes up the staircase.

"Please don't hit me, anymore. I'm sorry, Jimmy. I didn't know."

"Bitch. How many times do I have to tell you? Huh? Stupid slut. What the fuck were you thinking?"

Russo grasps her hair. He raises his arm to strike her.

Rage boils Stanley's blood. A lifetime of watching a woman mercilessly beaten by a man has taken its toll on his psyche. It isn't something he's willing to overlook anymore. He taps the walking stick against the doorway.

"You love bullying little girls, don't you Jimmy?"

Russo drops the woman. He panics, his eyes dart towards the window, then to the door, then back to the window. He desperately attempts to open the window to no avail. "Who the hell are you? How did you get in here? Do you know who I am?"

"Where you going, Jimmy?"

"Wait. I know you. You're that ugly fuck from Bellamy's. You didn't learn your lesson, huh? You're *dead* asshole."

"Yeah, so you keep telling me. Yet here we are." He looks at the woman and motions for her to leave. She leaps to her feet, grabs her clothes and races out the bedroom door, down the stairs and out the front door.

Stanley closes the bedroom door behind him and walks around the bed where Russo stands cowering in the corner.

Russo whimpers. "Look … we can work this out. I can pay you. I'm really sorry about that night … please … now just wait a minute here."

Stanley places the walking stick and the revolver on the dresser and grins. Russo seeing his chance, lunges at Stanley, trying to reach for the revolver. Stanley coldcocks him knocking him to the ground. Russo, rattles his head and glances up. His eyes are glazed over. A trickle of blood runs from his swelling nose.

"Get up you little piker." Russo stands and raises both fists.

"The boss is going to put you in a ditch you bastard."

"Bushwa. Your boss is looking the other way, Jimmy. You're all alone. He knows you're a coward. A piker. You like to hurt girls. He doesn't respect you." He grabs Russo by the throat and delivers a head-butt sending the thug crashing into the wall.

Russo's body slides along the wall to the floor. He grabs a vase off a night table and throws it at Stanley but misses.

Stanley grabs him by the shoulders and stands him up. He unloads a series of body shots that crumple Russo like an old paper bag. Moaning and whimpering, Russo tries to fight back.

"No backup today, Jimmy?"

Stanley smashes the heel of an open palm into Russo's face and breaks the thug's nose spattering blood all over the room and sending him to the floor once again. Russo grabs hold of a bedpost and pulls himself onto the bed. He spits blood towards Stanley in defiance.

"One more thing, Jimmy." Stanley takes a step back and grabs the walking stick. He cracks Russo across the ribs.

Russo collapses in agony, staring up at Stanley, wide-eyed and wheezing as he tries to breath—blood drooling down his chin.

Stanley breaks the walking stick over his knee and tosses it at him.

"Make sure you take deep breaths Jimmy. You don't wanna catch pneumonia. It's important." He picks up the revolver. "Just remember, I know where you live Russo. I better never see your ugly mug again. I better never hear another peep about you beating up a woman. If I do, I'll be back to visit."

***

So much for bathing and cleaning up. Sweat drips from his face all the way down to his heels. The muggy Ohio weather has a way of doing that to you.

Stanley spots a flower vendor on the roadside. "Can I get a dozen pink and a dozen red roses? Thank you. Keep the change."

He parks near the front curb of EmmaMae's home. He closes his eyes and pictures her face. Eyes green as Irish moss, flecked in nutmeg. Lips, soft and delicate. He fills his lungs with air and slowly exhales helping to calm his nerves.

He steps onto her porch and stares at her door. He hides the roses behind his back and taps on the door. Moments go by. He sighs. *Guess she isn't home.*

He places the roses on a small table by the door and turns to walk away. The creaking of a screen door gives him pause. "Stanley?" His heart leaps.

He turns. EmmaMae steps out onto to the porch. She has a bounciness in her step like a school girl today. An orange floral peplum summer dress clings to her body, revealing feminine curves. Her wavy chestnut curls flow softly in the gentle breeze, kissed by the afternoon sunlight creating shimmers of auburn highlights in her hair. He's mesmerized by the vision.

"Hi doll." He can sense the big dumb smile stuck on his face like a Halloween mask.

She rolls her eyes and crosses her arms. *Is she annoyed? Or just teasing?*

"What are you doing here, Stanley? Did you miss me that much?"

She notices the roses and places her hands on her hips. "Are these for me? They're beautiful." She gathers the roses and presses her nose against the Bouquet. "Mm. I need to put these in water." Her screen door creaks as she swings it open. She pauses and turns towards him.

"Well. Are you going to come in, or are these beautiful roses from someone else? And wipe that dumb smile off your face."

"Um, yes. They are from me and I'd love to come in." He follows her into her living room.

"Have a seat. I'll be right back." She walks towards her kitchen, then pauses. "Can I get you some lemonade or tea, maybe?"

"Sure. I'd love some lemonade." She shakes her head and laughs to herself.

He can't stop fidgeting. He taps his fingers on the coffee table. *Why am I so damn nervous?*

He takes a gulp of lemonade and wipes a few sticky droplets off his chin using his sleeve. She stares at him with a slight frown, furrowing her brow.

Aware she's staring at him he glances around the room. "What?"

She shakes her head. "Um, do you need a napkin or something?"

"No thank you. I'm good."

She opens her mouth to speak then just rolls her eyes, choosing to refrain.

"So. Why the visit, Stanley?"

"I-I'd like to kidnap you…. Take you to the lake. Maybe … have a picnic. Just you and me." He said the first thing that came to his mind. He didn't really have a plan at all. He didn't think past the flowers. He simply wanted to gaze at her beauty. Listen to her soft voice. Breathe in her scent.

"Wow. You really have this all planned out, don't you? Well, I am off work today. I guess I'll allow you to do that."

The realization of what he just proposed hits him like a mud pie in the face. Sweat seeps along his collar. His face and neck heat up and prickle. "So, do you have anything to put in a picnic basket? Any food?"

She glares, speechless for several moments. "What? You mean you didn't bring a picnic basket or any food when you were planning this all out?"

He looks away from her glare, nervously tapping the coffee table with his fingertips. "Yeah, I guess I kind of overlooked that small detail. I'm kind of winging it here."

She sighs, slightly shaking her head. "Wait here Casanova. I'll be right back. Do you need any more lemonade? Or anything else you might have forgotten today … or maybe a napkin …?"

EmmaMae returns with fully-packed picnic basket, a folded tablecloth and a camera. She holds up the camera and smiles. "Just in case I want a picture of you and me to put on your mantle."

They drive a couple miles, mostly in silence to Meyers Lake and park in a pleasant secluded spot. They spread a large green and white plaid tablecloth over the green clover and grass. A fifty-foot oak tree casts shade over them and softens the light. EmmaMae tilts her head back and closes her eyes, breathing in the moist summer air. So much beauty in the curves and details of her face and neck. The fullness of her lips …

A young couple walks past them. EmmaMae turns to them and asks, "Could we get one of you to take a photo of us?" The young woman smiles and takes the camera from EmmaMae and snaps a photo of EmmaMae and Stanley sitting, hugging and each of them making their own silly face.

He caresses her face, barely brushing his fingertips along her cheek. His lips brush against the softness of hers. She pushes him away. "I thought you wanted to have a picnic?" She playfully glances at him. The left corner of her lips gently smiles. A single curl falls over her eyes. Eyes now locked on his, slightly squinting, catching tiny rays of sunlight and reflecting shimmers of aquamarine.

The rustling of leaves in the trees relaxes his soul. He's where he wants to be. The sky has never looked so blue. The sun has never shined so bright. The summer breeze has never felt so gentle.

"I'm beginning to think you have a crush on me, Stanley." She lays her head on his chest. He didn't expect that. She closes her eyes. The corners of her lips curl with the hint of a peaceful smile.

Two people have never been more perfect for one another. He gazes at the woman he has fallen in love with. Watching her sleep. Her head pressed against his heart.

You are the dream I dreamt. A wish fulfilled. My hope for salvation. My love for you knows no boundaries. No beginning and no end. It has always been there. Waiting to be realized. Waiting to be found. And now that I have found you, I can never let you go. This beautiful love we created together grows deeper with each breath. And from this day till the day I breathe my last breath, I will love you with all my heart and never leave your side.

CHAPTER SIXTEEN

Early Sunday morning seemed like the perfect time to make a quick stop at a local jewelry shop. A beautiful square cut diamond ring mounted on a platinum band grabs his eye. "Look at that thing sparkle. Damn." The price tag takes some of the sheen off. $365.00.

A clerk walks up and stands beside him. He points at the ring. "That's a full karat. A very nice ring for a special lady."

Stanley purses his lips and crinkles his brow and mutters. "I can give you three-hundred."

"What? I can get full price for this ring. It's worth over five-hundred. Easy."

Stanley, grimaces, and starts to walk away. "Good luck."

"Alright. I can go as low as three-fifty for you today. It's a beautiful ring. Any woman would be proud to display it on her finger. A special price, just for you, today."

"Three-twenty-five."

The clerk frowns and exhales like the air let out of a balloon. "Okay. Three-twenty-five. Only because I'm feeling generous today."

***

EmmaMae sits waiting on his porch. Tools in hand he stands on the steps shaking his head in disbelief. *She's up to something.* She smiles and crosses her arms.

"Get yourself cleaned up. I'm taking you to church today to attend Mass. I'm sure your soul could use some redemption. I'm also sure you have lots to confess."

He sets his tools on the porch rubbing his chin. "As long as I can take you for a vanilla shake afterward, I'll endure it."

***

Mass was long and boring. But if attending makes EmmaMae happy, then the sacrifice is worth the boredom.

"Let's swing by Heggy's for caramels and a shake."

They push open glass double-doors and step across bright red and white tiles to reach the candy counter.

"What can I help you with today?"

"A vanilla shake, two straws and a handful of those caramels. Please."

They sit in a cramped booth enjoying the rest of their Sunday afternoon engaged in small talk and playful banter. Hours quickly pass.

"Why the frown, doll?"

"It's getting late. Can you take me home, Mister Miller?"

He sighs. "Where did the time go? Of course. On the other hand, I live so close and you live so far. Maybe you can come home with me and spend the night. I can take you home in the morning."

Did I really just ask her that? What am I thinking?

She scowls and wags a scolding finger. "Why Stanley Miller. We aren't even married. I can't spend the night with you. How would that look?"

"I ... I'm sorry. You're right. Let's get you home."

They stroll along the sidewalk. Her hand fits perfectly into his. Her fingers slip and slide from moisture on his palm. She pulls her hand away and wipes it on her skirt. "You're sweaty. Ew. And you're acting very strange."

Stanley stops walking and grasps both of EmmaMae's hands, pulling her towards him. He pauses and stares at the ground. Then he focuses his eyes on hers. Staring deeply, lovingly.

"Marry me, EmmaMae. Spend every night and day with me for the rest of your life."

Her lips part and her eyes widen. She blankly stares for a moment, then gently shakes her head. "What was that? What did you say?"

He slips the ring box out of his pocket and opens it.

"I said, marry me. Please spend the rest of your life with me. I love you, EmmaMae. I can't breathe. I can't sleep. Just please say yes." He kneels in front of her, staring up into her eyes, holding the ring in both hands. His heart pounds from the surge of adrenaline coursing through his veins. Her silence is a grueling eternity of anticipation. *What if she says no?* Every hope and dream for his future will be washed away like tiny petals of orchids swept into the ocean. An ocean of his own tears.

She gently pulls the ring from the box and glides it onto her finger. She examines it in the light. "It's absolutely beautiful. Oh, my goodness. How did you ever afford such a beautiful ring?" Her eyes widen and glisten with moisture. Her lips part as she gazes at the gem's fiery beauty—mesmerized by the flickers of rainbow.

The hard sidewalk isn't an easy place to rest his knee. He winces from the penetration of concrete and pebbles jabbing and digging into his flesh.

He meekly whispers. "EmmaMae?"

"Yes. Yes. I *will* marry you, Stanley."

He exhales and stands allowing blood to reenter his burning kneecap.

She hugs his neck then pushes him away. She plants her index finger into his chest. "Don't think this means I'm going home with you tonight."

"Um ... no, not at all. I wasn't thinking that. I-I wouldn't think that."

She admires the diamond on her finger the entire ride home. Never seen her smile so much or look more angelic. Stanley opens the door for her and takes her by the hand. The couple walk to her front door holding hands and locking arms.

When they reach the door, Stanley softly places his hands on her shoulders. "EmmaMae. Can I kiss you? Would that be ..."

She wraps her arms around his neck, pulling his face towards hers. She presses her lips hard against his. Her lips. Lips plush and gentle. Subtle in their sweetness. Plump like fresh ripe berries. His heart pounds against hers. His body surges with adrenaline and erotic excitement, intoxicated by the taste of her breath. She pushes him away and disappears through the door. Gently closing it behind her.

He catches his breath and steps backward, his mind caught in a whirl of emotion. He turns to walk down the steps and catches his pant leg on the last step and stumbles. This time he manages to stay upright. He glances at her window. "Damnit. Not again you idiot."

She giggles, shakes her head then disappears behind the curtains.

***

Sunrise by the docks near 55th street on Lake Erie comes early. He parks his automobile near the pier and walks along its wooden docks. The air smells salty and fishy. The humidity is thick causing his clothes to stick to his body.

"None of these boats are called *Time Bandit*. Maybe it ain't here yet." He sits on a wooden bench and waits.

Gulls swoop in and out of the bay searching for an easy meal. Fishermen stand in small boats whipping fishing rods and casting lines into deep waters. He closes his eyes and takes in the salty air.

Papa took him fishing when he was a small boy. By the end of the day Stanley hooked him over a dozen times. It was one of the few times Papa didn't lose his temper. He'd curse in Polish as he yanked the embedded hooks from his flesh. Then patiently bait and reset them.

"Are you Miller?" Stanley opens his eyes. A heavyset Italian, wearing overalls, a ball cap and a black wool sweater stands over him. *Wait. The sweater is hair. This guy looks like a gorilla.*

"Yeah, I'm Miller. You have a package for me?"

"Follow me."

He follows the man along the dock towards a small commercial fishing boat. The weathered boat is white with a large blue stripe. On the side of the stripe are white faded letters. *Time Bandit.* Another man is waiting on the dock with a dolly stacked with wooden boxes. The boxes are stamped, *Fresh Produce.* The men follow Stanley to his automobile and stack the boxes in the back seat. He covers the boxes with a gray canvas. Ready for delivery.

***

Bellamy's rear parking lot is mostly empty today. Max sits among several wooden pallets smoking a cigarette and humming.

Max grins. "Hey lover boy. Whatcha got for me?"

Max jumps up, crushes his cigarette under his boot and helps unload the stash. "Here's some jack for your troubles, sheik. Nice work."

Max, places his arm around Stanley. "Why not come in for a brew and shoot the shit for a while? Get a little pie-eyed with me."

"Throw in a burger and I'm in."

"You got it buddy. I want to hear all about your dame and when the wedding is. You better invite me. I'm the Best Man, right?"

There's a small crowd in Bellamy's today. Mostly businessmen grabbing a quick lunch and a beer. Stanley takes a gulp of his brew as Max sets a plate with a large burger, fries and bottle of ketchup next to him. Max wipes the bar top and sets a plate on it for himself.

"You'll make someone a great wife, Maxie, if you weren't so fucking ugly."

Max grins. "Yeah, well, I'm saving myself, so you're out of luck. So... What's the story on you and your gal?"

"I love her. I'm going to marry her."

"That's it? You love her and you're going to marry her?"

"Yeah. That's it."

Max shakes his head. "Well woopty do. Thanks for the scoop. I can't wait ... hey, does she have any sisters?"

"Yeah Max. She has sisters. They're too good for the likes of you, so lose the thought."

Stanley finishes his brew and wipes his mouth with his sleeve. "I gotta go Maxie. Thanks for the brew and the burger."

"Yeah, well don't let the door hit you in the ass on your way out, pal."

***

Stanley picks EmmaMae up from work. They drive to Myers Lake and park close to the water. "Do you want to go for a walk, doll? Let's go take a look at all the construction around the lake. I hear they're adding more rides to the amusement park soon. Why not take a gander?"

"I'd love to."

The evening is warm, the air muggy and the mosquitos are savagely biting. The lake is calm and glasslike. A soft breeze blows through the trees rustling the leaves and adding to the peacefulness of the moment. Children are enjoying the park running around playing kickball. Others feed bread crumbs to the many ducks swimming in the lake and waddling along the shoreline.

EmmaMae points. "What's that?"

"That's the *Moonlight Ballroom*. We should come listen to some jazz music one of these nights. They're pulling in some really big bands."

"What are they building over there, darling?" Stanley squints to focus in on all the activity. "I think those are the new rides going in. This is going to be a swell place by next year."

She spontaneously grabs his hand and pulls him behind a large sycamore tree and kisses him. He's caught off-guard by the advance. But he welcomes it and embraces her.

A huge splash sprays water on the bank and all over the couple, interrupting the moment. "Your Sheba's got some great gams, sheik. What's her name?" Stanley steps around the tree followed by EmmaMae. Two young men are throwing rocks into the lake.

Stanley is furious but keeps his cool as he approaches them. EmmaMae wipes lake water from her legs with a handkerchief.

"Stanley. Let's just go."

The men laugh. "Who's your girlfriend, *Stanley*?"

Stanley doesn't say a word. He approaches the bigger man and lands a ball-crushing kick to his groin, doubling him over.

Sucker punched! *Where did that come from?* Stanley's ears ring and the world is spinning. His arms are being held from behind. The big man recovers from the kick to his groin and lands a blow to Stanley's ribs taking his breath. With all his strength Stanley smashes the back of his head into the face of the man holding him. He's free. He tackles the bigger man, wrestling him to the ground.

The other man steps toward Stanley and readies a kick. He's met by a solid purse to the face, sending him backwards into the lake. "You stay right there, buster! Unless you want another one." He holds his nose and upon seeing blood running through his fingers, he curses and retreats.

Stanley sits on top of the big man. "You're going to apologize to the lady." He punches him in the face repeatedly.

"Stanley! Stop! He's had enough." She hugs him, pulling him away. She grasps his face staring into his eyes. "Calm down. It's okay. Calm down."

The man staggers to his feet, wiping blood from his nose with his sleeve. He stumbles away.

Stanley's heart is raging. His breathing is rapid like a cornered wounded animal. She caresses his head and face. "They're gone, sweetheart. It's okay now. Just breathe. Relax."

"I wanted to kill him. I lost my head, I guess."

"It's okay. You whipped his butt, good." She opens her purse and pulls out a rock the size of a baseball and drops it on the ground. She cocks her head and innocently grins.

His face contorts, then breaks into a smile. He takes her by the hand. "I'll take you home now. Just … leave the rock, okay?"

He's troubled by the temper he can't control. It's Papa's temper. A temper he never asked for. It resides deep in his soul. He doesn't know why or how it got there. It gives no warning. It brews and boils like a dormant volcano ready to explode at any given moment.

Stanley leaves EmmaMae at her home and drives to Bellamy's. Maybe a shot of whiskey can quench the thirst of his demons and numb his torment.

"Set me up with some panther piss, Max."

"Whoa. The hard stuff. Bad day, buddy?"

"Just need a jolt to calm my nerves. I've been thinking Max. I have something I want to talk to you about. I need your help. I need a partner."

CHAPTER SEVENTEEN

SEPTEMBER 13, 1925 - Today is the fifth anniversary of the murder of George Puchalski. Stanley is restless. Agitated. Images of the past haunt his memories today more than any other day of the year. He cranks the engine of his Chevy and drives off. Maybe some fresh air and scenery might take his mind to a more pleasant place.

He drives along Cherry Street into the seedy areas of Canton. A large sign catches his eye. "Hm. For sale, huh? Flora's Market." He pulls into the empty gravel parking lot.

I know this place. I think it has a blind pig below.

He leans against aged red bricks and glances through the large plate glass window. Wooden baskets of fruit and vegetables sit on the floor. A sign on the wall with an advertisement of today's special reads: A dozen eggs for forty-five cents, a quart of fresh milk, fourteen cents, a pound of butter for fifty-six cents.

He turns the knob of the front door. It's locked. He jots the telephone number inside a book of matches. *This is exactly what I'm looking for.*

He drives to Bellamy's. If there is anyone who would know something about this joint, it would be Max.

"What's the password, shithead."

"Your mother's ass." He hears a bellowing laugh from behind the door. The door flies open. He stumbles forward with the help of Max's grasp on the front of his shirt yanking him inside.

"My mother's ass is too good for the likes of you."

Max hugs him. "What the hell are you doing here? Did your gal dump you already? Need to cry on my shoulder? Want a tissue?"

"No, dumbass." Stanley takes a seat at the bar. "You know anything about a small market store for sale up on Cherry Street? Flora's Market?"

Max crinkles his brow. "Yeah, I know it. Why? You wanna buy it?"

"I'm thinking I need something steady. Something to support my new wife. Like my own joint."

Max jerks his head back. "You really want to open your own joint?"

"Do you know the owner? I have some money itching to spend."

Max crosses his arms. "Let's say, I know of him. But I can ask around and see what I can find out. Do you have a telephone number or address?"

He tosses Max the matchbook. "Number's inside."

"You wanna beer, boss?" Max slides a frothy cold brew down the bar into Stanley's hand. He sips the foam. A painful jolt of electricity hits a molar.

"Shit. Son of a bitch." He slams the mug onto the bar, spilling foam.

Max throws him a towel.

"What the hell? You bite your tongue or something?"

He wiggles one of his teeth. "This damn tooth. Do you have some pliers?"

Max raises an eyebrow ready to laugh. "You going to pull your own tooth, Miller? What kind of moron, pulls his own tooth? You can afford a dentist, man."

Stanley lays an open palm across the bar and wags his fingers. "Don't worry about it. Toss me the pliers."

Max reaches under the bar and slides an old pair of rusty pliers along the bar surface. They spin and slide to a stop in front of his half-empty mug.

He grips the sore tooth, gives it a quick twist and yanks it out with a crunch. He shoves a corner of the towel into the gaping bloody hole. He examines the tooth. Turning it. Inspecting each side. "I hate dentists. They scare me."

Max approaches with a napkin. Stanley deposits the tooth.

"You want me to save this for the tooth fairy, buddy?"

Stanley's laugh is muffled. He slides the pliers across the bar towards Max and tosses him the bloody towel. He swigs a mouthful of beer, swishes and swallows.

"Shit. I don't want your damn bloody rag." Max gingerly grabs the blood-soaked towel with the pliers and tosses it into the garbage.

"You're a sick bastard, Miller. Real sick. I've never seen shit like that before. You learn that from your days on the farm? You and your family have to pull your own teeth? What the fuck?"

He slides the mug down the bar to Max. "Let me know what you find out about Flora's. I'll swing by tomorrow. I want to move on it fast."

Max winks. "Only for you sweetheart. Only for you …"

The drive home was uneventful. He grabs a coke from the ice box in the kitchen and plops into his easy chair. He flips on the radio, stretches his legs out. He listens to the sounds of the Indians at Detroit. It's the bottom of the eighth and the Indians are up four to three. *"Ty Cobb at the plate. It's a two-one count. Uhle hits Cobb in the back and walks him. Now with a runner at first ..."* The sound of the announcer's voice fades into blissful silence.

***

"You're not your usual jolly witty self this morning, Max."

"Sit down, man. I have the full story on this joint and some things you might wanna think about before venturing into this business endeavor." Max projects a thoughtful stare.

"I'm all ears Maxie. What do ya got?"

Max, rubs the back of his neck and loosens his collar. "I did some checking around. The joint is owned by a mick bootlegger from Cleveland with some bad connections by the name of Johnny Joyce. The guy is an Irish thug. I heard he murdered a car salesman five years ago and got away with it. He's looking to sell the joint for a reasonable price, but he wants a little take for himself. Basically, you're in bed with this mick if you make a deal"

"Well, I won't make that kind of deal. I got nothing to lose."

Max's face relaxes and forms a grin. "Well, okay then. I can set up the meeting. If you can make the right kind of deal, this could maybe benefit us both."

Max has this unique grin when the gears are grinding in his head. It's the sort of grin where he has a crazed look in his eye like he's about to piss on your shoes. He'd be the perfect partner in all of this. He has a lot of connections. He's the best bartender I've ever been around. Men love him. Women love him. It's sickening.

"One more thing, boss."

"I knew there was something else. Okay. What?"

Max glances at the bar and rolls his lower lip under his teeth and bites down. "You have to hire me to run your bar. Otherwise, I ain't introducing you. No dice. And, I ain't cheap."

Stanley shrugs and shakes his head. "The job was already yours, dumbass."

Max kisses him. Stanley spits at the ground. "Dammit Max. I always knew you were light in the shorts."

Stanley vigorously rubs his mouth on his sleeve. "One more thing. I'm going to bring in my younger brother Frank and teach him the biz. He's fifteen. A perfect age to indoctrinate into a life of crime. Ha-ha."

Max rubs his chin. "I don't think I'd want my little brother mixed up in this shit. But hey, you're the boss. I'll let you know when I have the meeting set up."

Stanley places Max in a headlock then releases him, dropping him to the floor. "What the shit?" Stanley bursts into laughter. "Don't ever kiss me again, Maxie. You, sick schmuck."

Stanley drives to the Telephone Exchange Office. EmmaMae is waiting by the curb. She smiles and waves with her fingers. *How the hell am I going to sell this idea to her? She's just going to have to trust me.*

The drive home was quiet. He pulls into the driveway and parks. "Darling, I have something I need to talk to you about."

"What is it, dear? You can tell me anything. You know that."

His lips are pursed as he grips the steering wheel. "I want to do something, sort of crazy. Something I've been thinking about for a while now. I need to take care of you, you know, and … and I've been thinking of how I can do that. So, I was out driving around and I came across this speakeazzz … well, uh, market place."

She stares intently. Her eyes connect with his. She slightly shakes her head and squeezes his hand. "Just spit it out, already. Say what you want to say. Stop beating around the bush."

Trickles of sweat bead and run down the back of his neck. "Okay. Here it is. I'm going to buy a market store."

"Well, I think that's wonderful. I'm excited for you."

The back of his neck prickles. "Well, that's not all. Um, the joint also has a basement."

"That's great. A basement can be a great place to store things. Is that it?"

He takes a deep breath. "The basement is a bar. A speakeasy. We could make a lot more money with a set up like that."

She sits in silence. She squints and tilts her head. "Well. I'm not so sure that's a good idea, Stanley. How is that going to work? You could catch a lot of hell if you get caught selling booze. It's still prohibition, you know. They'll give you a ticket straight to the big house."

He pats her hand. "I know dear. And that's why we can make so much more money. Just trust me on this."

She shakes her head and throws up a hand in surrender. "Let's talk about it more tomorrow. I'm really looking forward to just relaxing on the sofa with you and listening to some jazz on the radio." She gives him a peck on the cheek and runs along the walkway, disappearing into the house.

"Whew. Not sure how that went."

He walks through the front door. She pats the sofa. "Come sit."

He tunes the radio to the first jazz station he can find. She snuggles into his body and rests her head on his shoulder.

***

Stanley pulls into the parking lot behind Bellamy's. A brand new 1925 baby blue Bugatti Grand Prix Roadster is parked in the lot. A thug leans on the Bugatti arms crossed, puffing on a cigar. *Why is this mug eyeballing me?*

Stanley whistles. "She's a beauty. She yours?"

"No. She belongs to the boss." A cloud of cherry-flavored smoke assaults his face and nostrils. He walks through the smoke into Bellamy's.

A hint of queasiness starts to grip his insides as he approaches the joint. I think I'm about to meet Mr. Joyce in person.

The green rear door allowing access to Bellamy's speakeasy is partially propped open by a wooden doorstop. Stanley slips through the doorway and descends the stairway. A muffled conversation becomes clearer as he enters the bar.

Max chats with a dapper young gentleman. Glistening jet-black hair neatly combed and slicked to the side. Early thirties maybe, expensive brown three-piece suit. Matching brown fedora purposely placed next to him on the bar. A large overcoat lays across the barstool. A lot of glittering jewelry. Gold ring on his left hand, another gold ring on his right pinky set with a large sparkling emerald. No doubt this is Johnny.

Max beams. He seems relieved. "Hey. It's Miller. Welcome, buddy."

The gangster spins around on the barstool.

"Miller. I'd like to introduce you to Mr. Johnny Joyce." Max turns towards Johnny. "Mr. Joyce, this is Stanley Miller. The interested buyer I told you about." Max takes a step back. "Hey. You two have a lot to discuss. I'll be right here if either of you need anything."

Johnny's eyes are dark like a predator. It's almost like he knows something, you don't. He's cocky. His presence is felt.

"Mr. Miller. Let's move over to that table in the corner and chat."

"Call me Stanley. Can I buy you a beer, or a whiskey?"

Johnny nods, purses his lips and turns toward Max. "What brand of whiskey do ya have, lad?" Max holds up a dusty bottle of Old Crow. Johnny nods. "That'll do just fine."

A small wooden table separates them. Max sets up two shot glasses and pours. He leaves the bottle. "This is on the house."

Johnny nods. His jaw juts and his razor-thin lips form a turned down smile. "A mighty fine gesture." Max lingers.

Stanley smacks him on the arm. "Max."

"Oh … I'm just going to leave you two alone now. Let me know if you need anything. Like a burger or a dog …" Stanley throws his hands up. "Max. Please."

Max raises his palms as he backs away. "You got it boss. I'll be over here." He pulls a towel from his back pocket and proceeds to clean beer mugs.

Johnny extends his shot glass. "Here's to business."

The clink of glass and a gulp of whiskey burns and warms his throat. Stanley quickly inhales through his nostrils in an attempt to regain his breath. He turns his shot glass over and slides it next to Johnny's.

Johnny folds his hands together and leans into the table. He has an intense dead stare that burns right through to the back of your skull.

Stanley takes a deep breath and locks eyes with Johnny, holding his stare. Papa taught him well. He understands the psychological strategy of fearlessly staring down an opponent.

"So. Stanley. I hear you are interested in my little business?"

"I might be interested if the price is right and the deal is good. Yes sir."

Johnny scratches his head. He pours himself another shot. "Another shot, lad?"

Stanley waves it off. "No thanks."

Johnny shrugs and sets the bottle down. "Are you only interested in the market store? Or are you also interested in the speakeasy sitting below all those groceries?"

"Both."

Johnny grins. "Okay. Here's my offer boy. I'm going to cut through all the bullshit and straight to the chase. I want three G's for the business. I want cash. No loans, no credit. I want twenty-five percent of the cut from downstairs. I'll supply and sell all the liquor. I don't want a cut for the market store. That's all yours."

Johnny grins. "Pretty good offer, right? Do we have a deal?"

Stanley's heart sinks at the initial offer. He leans back in his chair placing his hands behind his head. He stares at Johnny without blinking.

Johnny sits with open palms, shrugging his shoulders and shaking his head. "What are we waiting for? I made you a great offer. Take the deal."

Stanley folds his hands on the table. "Here is my counter to your generous offer, Mr. Joyce. I can pay you two-thousand in cash for the business. I can offer you a five percent cut of the liquor profits for one year only, and I'll supply my own liquor. I also need to inspect the property before I can agree to any terms."

Johnny glances around the room. His eyes widen. His jaw tightens. He looks at Max. "Can you believe this bloke?"

Max continues to polish glassware, avoiding the question.

Johnny takes a deep breath. "Okay, lad. I can see you are a man to be bargained with. So, I'll tell you what I'm going to do. I'll sell you the business for twenty-six-hundred in cash. I'll take a twenty percent cut of all liquor sales and you can supply your own spirits. Now that's a generous deal. I need an answer right now. No more bloody shenanigans. What do you say?" Johnny offers his hand.

"Mr. Joyce, with all due respect, you need to understand something. I do not have to make a deal today on your business or any other business. I'm in no hurry. Here's my final offer for you, sir. I'll give you twenty-five hundred in cash for the business. I'll pay you ten percent of my liquor profits for one year. I supply my own liquor. That's it. If my offer offends you, I apologize and we're done negotiating. If my offer is acceptable, then let's go look at the property."

He extends his hand to Johnny. "Do we have a deal, sir? Can we take a ride and look at the property?"

Johnny rubs the back of his neck, then scratches his chin. He glares. His face turns flush. He pulls a cigarette from his shirt pocket and lights it. Stanley chokes from the puff of smoke engulfing his face.

"Aye, lad. So ya drive a hard bargain, do ya? Alright then. If it's a ride ya want to take, then let's take a ride."

On the way out, Johnny tosses Max a wad of cash. "Thanks Max. You were a fine host." Max's eyes widen. He pockets the cash. "Thank you, Mr. Joyce."

Stanley crosses his fingers and shrugs as he walks past Max.

"That's a mighty fine-looking automobile, Mr. Joyce."

Johnny grins. "Jump in lad. We'll take my car." Johnny turns to his driver. "Wait here. I'll be back shortly. Go have a pint." The thug leers at Stanley. "Yes sir Mr. Joyce."

Johnny tosses Stanley the keys.

"Holy shit. You're gonna let me drive her?" He takes a deep breath and fires up the engine. The two men drive off.

"Damnit, she drives smooth."

Johnny removes his fedora. "It's a brand new 1925 Type 35 Grand Prix Roadster. It fetched a hefty price tag, but she's my baby blue. I had the paint job custom ordered."

"She's a beauty Mr. Joyce. I would love to own a gem like this someday." He turns onto Cherry Street and rolls into the market store parking lot. "Thank you for allowing me the pleasure of driving your baby blue, Mr. Joyce."

Johnny grins and nods. "Call me Johnny." He fiddles with the lock for a moment and swings opens the door. "After you, Stanley."

The floor is tiled in four inch black and white ceramic tile. The tile job is flawless. The walls are painted mint green. A small register sits on a counter facing the front of the store. On the counter sit several jars with a variety of sweets. To the right are several shelves stocked with flour, sugar, cocoa, cereal, bread, and canned goods. On the back wall is an electric ice box housing blocks of ice, quarts of milk and blocks of cheese.

Behind the counter is a small cellar door. "The store is just a cover for the blind pig below, lad." Johnny opens the cellar door and descends a set of creaky wooden stairs.

At the bottom of the stairs, he stands in an eight-foot by twelve-foot cellar. The floor is dirt. A shelf covers the back wall where bags of rice, beans and potatoes are stored. He notices a couple rat traps on the floor. One of the traps holds the decayed corpse of a dead rodent. The air is musty and cool. A string dangles from the ceiling leading to a single light bulb illuminating the room.

Johnny swings the shelf away from the wall revealing a doorway and a sturdier set of stairs leading downward. He winks. "Ready yourself for the big reveal." Johnny flips a large circuit breaker on the wall, illuminating the stairwell. "The lights are on, lad. Follow me."

The joint emits a concoction of aromas. Mildew, cigar smoke, liquor and stale perfume are a few he can identify. There's a small bar towards the far wall. Behind the bar is a large mirror. Bottles of whiskey, rum, gin and other indistinguishable liquor bottles are lined up in front of the mirror. Dirty beer mugs sit on the bar top along with a small plate of moldy cheese.

Round wooden tables are scattered around the floor. A few of the chairs are knocked over. There's a small stage in the back. The walls are made of aged dirty red brick. Sports banners hang on the walls. Cleveland Indians, Ohio State Buckeyes, and Canton Bulldogs.

Tattered photographs of young naked flappers are tacked on another wall. Strewn across the floor are old playing cards, cigar butts, scraps of paper and crushed peanut shells. There are a couple electric fans on either end of the room and a large cathedral style radio sitting on a small round table against the wall by the stage.

Johnny opens his arms. "So, this is it. The place has avoided the coppers for years and turns a fine profit when it's open. To be honest, lad, I have too many irons in the fire, and I want to keep my focus on my businesses in Cleveland. This is why I'm willing to sell the joint to you for such a bargain. You caught me in a generous mood. I usually have a way of forcing anyone I want, to do exactly what I want, when I want. Maybe this is just your lucky day."

Stanley's mind screams with excitement. He clears his throat "Do we have a deal then?"

"I'm going to accept your offer, lad. With just one more concession on your part. I have three girls who I have employed here the past several years as flappers. They're good girls. I don't want to see them lose their jobs, so I want you to keep them on. I pay them two dollars per night and any tips they can score."

"You have a deal, Johnny." A firm handshake seals the bargain.

"Meet me at Bellamy's tomorrow morning. Nine o'clock. Bring the cash. I'll sign over the deed and give ya the keys."

"Now let me give ya the full tour." Johnny leads him behind the bar. "See this switch? If ya get wind of a raid, flip it. It flashes red lights in the bar. Your customers will know to high tail it to the exits." Red light pulsates off the walls when Johnny hits the switch.

"Follow me. I'm going to show ya the backway out of this joint."

Johnny walks past the stage to a wooden door against the wall. It's a small closet containing cleaning materials, a broom and other miscellaneous items. Johnny places both hands on the back wall of the closet and slides it to the right. Behind the wall is a set of red brick steps leading up. "Let's go up the stairs."

At the top is a set of wooden shelter doors. Johnny slides a lock and pushes the doors open allowing access to the rear lot of the building.

"Guests can exit into the woods or down the street far away from the speakeasy. Ya want to keep this door locked from the inside to keep people from entering from the outside." Johnny pulls the door closed, slides the lock back into place and the two men return downstairs. Johnny slides the fake wall into place and closes the closet door.

"There's a small wine cellar below the bar where you can store your most expensive wines and liquors and keep them safe." Johnny walks around the bar and rolls up a large rug on the floor, revealing a small trap door. He lifts the door and walks down a small set of wooden steps and flips a light on.

The room is very cool. The floor is clay. Empty wooden wine racks line the walls.

"The temperature is perfect for storing your fine wines."

They exit the wine cellar. Johnny flips off the flashing red lights.

Johnny walks toward the left side of the stage and opens another small wooden door. "This is where ya piss and shit. It's connected to a cesspool."

"Well. There ya have it. That's the grand tour. Any questions? You can lose the poker face now, lad. She'll be all yours by the morrow. Just bring the cash and we're square."

CHAPTER EIGHTEEN

Stanley taps his fingers on the table. The anticipation has slowed the minutes of his timepiece so they pass like hours. If patience is a virtue as they say, it isn't a virtue he possesses. What if Johnny changed his mind?

"Maybe he's running a late, Max."

"He'll be here, Miller. Just relax." Max drums a beer mug with his fingers.

A knock on the rear door. Twelve minutes past the hour.

"God, Mary and Joseph be with ya, lads."

"Good morning Johnny. Can I buy you breakfast?"

"No thanks. Not hungry, really."

Johnny seems almost too happy. Way more energy in his step this morning. Is he up to something? He neatly lays the deed and a contract on the table. He has a suspicious twinkle in his eye as he slides them over to Stanley.

"Here's the deed. And here's a small contract between you and me, lad. For the ten percent, ya know."

Wait a minute.

"Excuse me Mr. Joyce, but the contract says, twenty-five percent. It should be ten percent."

Johnny smirks. "I was just testing ya, boy. I need to be sure the fella I sell my joint to pays attention to detail." He lifts the pen and draws a straight line through the verbiage then corrects the error.

"Here goes." He signs Stanley W. Miller. He slides the contract and along with twenty-five-hundred dollars cash to Johnny.

Johnny counts the money twice. He tosses the keys across the table. "Pleasure doing business with ya. Best of luck. I'll be by at the end of the month for my cut." He stashes the cash into a small leather wallet and walks towards the exit. He pauses and turns and tips his hat. "Stay in the company of angels, lads."

It's just a piece of paper. But a sense of pride and accomplishment accompanies the deed he holds in his hand. He smacks the table and waves the deed in the air. "We did it, Maxie."

Max bull rushes Stanley and puts him in a headlock. "Dammit man. You did it. You actually did it. You, shrewd son of a bitch. Your very own blind pig … and you negotiated the shit out of that deal. Weren't you scared he was going to whack you or something?"

"Get off me. Shit" He shoves Max into the tables. "We have a lot to talk about. A lot of work to do. Sit down for minute."

Stanley strokes his chin and squints. "Max, I need you to set me up an account for liquor and beer."

"You got it boss. Consider it done."

"I need to clean up the joint and have everything ready for the weekend. Put out the word we are open for business on Saturday. I'll pay you twice what they're paying you here."

Max grins. "They don't pay me shit here. So, you're gonna pay me double shit? Sweet deal."

"I gotta go. I gotta pick up Frank. He's got a lot to learn in a short time."

***

The drive to Lisbon is quiet. It's a cool seventy-five degrees and cloudy as he pulls up to Aunt Mary's home. His timepiece reads, 2:17 p.m.

Flowers in hand, he walks along the sidewalk towards the porch. "Serduszko. Oh."

"Geez Mama, you're squeezing the shit outa me."

She slaps him. "Watch your language."

"Look who's here, Mary."

Aunt Mary pulls a chair out from the kitchen table. "Sit sweetie. I'll make you some coffee. Are you hungry?"

"Starving. Cream and some sugar, please. What do you have to eat around this joint, Aunt Mary?"

"How about some hot apple pie with vanilla ice cream?"

His eyes widen. "Hell ya … I mean, yes, please."

Stella kisses his hand. "Such a nice surprise."

"Ah, I just wanted to see you all. And … I want to talk to Frank. I have a job for him." He reaches into his pants pocket and pulls out a small wad of cash. "This is for you, Mama. To help with the kids."

"What is this, mój syn?" Mama's eyes water. "Thank you, thank you, my boy. This will help out so much. Annie needs new shoes for school and Billy wears out every pair of pants I buy him. He's growing so fast."

Aunt Mary sets a plate in front of Stanley. The combined scent of cinnamon and vanilla excite his senses. Ice cream melts over the sides of the steamy pie, creating small pools of cream.

The door bursts open. Annie and Billy rush into the kitchen.

"Stanley!" He kneels with open arms, readying to catch them both. The children knock him to the floor. "Ah, Billy. You're breaking my ribs with those punches. Hey, that's my stomach. Ug."

"Annie, you're choking me to death. How'd you get so strong?"

A familiar voice resonates from the living room. Although the voice is several octaves deeper now. "Kick his butt Billy. Don't let him go Annie. Hold him down. Kick the shit out him."

Mama slaps the table. "Frank. Watch your mouth."

"Ha-ha, sorry Mama. We're all getting too strong for you to handle, big brother."

"Okay, you guys win. Let me up."

Frank stands six-foot-two and a solid two-hundred pounds. "What have you been feeding this kid, Mama? Holy shit ... uh, I mean holy crap."

Frank flexes his biceps. "Nice to see you, brother. Yeah. Go ahead, feel these solid biceps and dream.

Annie tugs Stanley's sleeve. "Stanley, will you play kickball with me and Billy?"

"I'll play with you both in a little bit, sunshine. Right now, I need to talk with Frank."

She frowns. A sharp pain strikes his calf, followed by a giggle and footsteps running out the door.

"O-o-o-ouch."

Frank bursts into laughter. "She's a little bearcat. She doesn't handle being told, no very well."

"Mama, I'm going to talk with Frank for a few minutes. We'll be right back."

"Where you two going?"

"Just up the street. We'll be right back."

He grabs Frank by the collar. "Let's go for a walk, Franky."

They stroll around the neighborhood. Frank swings his arm around Stanley's neck. "I've missed my big brother. It gets real boring around here. Mama and Aunt Mary talk a lot about moving. I also heard them saying something about wanting to make moonshine. To make extra money, I guess."

Stanley shakes his head and laughs. "Well, Mama knows how to brew it. Maybe I'll buy some of her first batch. Man, I'm going to have to get used to looking up at you."

Stanley plops on the raised bank of a neighbor's front yard. Frank sits next to him.

"I want you to come live with me. I've got a job for ya."

"A job? What kind of job? Sweeping your floors and cleaning your shitter? No thanks."

"A real job, jackass. The kind that's going to make you a rich man."

"How long do I have to think about it?"

"I'm here to pick you up and take you back today. So, no pressure or anything."

"I was afraid you were going to say that. So, what exactly is the job?"

"I bought a market store."

"So, you want me to bag groceries?"

"Not exactly. Under the store is a speakeasy, ya know, an illegal tavern."

"So, you want me to be the muscle to keep everyone in line?"

"I want to teach you to rum run. Pick up packages for me and deliver them to the joint."

"Oh … a bootlegger."

"You got it. Rumrunner … bootlegger. I want you to know your onions when it comes to the business. Make a lot of dough. Maybe find a little hotsy-totsy to spend all your money on."

Frank's face flushes. "You make it sound swell. I'm ready to leave here, anyway. There's nothing to do in Lisbon. Okay. I accept the job."

"Great. Go pack your crap and let Mama know you're leaving with me."

"Me? You tell her. I'm not telling her."

They walk back to the house slapping each other trying to decide who's telling Mama. Stanley points. "Well, there's Mama and Aunt Mary on the porch. So, think of what you're gonna say. Make it good."

Mama waves. "You boys want some lemonade?"

They respond in unison. "No thanks Mama." They sit on the top rail of the porch still slapping each other.

Mama frowns. "Okay, what's up with you two?"

Stanley stares at Frank and raises his eyebrows. "Tell her."

"Ahem … Mama, Stanley has offered me a really good job in Canton. I'm going to be sixteen soon, and I really need a change of scenery. Would it be okay with you if I go with him? I'll finish school. I promise."

Mama places her hands over her mouth. Here come the tears. Her voice trembles. "My boys, my boys. What can I do? What can a mother do?" She walks over to Frank and places both hands on his face. "Is this what you really want my sweet boy?"

Mama lays on the guilt heavily and it always seems to work best on Frank. "Yes, Mama. I'm almost a man now and I want to go with him. As long as you're okay?" He hugs her. The gesture has the effect of giving Mama permission to let loose and cry. She sobs, then steps backward in melodramatic fashion.

"Stanley, I know you'll take good care of your brother. Promise me he goes to school. And promise me you'll bring him home to visit often."

"I promise. And I will."

She nods and returns to the porch swing. Mary pats her on the thigh, reassuring her.

The front screen door bursts open. It's Annie. She screeches like a banshee in the night. Something smacks Stanley in the face from out of nowhere. The sting is followed by a swoosh of water that drenches Stanley's hair and shirt. "What the fuck just happened?!"

Annie shrieks and runs back into the house closely followed by Billy.

"Are you kidding me? I've been hoodwinked by a twelve-year old."

Frank doubles over with laughter. Tears stream down his flushed face. Mama and Mary giggle with amusement. Mama stands up and slaps Stanley hard on the shoulder adding to the shock. "I told you boys to watch your mouths around Aunt Mary's home. It's disrespectful. I didn't raise you like that."

He removes his soaked shirt and wipes his face. He pauses momentarily. "I apologize Aunt Mary. Just wasn't quite expecting that."

Stanley strips down to his skivvies and lays his clothes across the top rail of the porch. Two little heads peek out from around the corner.

"Okay, I surrender. You can come out now."

They slowly emerge. Annie wags a scolding finger. "That's what you get, Stanley."

"What? What, did I do to you?"

"That's what you get for not playing with us"

He laughs. "Okay, get your ball and I'll play. Then Frank and I have to go."

Ten minutes pass. Frank emerges from the house with a bag over his shoulder. "Let's go. I'm ready."

Annie stops. The ball rolls past her feet. "Where you going? Why are you leaving?" She frowns and lowers her head, then looks up wide-eyed with tears rolling down her chubby cheeks.

Frank hugs her. "I'll be back soon, pumpkin-eater. You take care of my room, okay? You're in charge of all my stuff. When I come back, I'm going to bring you the biggest teddy bear you've ever seen."

She sniffs and wipes her eyes. She stares at him. Her little nose is red and her lower lip protrudes. "You promise?"

"I promise. Be a big girl. I'll call ya on the telephone when we get there. Okay?"

She squeezes him, burying her face in his chest and closing her eyes. "I love you Frank. I'll miss you."

Billy latches onto Frank's leg. "Stay here, Frank. Don't go."

"I gotta go Billy. Take care of Annie, okay? You two be good for Mama and Aunt Mary."

***

Aunt Mary's home fades in the distance as they turn onto the highway. "Are you okay, little brother?"

Frank nods and smiles. "I'm good. I'm ready to do this. Just getting out of Lisbon is a load off my mind. I'm mean, I miss Mama and the little ones, but I was going stir crazy back there."

"Pull over for a minute. I gotta piss." Stanley steers the automobile onto the shoulder of the highway and rolls to a stop. Frank jumps out and jogs a few feet down a grassy bank and hides behind a bush.

Frank jumps. "What the shit?"

Stanley chuckles after seeing Frank stumble backwards, pissing in the wind. "What happened Frank? Piss on your foot? See a little spider or something? You scream like a girl."

"Oh really? Do I, now?"

Frank hurls something into the air and into the front seat of the automobile. It lands in Stanley's lap.

"What the hell? What the hell *is* that?!" No one has ever dived out of a window with such speed and complete abandon.

Frank is hysterical with laughter. "Yeah, I scream like a girl, but you run like a piker."

Stanley creeps over to his automobile and eases the door open. A black snake. Coiled on the floorboard. "You little asshole." He grabs the snake by the head and tosses it toward the brush. "Let's go shithead. You think you're funny, huh?"

A cloud of dust and they're back on the road. "That was a good one, little brother. Yeah, ya got me good on that one." Frank nods his head. "Yeah, that *was* good. You should have seen your face." Frank slides back into his seat placing his feet on the dashboard and sighs.

Yeah, get nice and comfortable, Franky. He patiently waits for Frank to get relaxed. Then he leans his head back and closes his eyes. The vehicle veers off the road towards a large oak tree.

"What's going on? You're off the road, man."

"Hey … wake up. What are you doing? Watch it … you're gonna hit that fucking tree!"

Stanley hollers like a crazed lunatic and veers back onto the highway.

"What the hell is wrong with you? I think I shit my pants."

"If you're gonna prank me, Frank, ya better get me good. Cuz, I will get you back, tenfold. Ha-ha. Remember that."

The brothers roll into Canton and into the driveway of Stanley's modest home. "We made it. This is home now. I have some colas in the ice box. Let's get you settled in and see if we can find a ballgame on the radio.

***

Thursday morning, Frank wakes to the aroma of bacon and eggs sizzling in the kitchen.

"Wake up princess. Time for breakfast." They sit at the kitchen table eating a breakfast of eggs, bacon, toast and jam, potatoes and orange juice.

Stanley wipes his mouth with his sleeve. "There's someone I want you to meet. She's special to me. I asked her to marry me."

"What? Are you kidding?"

"No. I'm not kidding. Her name is EmmaMae Flagg. She's the reason I bought this joint."

Frank places his hand on Stanley's forehead. "Well, you aren't running a fever. You're serious?"

He nods. "I fell in love with her the moment I saw her. She's strong willed, she's funny, she's not afraid of anything. The way she carries herself ... so confident and smart. I can't get her out of my thoughts. I spend all day dreaming about a life together with her. Am I crazy?"

"I don't think you're crazy. Can't wait to meet her. Should be interesting. She must be an amazing gal. Never seen you act this stupid."

"Alright, enough about that. I'm going to take you to Bellamy's after breakfast to introduce you to Max. Then we'll head over to the new joint and get everything ready to go for Saturday."

***

"Holy shit. Is this your little brother?"

"This is Frank. Frank this is Max."

"Nice to meet you, Max. Heard a lot about you. None of it good."

Max grabs Franks hand and gives it a firm shake. "No doubt you two are brothers. The joint isn't open yet. Let's move to the back of the bar. I have the perfect spot for our little sit down."

"This is the *Rumrunner's Den*, Frank. It's a small poker room. Local mobsters and businessmen hang out, play poker and drink. Some of the games are high stakes. There're a few heated arguments that break out and even a brawl once in a while. There's always a game manager overseeing the activities and packing heat. A lot of cash changes hands in here."

They sit around a small square wooden table. The walls are wood panel board. The floor is concrete, painted brown. A few pictures hang on the walls below light fixtures. A mini bar sits towards the far wall. Cigar smoke lingers in the musty air.

Stanley places his hand on Frank's shoulder. "I'm going to show you how to make our liquor runs. Our supplier smuggles product across Lake Erie from Canada. We pick up the shipments on the docks."

Max interrupts. "I'll be running the bar and you'll help me keep things running smooth. Also going to be some flappers dancing and singing and waving their little asses around. But your eyes are too young for that shit. So, I'll keep you busy."

Frank chuckles. "I appreciate that. I'll do my best to keep my eyes on my work." Frank turns towards Stanley. "I'm ready to work, brother."

Max brings three shot glasses from the mini bar to the table along with a bottle of bourbon. He sets a glass in front of Stanley and Frank and one in front of himself. "I know it's way too early for this, gents, but we have to consummate the marriage." Max fills each glass with the brown liquid. "Cheers boys. Here's to money, booze and women and lots of success." The three tap their glasses and down their shots.

The bourbon hits Frank's throat with a nauseating warmth causing him to choke. He spews the shot all over the table. Stanley and Max burst into laughter. Max pats Frank on the back. "It's okay kid. It's an acquired taste as they say."

"Frank and I are going to head over to the joint and start cleaning up and getting things ready by the weekend. Come by when you get off work."

Max, nods. "I'll be there, boss."

***

The brothers roll into the gravel parking lot of Flora's. "We have to come up with a better name than Flora's for the joint, Franky. How about, Sophie's Fine Foods?"

Frank laughs. "Yeah, Sis will love that until she finds out what's going on beneath the store."

Stanley jingles the keys. "Let me give you the tour. Then roll up your sleeves. We gotta a lot to do today."

Frank glances around the store with his hands on his hips. "You'd never know this was a speakeasy. This is a swell little store if you plan on making your fortune selling potatoes."

Just as Frank finishes his sentence, a hard blow hits him square in the chest. He yelps and staggers backwards and falls into a half empty barrel of navy beans. He's stunned. Pieces of potato are everywhere. A rotten odor fills his nostrils and the sound of his brother's booming laughter fills the room.

Before Frank can move, Stanley fires a barrage of old rotten potatoes at him, nailing him on the head and all over his body. Frank squeals and laughs hysterically struggling to get out of the barrel.

"Truce. I'm stuck in the barrel. No fair man. I'm defenseless." Stanley helps Frank out of the barrel.

He hugs Stanley. "Man, I've missed you so much."

Stanley pushes him away sensing the wet sticky plum juice running down the back of his neck. "Shit. And I fell for that."

Stanley opens the cellar door. "Be careful. These steps are a bit shaky. We'll need to either replace them or sturdy them up. He pulls a string illuminating the walls and revealing the small dirt-floor cellar.

"Wow. What a great speakeasy. Where's all the broads?"

"The broads are this way." Stanley moves the false shelf, revealing another set of steps leading downward into the speakeasy. He flips on the lights. "Here's our money maker. Follow me."

Frank's eyes widen. He gazes around the room. "Dang. Look at this place. This is going to be a lot of work brother, but man this place will be the bee's knees when we're done."

Stanley removes a push broom and cleaning supplies from the closet. "You remember how this works, right? You're on the clock. Start dancing with the mop. I'll start working on the upstairs."

They work nonstop throughout the day. Stanley has cleared out all the rotten fruit and vegetables, swept the floors, cleaned walls and windows and fixed everything that was broken. The store is ready for business again. All it needs is some fresh goods to fill the shelves and some fresh produce to fill the baskets. A respectable cover for any speakeasy.

Meanwhile Frank has cleared out all the garbage from the bar. The floors are swept and mopped and immaculate. The bar area is pristine and orderly. He tests the fans and the radio to ensure they're in good working order.

"Frank. Let's go get some grub."

"Sweet. I could eat an elephant's ass right now."

Before the two can exit the store, a beautiful young woman steps through the front door. She has to be around nineteen or twenty. Five foot three. The sleek muscled body of a dancer. Flawless ivory skin. Eyelashes that flutter like tiny butterflies drawing attention to her sultry nut-brown eyes.

She sports a bob of thick wavy black hair complimenting a sporty lace dress with a pink silk crepe underneath. Her dress conforms to the shape of her body revealing deadly curves. Her plump lips glisten with crimson lipstick. The scent of flowery perfume permeates the air with a seductiveness that's hard for Frank and Stanley to ignore. She carries herself with poise and grace like a model.

She places her left hand on her hip and tilts her head and smiles. "Hey boys. Johnny said there was a new owner in town. Which one of you is Stanley?"

"That would be me."

Frank points. "Uh … that's him."

The young woman giggles. "Ooh, don't you both look hard boiled. Let me introduce myself. I'm Rose." She presents her hand to Stanley. He gently grasps her fingers.

She presents her hand to Frank. He takes her hand and kisses it as if he were meeting royalty. Rose giggles and swipes her fingers across Frank's arm. "You're a big boy." Frank blushes.

Stanley shoves both hands into his trouser pockets. "Johnny said there's three of you."

Rose nods. "Uh-huh. That's right. Let's see. There's me, my younger sister Ruby and my best friend, Lily. Anyway, I was just passing by and noticed you boys working, so I thought, 'Why not introduce myself?'"

"It's a pleasure to meet you Rose. I did promise Johnny I would hire you all." Stanley removes his hands from his pockets and places them on his hips. He glances around. "We're kind of in the middle of renovations at the moment, but we should be open for business by Saturday. Why don't you bring Ruby and Lily and stop by on Friday afternoon … say around six o'clock and we can all chit-chat. Work out all the details.

Rose runs her sleek tongue across her top teeth, grinning coyly. "Ooh. That would be so nice. We'll see you on Friday then. So nice to meet you both." She glances at Frank and winks as she walks away swinging her hips in perfect rhythm.

Frank's mouth is agape. "Did that really just happen? Punch me in the face."

Stanley shakes his head. "Yeah. It did. That looks like a whole lot of trouble if you ask me. But I made Johnny a promise."

"Hey, with all you have to worry about, why don't you let me manage the girls? Great idea, right?"

He draws in a deep breath and exhales. "You know what, Frank? Sure. Why don't you line up the girls and manage them? Just strap down that boner when you do. Let's get cleaned up. I have someone very special I want you to meet."

***

EmmaMae emerges from the telephone company. She curiously squints and slightly shakes her head as she approaches. "Who's this nice-looking young man, Stanley?"

Frank steps towards EmmaMae and offers his hand. "I'm Frank. I'm Stanley's younger brother. Very nice to meet you. I've heard a lot of nice things about you."

"Thank you. Very nice to finally meet you too Frank. What are you two stiffs all spiffed up for? Do you have dates or something?"

Stanley nods. "Um. Yeah. You. You're our date. I'm taking you and Frank to dinner."

"Ooh. Where are you taking us? I'm starving."

"I'm going to buy you two the best burger in town."

The *Canton Brewing Company* is a fine restaurant in an area of Canton called *Little Chicago*. It's also a well-known speakeasy on Stanley's route of distribution. A short balding German man wearing an apron greets the trio. He speaks in a thick German accent. "What can I get you folks?"

"Can we get three deluxe burgers with everything, some fries a couple sarsaparillas, and one Cascade beer?"

EmmaMae waves her hand and buts in. "Please, no onions on mine thank you."

The waiter bows his head. "Coming up."

EmmaMae slides her chair back. "Will you both excuse me a moment? I need to go to the powder room."

Stanley's arm stings from Frank's slap. Frank doesn't realize his own strength at times. "Wow. I'm really happy for you. She seems like a fine dame."

"She is. But you have to help me out here. Help me tell her about the speakeasy and help me convince her what a great idea it is."

Frank jerks his head back. "What? You haven't told her yet? How do you expect me to convince her? No, no. That's your job. And I'm gonna enjoy watching this."

Stanley's chair suddenly becomes uncomfortable. "Alright. Just … back me up or something."

The waiter serves the table its order of burgers and drinks. Frank snatches his burger ready to devour it.

"Frank. Wait for EmmaMae. Bad manners."

He drops the burger on the plate. "Oh, sorry. You're right. Here she comes."

EmmaMae places a napkin on her lap. "Bow your heads, boys."

"Lord, please bless this meal. We thank you for its bounty. Bless these two handsome men I am sitting with. We ask this in your Son, Jesus Christ's name, Amen."

Frank smiles. "Can we eat now?"

EmmaMae nods. "Yes, we can eat now."

Frank stuffs his face with the burger in one hand and crams fries into his mouth with the other. He washes it down with the sarsaparilla. "So, Stanley, are you going to tell EmmaMae about the speakeasy you bought?"

Frank nods his head and grins as if to say, you're welcome. He actually seems to think he just helped Stanley with his dilemma.

Stanley's neck is tingling with a sudden itch. His knee inadvertently bounces up and down beneath the table.

She's scowling. "You bought the speakeasy bar? When were you going to tell me?"

"I ... I was going to tell you tonight ... here. At dinner."

"Thanks a lot Frank."

"Don't blame Frank. I thought you would discuss this with me a little more before you made a decision." She places her burger on her plate and wipes her mouth with her napkin. She sits quietly and pouts.

EmmaMae glares. "Stanley, we can't have secrets in our relationship. You should have talked to me first. I don't know what to say."

He turns his chair and faces her. "My love, I'm sorry. I would give you the world if it was in my power to do so. You mean everything to me. All my hopes and dreams have only one purpose. You."

Her face softens from the tender words and her eyes mist.

"I didn't have much time to act. I had to make a quick decision or risk losing out on the opportunity. An opportunity for me to give you the life I want to give you. A life you deserve. I want to buy you everything your heart desires and take care of your every need. I adore you. I didn't mean to hurt you or not to include you in my decision ... and I promise it'll never happen again. Can you forgive me ... and maybe finish eating your burger?"

She softly takes his hand. "I forgive you. I'll just have to trust that you know what you're doing."

Franks leans back in his chair and folds his arms. "Wow. That was beautiful. Ya, might tell her about Rose too." He glances at Stanley and nods. He must really think he's helping the situation.

"Who's Rose?"

"She's just someone who came looking for a job today. I think she was sweet on Frank. Probably stopped to talk because he had his shirt off trying to impress her. He thinks he's a sheik or something."

She laughs. She bought it for now. He's going to have to tell her the full story about Rose and her girls at some point. Maybe when the time and place is right. The dishonesty nags at him, but getting her to accept the speakeasy itself is enough honesty for today.

Frank mumbles. "Nice recovery."

After dinner, Stanley drives EmmaMae to her sister Betty's home. "Frank, it was such a pleasure to finally meet you." EmmaMae walks towards the house. "Drive safe and stay out of trouble—both of you."

***

Friday morning couldn't come soon enough. Hammers pounding, nails flying. Motes of saw dust swirling around the air. The scent of fresh wood. It feels good to sweat and put your back and hard work into doing something for yourself.

Stanley steps back and admires their work. "As soon as we finish this staircase, let's give it a couple coats of varnish."

Frank nods. "Sure thing. It looks great. You really inherited Papa's skills on building and fixing shit up. You remind me a lot of him."

"Papa was a wife beater. And a child beater. And a drunk. I'm nothing like him, Frank." He points his finger at Frank. "Don't ever say that shit again."

"I'm sorry man. I didn't mean it like that. Papa was a skilled builder and successful farmer ... and a smart businessman. I only meant you inherited the good things he was. Not the bad."

"I'm sorry. I know you didn't mean it like that. I can't think about Papa. I can't think about what Mama did. I don't want to talk about those things. They're in our past. Let's you and I build a future right here. I'm proud of you, Frank. And I'll always have your back and be here for you."

"I know that. You came back and got us out of that shithole orphanage and took care of us. I'll never forget that. You taught that punk Marco a lesson that night when you left him naked as a hairless dog in the hallway."

They burst into laughter. "Marco and his crony little brother never bothered any of us again, after that. They even left Eddie alone."

"Let's finish this staircase before it gets any later. Plus, you need a bath, Frank. Damn. You smell like pig shit." Frank sniffs his armpits. "Nah, I think that's you."

"Are you ready to become a professional bootlegger, Franky?"

CHAPTER NINETEEN

"Ah, it's the Miller brothers. Get your asses in here. Follow me to the den."

"The run is set. You're picking up eight cases of Seagram's and Canadian Club whiskey. Good stuff. I also have five kegs, some raisin jack, rum, wine and gin. That should get us started, gents."

Max punches Frank in the shoulder. "You ready for your first rum run? You look nervous."

"I got this, Max, thanks."

Max leans back in his chair, puts his hands behind his head. "The stash will be loaded and ready for you in the back of an ice cream truck. The truck will be parked near the dock at Lake Erie. One of the Semple brothers, probably Ed will be waiting in the truck until you arrive. The pick-up time is two a.m. Don't be late. All you gotta do is drive the truck back here and unload it. Simple enough?"

Frank grimaces. "An ice cream truck? Are you kidding?"

"I'm going with you on this first run little brother. So, don't be nervous.

But, yeah, Max. An ice cream truck?"

Max stands and stretches his neck. "Hey, last minute arrangements. It's the best I could do. You'll be fine. I'll come to work early tomorrow morning, around eight. I'll have the bar all set up and ready for business. Assuming Frank here can deliver. I'm sorry the pick-up spot is all the way in Erie. I'll get a closer location on the next run, boys."

Stanley rises and places both hands on the table. "Let's go, Frank. We have some things to tend to before we get ready for tonight."

***

The sound of a horn directs the boy's attention towards the street where a yellow cab has arrived.

"Where ya headed, fellas?"

"To the docks at Erie, please."

"Erie? Long drive. That's going to cost you boys fifteen for the ride."

"Here's twenty. Keep the change."

The drive was long and boring. The squeak of the taxi's brakes jars Stanley from a nap. Frank grins. "Have a nice sleep?"

"You boys going to want a ride back?"

"Nah, we have a ride." The cabbie peels out leaving a dim cloud of dust particles dissipating into the cool night air. It's dark and quiet. Almost too quiet.

They walk towards the black shimmering water of Lake Erie. The shadowy image of a square truck sits alone near the docks.

A voice breaks the silence. "You boys picking up ice cream?"

"We are. Are you Ed?"

"That's me. Here's the keys. Everything is inside under a false floor. Access it here, under the truck." He points under the rear of the vehicle. "See, that part of the fuel tank is fake. You want to inventory it?"

"No, we trust you have everything in order. We'll do inventory when we reach our destination."

"Fair enough. Have a nice trip. I'll have one of our guys pick up the truck tomorrow."

Stanley hands Frank the keys. "Get in the driver's seat. You know how to drive a Model T?"

"Um ... no. Not exactly."

"Okay. Get in."

"Put the key in, retard the ignition, and turn the key to *Battery*." He points. "Push the ignition, use the throttle to speed it up."

The engine fires. Frank turns the key from the *Battery* position over to the *Magneto* position. He grins. "I remembered that part."

"Good. Now move the hand brake into neutral. The clutch is on the left, reverse is in the middle and the brake is on the right. Got it?"

"Got it." Frank puts the automobile into first gear, then uses the hand throttle to get the truck moving forward.

"Frank, at this rate it's going to take us a week to get back. Push the clutch in and put it in second gear so we can hightail it out of here."

The ride back is as quiet and uneventful as the ride over. They turn onto Cherry Street.

Red lights flash. The shriek of a siren echoes.

"Pull over Frank. Let me do the talking. Switch seats."

"I told you an ice cream truck would stand out like a sore thumb. Damnit."

"Relax. Everything'll be fine."

A pair of hands rest on the driver-side door.

"What are you boys doing driving around in an ice cream truck in the middle of the night like this? Is this truck stolen?"

"No sir. We bought it in Pennsylvania earlier today and it took a while to drive it back here to Canton. We're going into the ice cream business."

Long silent stare. "Uh hmm. I see. Mind if I take a gander in the back?"

"Not at all, sir. There isn't any ice cream though. Not yet."

"Step out and follow me." He opens the door to the rear cab. He shines his flashlight, panning over the walls and floor. A few empty ice cream containers and cardboard boxes lie scattered on the dusty wooden floor. He shines the light under the vehicle. "Looks like you're leaking something. Might be a gas leak. Could be dangerous."

Shit.

A bright light in his face momentarily blinds Stanley. "You boys wouldn't happen to be transporting any illegal liquor, now would you?"

"No sir. This truck is only for ice cream."

He clicks off the light. Another long stare. "U-huh ... ice cream. You have any paperwork proving you own this truck?"

"The previous owner is bringing the title tomorrow. So ... uh ... no sir, I don't have any paperwork yet."

Stanley's heart pounds. His stomach tightens. The officer bends over and touches the leak with the tip of his finger. "Smells like hooch to me, boy." He pulls his revolver. "Turn around. Both of you."

"Sir, I swear, there's no hooch in there. Maybe that puddle was already there."

Cold steel bracelets lock on both his wrists. A tingling burn shoots all the way to his fingertips.

"You know bootlegging is a federal crime? The both of you could end up in the big house for a very long time."

"Sir, there has to be a way to resolve this."

Stanley feels his wallet slip out of his back pocket. "There is. Looks like you have around four-hundred *ways* here. You might want to report that missing. A lot of crime in this part of town. You should be more careful."

Blood returns to his hands. He rubs his wrists. Frank's eyes are wide and unblinking.

"You boys have a nice evening. And have that leak looked at." He walks back to his patrol car.

Without saying a word, they climb into the truck. Stanley slams the vehicle into gear.

Frank stares straight ahead. "Holy shit. I thought we were dead for sure."

Stanley heaves a breath. "You did good, Frank. Got to keep a cool head, so you can think straight."

The boys pull into the parking lot at Sophie's Fine Foods. "Six-twenty-three in the morning. Okay, climb under there and get that stash out and move it downstairs."

***

Shelves stocked. Icebox stocked. Cash in the register. 7:57 a.m. Stanley stands behind the market counter when Max arrives.

"Morning, Max. Frank has the stash downstairs. It's all ready for you."

Max grins and places his hands on the counter. He glances right, then left as if to see if anyone is listening. "So, you two buffoons made it back here in an ice cream truck? Without anyone noticing?"

"Ya. We did. Was that your idea, asshole?"

"Nah, but I'd love to take credit for it."

"We got pulled over by the fuzz up the street. I'm four-hundred dollars lighter. No more ice cream trucks. Okay?"

Max smirks. "Ouch. Yeah, sorry about that, buddy. Our next drop will be a lot closer. And no more ice cream trucks."

"Oh, by the way, I assigned Frank to take care of the girls."

"Now that'll be fun to watch. Those girls will kick his ass for sure."

Max follows Stanley downstairs.

"I'm right behind you. Let's see if Frank has everything unloaded."

"What's that? A house of cards?" Max pulls a towel from his back pocket, balls it up and launches a direct hit from the stairs.

"Shit. I was almost there. Why would you do that, Max?"

"We ain't paying ya to sit around and build houses out of cards. Help me set up the bar. Ya might learn something."

"Frank. What happened to these two bottles of whiskey?"

"They were already broken when I opened the crates. Probably the leak the copper noticed that almost got us sent up the river."

Max strokes his chin. "Hmm. I'm going to ask for a credit for those."

By ten a.m. Sophie's Fine Foods is ready to open up for business, liquor and sin.

Stanley claps. "We're ready to open, boys. Let's make lot of cabbage. Meet back here at five o'clock. Maxie, can you give Frank and I a lift home?"

"Sure thing, boss. But I want a raise."

Max drops them off at the curb in front of Stanley's home, then peels out down the road.

Stanley places his arm around Frank. "I want you get yourself slicked up for tonight. Manage Rose and her girls. Keep a close eye on them. Make sure they don't try to steal from us. Watch the customers too. If arguments break out, handle it. Other than that, have fun, stay away from the beer. Do whatever Max needs you to do."

"Okay, got it."

"Now go out back and feed those chickens."

"What chickens?"

"I bought some hens so we can have fresh eggs in the morning. Go feed 'em. You know I can't stand the smell of chicken shit. It's part of your new job."

Frank rolls his eyes and shakes his head. "Alright, alright, I'll feed them."

"Good man. I'm going upstairs to take a hot bath."

Stanley's rendition of *Sweet Georgia Brown* is off key, but the echo in the bathroom makes up for it. The warmth of the water relaxes his aching muscles. He lights up the stogie Jumbo Crowley gave him and closes his eyes. He blows puffs of smoke and slides into a deep meditation. He's the boss. On top of the world. He runs all the details of the operation of the speakeasy through his mind, over and over, until every detail is worked out.

Strange. A soft creaking. Is the door opening?

"This one was thirsty too, brother!"

His eyes pop open. Flapping wings, flying feathers and an ear-piercing squawking, followed by hysterical laughter sends his heart into pounding palpitations. A chicken lands on his chest.

"Frank! What the fuck are you doing? You son of a bitch."

The roar of laughter vibrates the walls. Frank's face is red.

Stanley grabs the bird. Water splashes everywhere. He can't see. He steps out of the tub and throws the bird towards Frank. The slippery wet tiles don't support his weight as his world appears to switch to slow motion. His tailbone hits the floor with a thud. Pain shoots up his spine. He stares at his feet pointing toward the ceiling.

Frank grabs the chicken and runs downstairs and out the back door laughing like a lunatic.

"What the hell just happened?" He sits in a pool of water on the tile floor. Feathers stuck to his body and a few floating in the tub. The stogie hangs off his lower lip soaked and broken. He spits it out.

***

Stanley emerges from the upstairs looking dapper in a pair of black dress slacks, blue shirt, suspenders, black bow tie, wing-tipped shoes, black fedora and his timepiece tucked neatly in his waist pocket.

Frank whistles. "You are one handsome devil."

"You can knock that shit off right now. You're lucky I'm all slicked up."

He points at Frank and winks. "Go get yourself ready, asshole."

Frank makes an entrance twenty minutes later dressed in brown slacks, a cream-colored long-sleeve shirt underneath a tan sleeveless sweater. He has a beige herring-bone newsboy cap on his head and brown wing-tip shoes and a big grin. Time to roll.

***

Max walks out from behind the bar. "Wow. You boys are some handsome sons of bitches."

Stanley hugs Max. "Not looking bad yourself, Maxie. Love the black vest and bow tie. Wow and a clean white towel in your back pocket for once. Is that a new bottle opener in your vest? Nice."

Max smacks his hands together. "This is our big night. Let's kick some ass."

Frank points at Stanley. "I better wait upstairs for Rose and her gals."

"You do that Frank."

Stanley takes a seat at the bar. "We're going to make a fortune, Maxie. Hold my spot. I just remembered I've got to unlock the door upstairs. And hell, watching how Frank handles the flappers should be entertaining."

Stanley emerges from the cellar door. "I'm unlocking the front door little brother, then I'll be here counting cash for a few minutes. So, don't mind me."

Frank holds a candy stick in his mouth like a cigarette. He taps his fingers on the counter periodically glancing out the front window.

"I'm excited for tonight. I'll make sure the ladies do their job."

"Start by relaxing. You're fidgeting. Take charge. Don't let these dames step all over ya."

The front door opens. Rose, Ruby and Lily stroll into the store full of giggles and energy.

This should be fun to watch.

Frank leaps from his seat, spits out the candy stick into a small garbage pail and makes his way around the counter. His grin is wide and way too eager.

Rose fills out a revealing silken pink evening dress that falls at her knees. She's wearing more rouge than the day they met, and a lighter shade of red lipstick. She wears a jeweled choker and ruby earrings that dangle to the base of her neck. Her raven hair is styled in a wavy bob, with a red headband and a fresh cut rose tucked in the right side of her hair.

"Hi Franky. Ruby, Lily, this is the young sheik I was telling you girls about." She smiles and places her finger in the middle of Frank's chest, batting her eyes at him.

Frank blushes. "Oh, Applesauce."

Rose licks her lips. "Don't be so modest, Frank. It's true. You *are* a sheik. And a real big boy." Rose winks at Ruby and Lily. They all giggle.

If Frank's face gets any redder it'll be darker than Rose's lipstick.

"Ladies, this is Frank Miller. We'll be working with him and Stanley over there tonight."

Geez, Frank. Say something instead of standing there like a moron.

Frank continues to awkwardly grin and stare. He glances at Ruby.

Ruby isn't exceptionally beautiful. Her skin isn't flawless, her eyes aren't extraordinary and her hair not above average. She's short and full-figured. But there's something beyond Ruby's ordinariness both stunning and intriguing. She has a captivating irresistible magnetism whose source is hard to put a finger on.

She has light brown wavy hair she wears in a bob. A silky gold evening dress clings to her curves. It has a revealing slit up the thigh and a low collar line accenting the cleavage of melon-shaped breasts. Her rouge covers a mildly ruddy complexion. Her eyes are bubbly and friendly and carry a certain irresistible radiance.

Frank extends his hand to Ruby. She delicately takes Frank's hand into hers.

"Very nice to meet you Ruby."

She softly pulls her hand back, but her fingers are stuck. She frowns, then giggles. "Frank, I think there is something sticky on your hand." She rolls her eyes at the other ladies. "Frank? What have you been doing? Why is your hand so sticky?"

Stanley snorts and tries hard not to burst out laughing.

Oh shit. Did I just snort? He's dying over there. I don't know if he can handle this. But I'm loving every damn minute of it.

Frank's face is almost purple. Beads of sweat drip off his brow.

"I am so sorry. I was eating a candy stick earlier and I must have gotten some on my hand."

Ruby giggles. "Mm. A candy stick. It's okay Frank. You don't have to explain yourself to me." She winks at Rose and Lily. They're all giggles and silliness.

Rose turns her attention to Lily. "Frank, this is Lily. Lily, this is Frank."

Lily runs her finger down the front of Frank's sweater. In a low sultry voice, she says, "So nice to meet you Mr. Miller." Frank takes a small step back and stumbles against the counter.

Lily appears to be a few years older than the other girls. She's the type women love to hate. Her long wavy blonde hair falls softly over exposed shoulders. Round mint-colored eyes and an innocent smile conceal an intellectual beauty.

She doesn't wear a lot of rouge. She wears pastel lilac lipstick on small full lips. She looks adorable in a short, shiny silver dress with frills along the bottom. Diamond earrings and a diamond necklace accent a long, sleek neckline.

Her skin is milky-white and flawless. A pair of silver heels raise her height to a mere five-foot-two. A tiny waist, large bosom and a full round bottom, she undoubtedly uses to her full advantage.

He nods. "Very nice to meet you Lily."

"The pleasure is all mine, Franky." She gently touches her right index finger to her lips. "Frank? Do you have a … candy stick for me?" Rose and Ruby snicker.

"Give them some candy, Frank. Nice to see you ladies. Excuse my manners. I have to concentrate on what I'm doing. I'll follow you downstairs in a minute."

Frank nervously grins. The right corner of his mouth trembles. He reaches into the candy jar and pulls out three candy sticks.

Get ready Frank. Here it comes, Ha-ha.

They lick, kiss and suck on the candy sticks both provocative and sensual. They try hard to make eye contact with Frank. But he's doing a good job of avoiding their stares. The three are merciless sirens luring their prey to devour.

Frank grins like a schoolboy focusing his eyes on the floor. "Would you ladies please follow me downstairs?"

Stanley holds the cellar door open for the group. "Frank. What's with the limp? Focus on the job, brother." He chuckles and follows the group downstairs.

Giggles and snickering echo down the stairwell as they ascend.

Frank wraps his arm around Stanley and whispers. "You wanna talk to the ladies and explain what they'll be doing tonight?"

He grins. "No ya coward. That's your job. Get 'em lined up. Oh, and try not to look so *happy* when you're talking to them."

Frank joins the trio at a table near the bar. "Ladies, I'm going to be in charge of you all, so if you run into any problems tonight or need anything, come see me and I'll take care of you."

All three smirk and chortle.

Rose places her hand on Frank's arm and mocks him. "Okay Frank. You're the boss."

"Okay then. Thank you, Rose. We'll pay you two dollars per night, and you can keep all the tips you make. Sound good?" The women glance at each other and cackle with laughter. Lily blows him a kiss. Rose whispers in his ear. "Okay. Sounds good Frank. Best to just let us do what we do. If we have trouble with any big lugs tonight, we'll be sure to fetch you."

Rose holds her hand out towards Frank forming a vee with her index and middle finger. "Butt me."

"What?" Rose impatiently shakes her head. "Butt me. Oh my God, Frank. Give me a ciggy."

"Oh, a cigarette. Sure. I'll be right back." He walks to the bar.

Max holds a cigarette and a box of matches. "I heard your conversation. Give her the ciggy and don't light it for her." Frank takes the cigarette and the match and nods. "Thanks Max."

Max grabs his arm. "Frank. You need to take control of these women. Don't let them walk all over you. You're the boss. Act like it. Be a man. You're embarrassing your brother and I."

Stanley nods. "He's right. They're kicking your ass right now. You're in charge."

Frank hands the cigarette to Rose. She holds it out waiting for Frank to light a match. Frank tosses the matches onto the table. "Have your ciggy, Rose. Then you three need to get to work if you want to get paid tonight." He walks back to the bar.

Rose rolls her eyes and glances at Ruby and Lily, her mouth agape. "Well. I never. So rude."

At six thirty p.m., Stanley walks upstairs into the store. He waits behind the counter anticipating a sizable number of patrons. Over the next couple hours, he allows dozens of men and women from all walks of life down the stairs into the speakeasy.

"Looks like we have a full house." He locks the front door and flips a sign around in the window. *Store Closed.* Sophie's speakeasy however is open for business.

The radio blares jazz music. The joint is humming with conversation, laughter and the clinks and clanks of liquor-filled glasses. Cigar smoke and perfume permeate the air.

Rose, Ruby and Lily dance on the stage shaking their behinds to the rhythm of the music. Poker games are in progress. Couples dance and laugh. Max serves up drinks as fast as he can.

"We're making moola, boss."

Stanley smacks the bar. "Max, pour us all a round of whiskey." He fills three shot glasses to the brim with Seagram's. He slides a glass to Stanley, then another to Frank. "Bottoms up boys."

The trio slam their shots in unison. Frank chokes.

The whiskey burns Stanley's throat. But his nerves relax. *Maybe this is why Papa loved his drink. It dulls the edges.*

"Max, pour us another shot." He pats Frank on the back. "Sit this one out."

"Salute."

Ruby spins Frank around on his bar stool. "Frank. One of the customers just slapped his girlfriend. The lug also keeps grabbing my ass. Can you please handle it?"

Frank nods and slides off his bar stool. Stanley stands, but Max's hand on his shoulder gives him pause.

"Hold on big brother. Let's see how the young Miller handles it."

They observe Frank.

"Is there a problem here sir?"

A stout young Irishman rises from his seat and stands face to face with Frank. He's sloshed.

"Who the fuck are you, lad? There's no problem here. Now mind yer damn business and fetch me another whiskey, boy."

The Irishman, belts out a bellowing laugh. He slaps Ruby on the ass.

"Touch me again and I'll stab you in the eye, you bastard."

The man's girlfriend cowers.

Frank puffs his chest out. "You need to leave. Now."

The man drives a fat finger into Frank's chest.

"I ain't leaving, till I'm ready to leave. And who's going to make me? You?" He guffaws.

Frank grabs the man's finger and yanks it. The Irishman yelps, swinging a clumsy fist that glances Frank's chin. The Irishman charges, attempting to tackle him to the ground. Frank spreads his legs giving himself a solid stance, preventing the take-down.

Frank wraps his arms around the man's body and drops to the ground, slamming the man's face into the concrete floor. The two grapple on the ground in a fury. Frank delivers several blows bloodying the face of the man. On the next punch, the Irishman isn't moving.

Frank takes him by the legs and drags him across the floor like a bundle of rags. When he reaches the steps, he throws the man over his shoulder and carries him up the stairs and out of the bar. He tosses him in a heap onto the gravel.

The man's girlfriend follows Frank up the stairs and into the parking lot. Stanley is right behind her.

"What did you do?! Leave him alone."

"Your boyfriend is no longer welcome here."

She kneels, shaking her boyfriend, trying to wake him. "Why did you have to hurt him, you bastard?"

Frank shakes his head. "I'm sorry, Miss. Just take him home. We'll help you carry him to your automobile."

When the boys reenter the speakeasy, the crowd cheers.

Stanley pats Frank on the shoulder. "Nice work, brother."

Max tosses Frank a towel. "Frank, that mick carrot top was Brian Murphey. He's a well-known wrestler in the Ohio circuit. That's why everyone is cheering you. He ain't very popular. He's a drunk and a bully. Nobody's going to miss him."

Here comes Ruby. Batting her eyes and rubbing Frank's back. "My hero. Just let me know how I can repay you, Franky." She kisses him on the left cheek, leaving a smudge of red, which blends well into his flushed face.

Poker games resume and Max continues to sell shots of liquor and mugs of beer. Frank sits on a bar stool sipping a cola. He belches. "Ahh. That hit the spot."

"Come on Franky. Dance with me."

Max chuckles. "Yeah Franky. Wipe the fear off your face and dance with the lady" Stanley shoves Frank towards Ruby.

"Ruby. I … I don't know how to dance." She giggles. "Oh, come on Frank. It's easy. I'll teach you." She takes his hand. "This is called *The Charleston*. Start with your left foot forward and go forward and a tap and a back and a tap, forward and a tap and a back and a tap. Good. Now, swivel your feet as you step and tap and swing your arms like this. You got it. Keep it up, woo hoo."

Frank returns to his bar stool. Stanley pats his shoulder. "You better watch out for that one, little brother."

"She's just a tease. Besides, Rose is the gal I'm interested in."

Stanley beams. "Here's to you. We're making you the official bouncer after kicking that bog-hopper's ass tonight."

A drunk man in a business suit staggers over and pushes his way into the brothers. Stanley spills his shot on the bar. The man puts one arm on Frank and the other on Stanley. His breath wreaks of eighty-proof. He spits, slurs and slobbers as he talks.

"Yeah, nice work throwing ole Murph out on his laurels. He had it coming. But if he weren't so drunk, he'd have wiped the floor with you kid."

Frank glances at Stanley. "I gotta piss."

Whiskey. It can numb the pain of a broken heart. It can fuel a fiery rage. The temporary insanity it creates is the cause of so much tragedy. It fueled Papa's temper. A son dreams of walking in his father's footsteps, but there are paths a father takes a son should never follow.

The drunk man's words turn to an echoing babble. His fat face begins to blur and become an annoyance. A shot glass shatters on the bar. "What did you say about my brother?"

He grabs the man by the throat and pounds his fist into his face. The man hits the floor. Max races around the bar and wraps his arms around Stanley from behind. "What's wrong with you man?"

Frank emerges from the toilet. "Shit. What did you do?"

Frank drags the bloodied and unconscious man out of harm's way. Stanley breaks free from Max's hold and rushes towards the man. He's met by Frank, who drags him to the other side of the bar.

Max helps the battered man into a chair. "Rose. Get some ice from behind the bar and bring a towel." The bar has gone quiet for the moment.

Frank keeps Stanley cornered. "What the hell is wrong with you? That guy was just drunk. He didn't know what he was saying."

Stanley's eyes glare wildly.

"I see Papa in you right now. You're acting just like him. I see that same demon in your eyes."

Frank's words cut deep. He's right. The fear and hurt reflected in Frank's eyes have a sobering effect.

"I'm sorry Frank. I don't know what came over me. Where is he?"

"Who?"

"The customer. Where is he?"

"No, no, no, he's had enough."

"I have to make this right with him. I owe him an apology."

Frank reluctantly let's go.

The man's eyes fill with terror as Stanley approaches. Stanley raises his palms. "I am so sorry, sir. I apologize from the bottom of my heart. Your drinks are on me."

The man's lips curl. His brow wrinkles. "Keep your cheap drinks. I'll never come back to this dump again. I'll make sure all my friends and acquaintances never come here as well."

Stanley pulls out a wad of bills. "Take this please. As my apology."

The man shakes his head. "Keep your money. Don't you know who I am? I don't need your measly little hand out, boy." The man glances at his table where his friends sit in sobering silence. "We're leaving."

Frank and Stanley escort the group to the parking lot. Frank removes his hat. "I'm really sorry this happened. I hope you can forgive my brother."

The man pauses. He glares at Stanley. "Your brother has a real problem. He can't handle his liquor. He's in the wrong business. I'll make sure he finds a new occupation." The man stumbles into the back seat of a 1925 Rolls Royce Silver Ghost. They drive away.

It's only two-twenty-seven in the morning. Early for a speakeasy to empty out.

Max grabs Frank's sleeve. "Frank, take your brother home. I'll take care of closing up and getting the girls paid. Let's meet back here tomorrow evening at five o'clock."

"Let's go brother. I'll drive you home."

Stanley closes his eyes. His head is spinning and his temples pound.

Stanley opens his eyes and Frank is carrying him to the sofa. He puts a pillow under his head, removes his shoes and covers him with a blanket. Frank collapses into the easy chair.

A shadow hovers next to Stanley. Its presence emanates a deep sadness. Stanley slides the covers over his face. "Go away Papa."

CHAPTER TWENTY

A rooster crows. A clock ticks. Stanley's head is throbbing. He forces his exhausted body to sit upright, then attempts to focus his eyes on the far wall. A stabbing jolt in both eyes quickly forces them to close. Frank's snoring is amplified and annoying.

He wreaks of cigar smoke and liquor. He pisses an endless stream of eighty proof into the porcelain bowl, then he fills the tub with warm water.

He stares at the sink, then the mirror. Reddened glazed eyes stare back at him. "You look like shit."

A shadow materializes in the mirror behind him. A haggard haunting face. Or is it his own face? He turns. No one there. A splash of cold water soothes his throbbing temples.

Warm bath water loosens his joints. Muscle fibers untangle and relax. The rim of the tub supports his head as steam evaporates creating a misty veil encompassing his body. Anxiety dissipates along with the steam. His mind drifts, spinning into nothingness. Fleeting thoughts come and go.

Flashes of blue light illuminate the darkest places of his mind. He's back in Southington. Papa stands next to him baiting a hook and handing him the rod.

"Son, you have to cast your line way out into deep water if you want the big fish." The rod is light in his hand. He casts. He becomes entangled in the fishing line. The more he struggles the tighter the line enwraps him. He falls into the dark waters.

He gasps for air, pulling his body over the side of the tub. He climbs out and reaches for a towel. *Shit. Just a dream.* He pulls a tee shirt over his head and slips his legs into an old pair of overall jeans. He slides on work boots and walks outside.

He leans on the fence of the chicken coop, tossing grain on the ground and watching the chickens scramble in a frenzy pecking at the dirt. He gathers a few eggs and returns to the house.

"Hey handsome. Are you done playing with your chickens? Nice eggs."

"EmmaMae? What are you doing here?" He sets the eggs on the table and wraps his arms around her. She's the ray of light he needed. A cure to all that's ailing him.

She pushes him away. "What the heck has gotten into you? You act like you haven't seen me in months."

He pulls up a chair, sits and admires her. He stares not saying a word.

"Are you okay? Did you hit your head or something?"

"No. I didn't hit my head. I just needed to see your beautiful face right now at this very moment." He takes her hand. "I just want to tell you how much I love you."

She blushes. She struggles not to grin. "Oh ... sweetheart. Stop. I came to make you and Frank breakfast. Give me those eggs and get your butt out of the kitchen. And wake up your brother. He snores like an old bear."

She sits between Frank and Stanley. "Well. How did it go last night? Your first night and all. How did the opening go?"

They both stop chewing and stare at each other. She stares at them staring at each other, waiting for a response. "Wow. Sounds like it was a huge hit."

Frank grins. "It was a good night."

EmmaMae smiles. "That's nice. And did everything go smoothly?"

Frank leans back and wipes his mouth with a napkin. "Yeah. Well mostly. I mean, we had a couple small incidents."

Stanley kicks him under the table.

"What kind of incidents? Stanley?"

Stanley glares at Frank. "We had a good night. We made a lot of moola, people had fun. Some fella got a little too sloshed, so Frank had to throw him out. Other than that, it was ... good."

EmmaMae squints and pushes her tongue against her cheek. "So, then you three will split the profits?"

Frank nods. "Me, Stanley and Max will get our cut. Then we have to pay the girls, of course." Stanley rolls his eyes and glares.

"Girls? What girls? You have girls working at the club?"

He waves his hands. "Sweetheart, we have three young ladies who have always worked at the joint. Part of the deal was, I had to promise Mr. Joyce I would let them continue to work. They just serve drinks and entertain the customers, that's all. I know. I should have told you. I-I'm sorry."

"Oh, I see. So, what kind of entertainment do they provide your customers? Do they sing? Dance? Do they tell jokes? Or do they shake their little fannies for everyone? What exactly? I'd like to know."

He sighs. "They just serve drinks and get the customers to dance. Sometimes they get up on stage and dance for the crowd. Ordinary dancing. Nothing … out of line."

She tosses her napkin on the table and stands. "Well I hope you two enjoyed breakfast." Her eyes dart between him and Frank. "I have to run some errands, then I'm going to Mass. But maybe tonight you can take me to your new club and show me around. Hm?"

"Doll, I will take you to see the joint. I promise. But until we can get things running smoothly, I don't think it's a good idea. Give us a week or so to get everything settled, okay?

She doesn't answer. She scowls, then storms out the front door.

Stanley chases after her. "Wait. Can I give you a ride? I can take you wherever you want to go?"

"No thank you. I can walk." She swiftly walks along the street and fades into the distance.

"Damn." He walks back in the kitchen and leers at Frank.

"What?"

"You talk too much. Stanley smacks him on the back of the head, then walks upstairs. Frank rubs his head. "Ouch. What'd I do?"

***

It's four o'clock. They head to Sophie's Fine Foods to meet with Max. It's a quiet ride. The weather is muggy and warm. The air suffocating. No matter how much you bathe or try to stay dry, it's impossible. Sweat leaks from every pore soaking your clothes causing them to cling to your body like a sponge.

A baby blue Bugatti sits in the lot. "What's Johnny doing here? He's supposed to visit at the end of the month. Hm."

"Who's Johnny? What a sweet looking set of wheels."

"Don't worry about it. I bought this joint from him. Probably just wants to see how things went last night."

They walk down the stairs into the club. Sitting at the bar is Johnny Joyce, having a conversation with Max.

"I'm sure you're surprised to see me so soon, lad. Is this Frank I've heard so much about?"

"Good to see you Mr. Joyce. Yes. This is my younger brother Frank."

Frank offers his hand. "Nice to meet you Mr. Joyce. Love your wheels." Johnny beams. "Thanks lad. She's my girl. You'll have to excuse me. I need to have a little chat with yer brother."

They sit at a table near the stage. "I'm sure yer wondering why the visit?"

Stanley's heart rate increases. "Would you like a beer, Johnny?"

"Not drinking today." Johnny's face loses all expression. "A little birdy told me things got a bit bold here last night. Ya punched someone in the face fer no reason."

Stanley takes a deep breath. "I did. I lost my temper. He was talking bad about Frank ... I just lost my head. I tried to apologize, but he wouldn't accept it."

Johnny leans back and crosses his arms. "Lad. This guy is a former customer, but not someone I'm friendly with. He's a fecking asshole. But. He's a powerful and very rich fecking asshole with connections. He could rain down a lot of hell on you and this joint."

Stanley rubs his face, wiping a few small beads of sweat from his brow. "I had no idea. Is there anything I can do to make it right?"

Johnny sighs. "I sat and had a drink with him. I convinced him to leave ya alone, granted you turn over all your profits from last night."

"What? No way. I have people I have to pay."

Johnny holds his hand up in a calming gesture. "Calm down, lad. I convinced him to only take half. Max tells me yer total take was over seven-hundred. That's a pretty fine night. I have his half in my pocket. He doesn't need the dough. He just wants you punished."

"Alright then. As long as we're square. We'll make up the difference tonight."

Johnny stands and lays his hand on Stanley's shoulder. "I like you lad. But you need to emerge into someone who knows who he is. If ya can't handle yer drink, then don't drink. If ya can't handle yer temper, take up boxing. A business isn't a place for either. I'll be back at the end of the month for my cut. Consider this a free favor. Just this once."

Stanley shakes Johnny's hand and nods. "Thanks Johnny. I appreciate the intervention."

"Frank, 'twas nice to meet you. Would have loved to see the scrap between you and ole Murph." Johnny exits the club through the back escape via the closet.

"How much do we have left Maxie?"

Max frowns and pulls an envelope out from under the bar and slides it towards Stanley. "We have nine-hundred and ten dollars and fifty-three cents."

"Wait. What? Johnny said we made over seven-hundred dollars last night and he took half of that. How can we have over nine-hundred dollars left from that? I'm not a genius but the math don't add up."

Max beams that old Maxie Grin. It runs from ear to ear with a sparkle of boyish charm in his coppery eyes.

"What the hell, Max?"

"Johnny asked me how much money we made at the bar last night. He didn't ask me how much we made with food and tips and gambling. So, I didn't actually lie."

"You are one ballsy son of a bitch." Stanley pulls the cash out of the envelope and hands Frank one-hundred dollars.

"Hell ya. Thanks brother."

He slides three-hundred dollars to Max. He slips the remaining wad into his shirt pocket and winks.

Around half past seven, Rose, Ruby and Lily enter the bar. All three seem to be in a bubbly mood. They hug Stanley and attempt to rub their bodies on his.

"Ladies please help Frank and Max with whatever they need."

"Boo. No fun. Let's go girls. Let's leave him to his business. Old bluenose."

The radio blares. The girls dance and sing. Max is busy behind the bar filling drinks. Frank trolls the joint making sure everyone is having fun and nobody is causing trouble.

A shot glass slides across the bar top. "Hey boss? You want a shot of panther piss?"

"I'm fine with my beer. Thanks. Don't let that stop you, though." They shoot the shit into the wee hours of the morning. Business in good. Another big crowd throwing down greenbacks like cards from a poker deck.

***

The evening ends uneventful and mellow. "Let's finish the rest tomorrow boys. Pay the girls Max, and let's lock up and skedaddle."

Frank has a permanent grin stuck on his face. Probably has something to do with Rose hanging all over him and biting his ear like a vampire.

A pair of feminine fingers kneed Stanley's shoulders. "Please don't do that. I'm engaged Lily."

"So, she don't need to know, baby."

He stares her directly in the eyes. "I would know."

He turns towards Max. "What's the take for tonight, big man?"

Max stacks the bills in denominations. One-thousand, two-hundred and fifty-two dollars and twenty-seven cents."

"Wow. That's a swell take."

Max hands Stanley the cash. Stanley pays the girls, then hands Frank and Max a wad of bills. He pockets some cash for himself, then opens the trapdoor to the hidden wine cellar under the bar and descends the steps. He deposits the rest of the cash into the safe. The wine cellar is a nice little escape room, to just step away for a moment. He sits in the confinement and coolness of the cellar, admiring the wine rack that is well on its way to filling up. He sighs, then stands.

Lily is standing at the top of the stairs with her dress hiked up. She isn't wearing panties. She doesn't even try to hide her intent to reveal her perfectly shaped, milky-white thighs. Thighs leading up to a well-groomed, vee-shaped blonde pussy. He pauses and looks away. *Damnit. I don't want that image in my mind.* "Excuse me, Lily, I'm coming up." He shakes his head and climbs out of the cellar.

Lily winks, but he avoids her glance.

"Let's go. Frank, hit the lights."

The group makes their way up the stairs and into the parking lot.

Max taps Rose on the shoulder. "You and your girls need a ride home?"

"Why yes, Max. That would be so sweet. Thank you, big boy." Ruby and Lily climb into the backseat of his Chrysler B-70. Rose jumps into Frank's arms and hugs him with her entire body, wrapping her arms and legs around his torso. She kisses him hard on the lips. "Be a good boy Franky." She hops off and joins her girls. Max shows off and screeches out of the parking lot and onto Cherry Street.

"Let's go home Franky."

"Look out!" A cloud of dust fills the air peppering their eyes and throats with grit. An old flatbed truck skids to a stop. Blinding headlights light up the lot.

Two men exit the truck. "How in the name of Jaysus are ya, lads? Hope it was a nice one fer ya." Brian Murphy. Accompanied by a goon. The goon has slick jet-black hair, a handlebar mustache and no neck. He's holding a small Billy club. This can't be good.

Murphy points his finger at Frank. "I've come to finish that fight we had last night, laddie. You took advantage of my ossified condition. Now let's see how you do when my sobriety isn't in question."

Stanley takes a step toward Murphy. "Who's Bruno over there?"

"He's here to see to a fair fight. Now mind yer business."

The goon taps his hand with the club. "My name is Tony, shit face."

"Your name is *Tony Shit Face*? Who named you that? Your mother?"

"It's alright brother. I can take this lug."

"As long as this is a fair fight, I'll let it happen. If your muscle-head over there tries anything, I'm going to knock his teeth out."

"My name is *Tony*."

"I know. Tony shit face. You introduced yourself already."

"Let's do this lad. Let's see what you got." Murphy bull rushes Frank, catching him off guard and takes him immediately to ground. He puts Frank in a headlock. "What's the matter lad? No fight left in ya?"

Frank struggles to get free, but every move he makes, Murphy counters. He's toying with him. Trying to humiliate him and doing a good job of it.

Murph pins Frank's face in the dirt, spewing continuous verbal taunts in his ear. "This is too easy. Put up a fight, man."

Frank manages to slide his right arm free taking advantage of Murphy's carelessness. He slams his elbow into Murphy's left temple. Murphy releases his hold and hits the ground, stunned.

Stanley shouts, "Get him Frank."

Frank pounces onto Murphy's back and places him in a chokehold. Murphy tries to flip him over, but Frank hangs on like a bulldog squeezing tighter and tighter until Murphy's eyes roll back in his head.

Tony steps forward but Stanley lunges and tackles him from behind. The two men grapple in the dust like junkyard dogs fighting over scraps.

Murphy taps on the ground. He wheezes. "Okay lad. Let me up. We're done here." Frank releases his hold. The two men dust themselves off.

"Laddie, you caught me by surprise with that elbow."

"Man, you are a helluva lot stronger sober."

Murphy puts his hands on both of Frank's shoulders. "What's your name, lad?"

"Frank. Frank Miller."

"Frank, you have the look and the strength of a wrestler." Murphy pulls a card from his pocket and hands it to him. "Call me. I might be interested in training ya. Always looking for fresh young talent on the circuit."

Tony has Stanley in a choke hold. His face is turning purple and his eyes are bulging. He desperately looks at Frank and Murphy and squeezes out a high-pitched, "Are we done?"

"Let him up, Tony. His eyes are 'bout to pop." Tony releases Stanley and stands up. Stanley sits on the ground catching his breath and rubbing his neck.

"Thanks, big brother for having my back. Ha-ha." Stanley coughs and chokes, then waves and nods. "Sure-thing little brother. That's my job."

Murphy slaps Frank on the back. Murph and Tony drive off and disappear into the countryside.

"What? So, you two are pals now?"

"I beat him. I earned his respect. He wants to train me to be a wrestler. I think it might be something I'm really good at."

Stanley shakes his head and sighs. "You wanna be a wrestler? Wear tight little pants? Roll around on a canvas with a hairy meathead putting his sweaty balls in your face? Way to dream big, Frank."

The two brothers head home as the sun begins to rise on a new day.

***

EmmaMae sits on his porch moving back and forth in a rocker, arms crossed. "What happened to you two? Are those fingerprints on your neck? Why is there blood on both of you? You know I needed a ride this morning? But I can see you two spent the night drinking and fighting again."

Stanley reaches for her hand but she pulls away from him.

"Sweetheart, just let me clean up some and I'll drive you."

Her eyes well. "Who are you anymore? You love this damn club more than you do me. I'll walk to work." She steps off the porch and storms off along the sidewalk.

"EmmaMae. Come back. EmmaMae." He lowers his head and throws his arms in the air.

Heartache. That lump in your throat you can't swallow. The deep breath that escapes you. Watching the one person you love more than anyone or anything in the world, disappear into uncertainty.

CHAPTER TWENTY-ONE

Stanley peers over his morning newspaper. "Maybe you should consider playing football for the Canton Bulldogs instead of wrestling. 27-0 win over Massillon last night.

Frank shakes his head. "I don't want to play football. No future in that."

Stanley folds his newspaper and places it on the table. "Frank, I think I want to replace the radio in the club with a live band. I found a group of guys advertising a band. Let's swing by and talk to them on the way to work."

"A band would be a swell addition. I like that idea."

***

It's a sweltering ninety-three degrees. Stanley spots a woman selling flowers and pulls over. "How much for a bouquet?" She pats her forehead with a handkerchief. "Seventy-five cents."

Stanley takes a detour to the telephone company. "I'll be right back. I have to drop these off."

Franks grins. "I don't think that's going to save your ass. But good luck."

They arrive at the speakeasy just before ten. "I'm sweating my balls off. Fetch us a couple beers from the ice box, little brother."

Frank wipes his brow with his sleeve. He hands Stanley a beer then takes a swig of his own cold brew. He picks up the broom.

A voice booms from the stairway. "Need some help carrying this load of liquor boys."

"Holy shit. I didn't even think about that Max. Where did you get all that hooch?"

"No worries boss. All my own stash. You can buy it off me, later. We'll send Frank again in a couple days. This should keep us in business for now."

Around two o'clock the band leader and his crew set up the stage. Tonight, is going to be a special night. Rose, Ruby and Lily walk in a few moments later full of piss and spunk.

Max announces, "The flappers are here. Keep that boner hidden Frank. It's going to get you in trouble. And close your mouth."

Stanley's eyes meet Lily's. She's a sultry and experienced seductress. She licks her bright red lips and blows a kiss. He pulls a photo of EmmaMae from his wallet. *It ain't happening, Lily. Ever.*

He opens the trapdoor to the wine cellar and descends the steps. He sighs. Nice to get away for a second. He opens the safe and counts out change for the till tonight. The cool air invigorates his overheated body. He lays out the bills on a small wooden crate and enjoys a moment of peace. He can hear conversations above him in the bar, but he blocks them out. He sits back and leans against the cool wall and relaxes for a moment.

"Hey Max. Where's Stanley?"

"I'm in the cellar. Leave me alone right now."

"Max. The girls and I have a great idea on how to make us all a shitload more cabbage."

Max raises an eyebrow. "And what would that be?"

"Show 'em ladies."

Their bodies writhe in perfect rhythm. They unbutton their tops. Milky white breasts and pink nipples burst from their shirts. Max backs up and gasps. "Holy shit."

Lily moves behind the bar and slides her body against Max's. She pushes her breasts together and bites her lower lip. Max is frozen. She caresses his chest with hers. Max raises his hands and starts to move in rhythm with Lily.

Rose grasps Frank's head and places his face into her firm round breasts. She caresses his lips with her nipples. Ruby pushes up against Frank from behind, rubbing her breasts on his back and biting his earlobe. "Ooh. Let's sandwich him Rose."

"Damnit. I lost count again. What the hell is going on up there?" Stanley slams a stack of bills on the crate and starts recounting them.

"So, is this what goes on here every night?! Is this why you stay here to all hours? What is this Frank? Max? Where's Stanley? Is he hiding?"

Stanley's eyes widen and his heart stops for a moment at the sound of EmmaMae's voice upstairs. "EmmaMae? Is that you?"

Rose, Ruby and Lily button their shirts and stare at each other wide-eyed. Rose's lips pucker.

Max glances toward the cellar door. "Uh … better get up here boss."

Frank raises a calming hand. "This isn't what it looks like … I … can explain all this."

Stanley climbs the cellar stairs and enters the bar next to Max. "EmmaMae? What are you doing here, sweetheart? And what the hell are you all doing around the bar? Get to work."

Lily smirks and eyes EmmaMae up and down then winks at her. EmmaMae cold cocks her. Lily falls backwards and crumples to the ground holding her nose and crying—blood running through her fingers and down her hands.

Rose runs to the toilet and locks herself in. Ruby climbs over the bar and hides behind Max.

Max shouts. "Calm down! It's not what you think."

EmmaMae's right eye is half-cocked, her left eye burning a hole through Stanley. "Don't even bother trying to explain this Stanley Miller. You lying bastard. Hiding like a coward."

He rushes around the bar. "I have no idea what's going on here." Knuckles slam into his nose stopping him in his tracks. He feels a warm trickle from his nostril to his lower lip. EmmaMae turns and storms up the back stairs, crying and blubbering as she leaves.

"Max? What the hell? Give me a towel." He squeezes his nose to stop the flow of blood and rushes up the back stairs to follow her. But she's gone. How could she disappear so fast?

"EmmaMae!" Gravel flies, clouds of dust and the stench of burning rubber fill the air. He zooms up and down the road searching for her. She's nowhere to be found.

He hits the brakes and skids to a stop. He pounds the steering wheel. "Goddammit. Why? What did I do? Why is she so angry?"

He returns to the bar. Max has a cold wet towel on Lily's nose. Rose and Ruby are sitting at a table nervously sucking and puffing on a cigarette. Frank sits in a chair next to them with his face in his hands.

Stanley pounds the bar top. "What the hell happened here? Why was EmmaMae so pissed? What's her beef with me? Somebody please explain this shit, now."

Frank looks up from his chair. "It's all my fault. I was talking to the gals and they had this great idea to make us all a lot more dough. So, I asked them to show Max their ideas to see what he thought.

It involved showing some bare bubs and dancing around. It got a little out of hand and EmmaMae must have walked in ... I'm so sorry. I didn't see her come in."

Stanley plops into a chair and hangs his head. Then he raises his eyes to the ceiling.

"Max, you and Frank need to run the place tonight. I have to go find her and try to explain all this to her ... somehow. My life, this place ... it all means nothing without her."

Max hugs him and pats him on the back. "Go do what you have to do boss. Frank and I will take care of everything tonight."

***

Stanley sits alone at his kitchen table. She wasn't home, she wasn't anywhere. A glint of sparkle catches his eye. It's a ring. A diamond ring. It barely fits over the tip of his pinky. Tiny flashes shimmer and dance around the room in a hypnotic pattern emptying his mind and replacing his thoughts with bittersweet memories. Memories evolve into tears running across his cheeks and dripping silently onto the table. *Why?*

He takes the ring and a small bottle of whiskey upstairs. He lays on his bed and blankly stares at the ceiling not thinking, not feeling. Just an empty shell of a man.

"God, if you really do exist ... if you can hear me ... I need you now. I've never asked anything of you. But I'm asking now. Please listen to me. Please don't take her away. I'll do whatever you ask. And if you can't bring her back, then just let me die here. Right now. I don't want to live without her. I can't live without her."

A soft knock on his door interrupts his prayer. *EmmaMae?*

"Stanley? Are you in there?" The door creaks as it opens. The mattress sinks from the weight of a body. "Can I get you something to eat? We had a good night. Made over fourteen-hundred dollars. Max took his cut. I paid the girls." Frank lays an envelope on the bed.

"If you need anything, let me know. I'll be downstairs. I got you brother." The door quietly shuts and Frank's footsteps fade away.

Two days come and go. Stanley lays in bed. No appetite. Sleeping a few hours at a time. Waking frequently to a dismal reality. He grasps the ring, staring blankly into its shimmering beauty. Beauty that's become a bitter reminder of what is lost.

CHAPTER TWENTY-TWO

The silence and emptiness of his home is an extension of the loneliness in his heart. Nothing has taste, or smell. His body is numb. He can't think or feel. A half a sandwich and small glass of milk is the only nutrition he has had in days.

A warm bath cleanses the pungent odor of his body and soothes the pain, if even for a moment. He has no desire to think. Decisions are impossible. Barriers of depression become unbreakable walls that close in like a prison. His very existence depends on breaking through these cold sterile walls. She has to give him a chance to tell his side … to let him plead his case.

Seven minutes after noontime. EmmaMae walks out of the telephone company building accompanied by a female friend. The desperation of a dying man will make him do just about anything to save his own life.

He exits his automobile and boldly walks towards her.

"EmmaMae. EmmaMae."

She turns and sees him approaching.

"Can I talk to you? Please?"

She ignores him and hurries across the street.

Dejected, he drives to Myers Lake. He sits on a park bench. Ducks quack and race through the water. Children laugh and play. He tilts his head back and closes his eyes allowing the sun to caress his gaunt face with its lifegiving warmth.

Hours pass. The sun fades. Darkness creeps over the landscape like the Angel of Death.

He drives to the speakeasy and parks. As he descends the stairs the band music blares, laughter echoes and the cigarette smoke is thick. He takes a seat at the bar.

A familiar voice from behind whispers in his ear. "How you doing boss?"

Stanley shakes his head then lowers his eyes.

"Well, you look like shit. She'll come around eventually."

Arms squeeze him from behind. "Let me get you a shot boss."

"No thanks Maxie. I'm done with whiskey for good. I will take a beer though."

Lily taps him on the shoulder. "I'm so sorry about your gal sweetie. We had no business doing what we did. It was way out of line."

"It's okay Lily. The damage is done. She's never going to see me or talk to me again. I've lost her."

"She'll come back. Give her some time. She has to know what an amazing man she has. She won't want to let that go. I promise. She's just hurting right now and not thinking straight. She'll realize soon enough that you didn't do anything wrong."

Stanley lowers his head. "Thanks Lily. But I don't think so." She pats him on the shoulder then rejoins Rose and Ruby.

***

The night ends. The bar is clear. The customers have all gone home. Stanley taps his empty beer mug on the bar top. "Everyone take a seat please. I have something I want to share. Please let me finish what I need to say and don't interrupt me."

His chest tightens. He takes a deep breath. "I'm turning the speakeasy over to Max."

Ruby, Lily and Rose stare at each other. Max's mouth is open, but no words come out. It's the first time Stanley can ever remember Max being speechless. Frank's eyes widen with concern.

"I mean I'm going to sell you this joint Max. For a great price. I want you to take it over. Frank? Pursue your wrestling career little brother. Rose, Lily and Ruby? You girls continue to work for Max and help him make this joint a fortune."

Stanley rises and places his hands in his pockets. "I'm quitting the speakeasy business. It cost me the one thing in this life I can't live without. I can make an honest living working with my hands and that's what I plan on doing. Maxie, I expect to always have a bottomless tab in this joint."

Max laughs. His eyes are misty. "You never had a tab, boss. But you always will here."

Stanley forces a smile and winks. "You bet your ass I will. Tomorrow Max and I will work out the details. He's your new boss. Have a great night and get home safe."

"Frank. You coming home tonight?"

"Um … don't wait up for me big brother."

Stanley nods. "Yeah. I kinda thought so."

"Goodnight ladies. It's been a real pleasure working with you." All three girls surround and hug him. Lily places her hand on his cheek. "Maybe what you really need is a foursome, baby."

He laughs a guttural laugh. "That's the last thing I need, Lily. But I appreciate the thought."

He glances at Max. They share a moment. Stanley nods and leaves the building.

The house remains empty and quiet. Void of all life. He sits on the porch swing. A few fireflies still linger late in the summer. They blink and flash like little stars burning out in the night sky. He dozes to the rhythm of crickets chirping and the touch of a soft warm evening breeze.

A dark specter stands before him. Eyes deep with sorrow. Staring but not speaking.

"Papa. I forgive you. I forgive you for all the hurt and pain you put Sophie through. I forgive you for all the hurt and pain you put Mama through. And I forgive you for all the times you hurt me, Frank and Annie. I love you Papa. It's okay for you to go now. I'll be okay. Go and find peace."

The specter lowers its eyes, then turns away and fades into the darkness.

***

Stanley opens his eyes to the light of a new day, finding he'd slept all night on the porch swing. Birds chirp. The air is humid. The early morning sun wraps his spirit in warmth and comfort. His heart is empty. A void remains. It was once filled with the love and life of EmmaMae Flagg.

He stretches his arms and yawns and takes in the peaceful quiet of the Saturday morning. A beautiful red robin stands still in the yard holding a large earthworm in its beak. It glances around making sure its surroundings are safe then flies off.

An hour passes. Max pulls up in his B-70 Chrysler. His old friend approaches the porch. "Hey. What the hell are you doing, loser?"

Stanley chuckles. More of a half-hearted laugh. A fat envelope lands in his lap.

"Thanks Maxie. Have a seat."

"Boss, I figured you needed to sleep on your crazy decision and maybe come to your senses today."

"No. I meant what I said. I'm going to sell you the business. I'm going to sell it to ya for one-thousand dollars. Of course, you owe me free drinks and food the rest of my life."

Max rubs his chin. His eyes tear. "That's a generous offer my friend." Max places his hand on Stanley's shoulder. "You're sure about this?"

Stanley nods. "I'm sure. Wait here." Stanley disappears into the house for a few moments and reemerges with the deed and a pen. He smiles and signs the deed.

Max reaches to grab the deed from Stanley's hand, but Stanley holds on tight. Max tugs and bursts into laughter. "Let go, ya cheap bastard." Stanley releases his grip.

"It's all yours, pal. Oh. And by the way, you need to work out a deal with Johnny Joyce."

"I'll take care of Johnny. Don't worry about that." Max sits next to Stanley on the swing and places his arm around him. "Well, you ugly son of a bitch, you finally have your tab."

Stanley chuckles. "Get off of the swing Max. I don't want the neighbors talking."

Max plants a big wet kiss on Stanley's cheek.

"That should give your neighbors plenty to gossip about sweetheart."

Max does a dance step off the porch and jumps back into his Chrysler. He flashes a mocking grin while pointing to the deed as he speeds off.

Stanley packs a suitcase. He leaves a note addressed to Frank on the kitchen table. He tosses feed to the chickens. He places a *For Sale* sign on his front lawn, then drives away.

CHAPTER TWENTY-THREE

In a small coffee shop EmmaMae sits with her girlfriend Hazel. Coffee isn't a cure for a troubled and broken-heart, but it soothes a hoarse throat.

Hazel taps her on the arm. "Hey. You still with me? Maybe you walked in on something that looked like something else but wasn't the something else you thought it was. Ever think of that?"

EmmaMae frowns. "What? I don't know. It looked exactly like … what I thought it was."

Hazel pats her hand. "Maybe you should go and talk to him. Let him tell his side of the story. Give him a chance. You're no fun anymore, goodness."

She glances at Hazel then nods. "Maybe. I don't know."

Hazel stands. "I'm going to call you a taxi. Go find him. Talk to him."

EmmaMae sighs. "Maybe I owe him that much. I guess I can at least listen to what he has to say. I just don't know …"

They sit in silence sipping their coffee.

"There's your taxi. Give me a hug. Be strong and listen to what he has to say. There's always more to a story than one side. Get the full story before you decide what to do. Then call me. I want to know every detail." She kisses EmmaMae on the cheek.

"Take me to Sophie's Fine Foods on Cherry Street please."

The market store is open, but empty. She browses around walking past the many shelves, picking up items and replacing them neatly. She pulls on the cellar door. It opens. She steps down into the dimly-lit cellar. Nothing but potatoes and sacks of rice and beans sitting on a shelf. She's unaware of the hidden entrance. She climbs the steps back into the store.

She walks outside and wanders to the rear entrance. The entrance she walked into that dreadful night. One of the double storm doors lays open on the ground. She steps quietly down the stairs, through the closet and into the speakeasy.

Frank is sweeping up. He leans on his broom and stares in disbelief. EmmaMae walks across the room and takes a seat at a table near him. She crosses her legs and sits with perfect posture. "Hello Frank."

He sets the broom against the wall and sits next to her. She smiles through watery eyes.

"Stanley isn't here."

"I'll wait for him. I want to speak to him one last time."

Frank's eyes lower. He takes her by the hand. "What you saw that night wasn't at all what it looked like. I mean, it was ... it's just Stanley had nothing to do with it."

She fights back tears and holds her hand up as a barrier between them.

Frank touches her arm. "Please just listen to me for one minute. I have no reason to lie to you."

"Okay. I'm listening."

He pauses. "What the girls were doing was my fault. They worked here before my brother bought this joint and they were explaining to me ... well, showing me, how they used to make more tips and bring in more business. I decided to take them to the bar and I asked them to show Max what they showed me. You know, to see if he thought it was a good idea. Stanley wasn't even there. He was down in the cellar under the bar counting out money for the till. He had no idea what we were doing."

She wipes her eyes with a hanky and shakes her head. She raises her finger and points at him. "I want to believe you Frank. But you'd say anything to protect your brother."

Frank leans back and stares at the ceiling. "You're not listening to me. He wasn't there."

Rose, Ruby and Lily enter the speakeasy. EmmaMae glares. Rose and Ruby swiftly walk to the other side of the bar. Lily pauses for a moment and stares at her.

EmmaMae stands with her fists on her hips. "What are you staring at, slut?"

Lily shakes her head and places one hand on her hip. She cocks her head. "You're a fool sweetie. Your daddy spurned my attempts to seduce him. Oh, and believe me I tried. All he talked about was you. And how much he loves you. Men like that are hard to find, honey. But if you're out of the picture, sugar, you can bet your sweet ass I'm going to keep on trying if and when he ever returns."

"Oh really? Well how about I ask him to fire you and your two hussies over there? Then you three can take your slutty little asses to some other joint to flaunt."

Lily's eyes open wide mocking her. "Sweetheart, your man ain't the boss here anymore. He sold this place to Max days ago. He's gone. He gave it up. Probably gave it all up for you. But you're too stupid to see he had nothing to do with what went on that night when you walked in. He did nothing wrong. But you're too blind in your own jealousy to see." Lily struts off in a huff and joins Rose and Ruby for a smoke.

EmmaMae turns to Frank. Her face is ashen. "Frank. Is that true? Did Stanley quit the business?"

Frank nods. "It's true. He did. He couldn't do it anymore. He blamed owning this joint for losing you."

"Where is he, Frank?"

He shakes his head. "I don't know. Maybe he's home, maybe he left. I haven't seen him in days."

***

The cab driver stops in front of Stanley's home. "Thank you. Keep the change." The sight of Stanley's home brings a wave of emotion into her heart, flooding every corner with precious memories of the love they shared here.

"For sale? Oh no. No, no." Her heart sinks. She gasps. His automobile is gone. She turns the doorknob to find the door open and walks inside. Everything is still in its place. A photo sits on the mantle. A black and white photo of their picnic in the park at Myer's Lake. *He framed it.* She runs her finger over the glass and gently smiles. Her reflection overlays the photo with a saddened face staring back at her. A tear leaves her eye and runs across her cheek. Why was she so hasty in blaming him? She knew he was downstairs and not involved, yet her anger wanted him to be guilty. She simply felt neglected from all the time he spent at the speakeasy and she didn't know how to express it.

She wanders into the kitchen. His pocket watch sits ticking on the counter. She gently picks it up and opens its case. *Why would he leave this here? He's never without it.*

A note on the table catches her eye. It's addressed to Frank. She sits and slowly picks it up. She unfolds the note unaware she's holding her breath as she focuses on the neatly written words. She never realized how nice his handwriting was.

Frank,

Please take care of the chickens and the house. I'm leaving you in charge of selling them both. You keep the money and find a place, little brother. Don't give up your dream of becoming a wrestler. I'll check in on you soon. I just don't know when. Not sure when I'll be back or if I'll be back. You take care of yourself.

Stanley

Her eyes blur from welling tears. Large droplets spatter onto the paper. She clutches the timepiece in her hand and lays her head on the kitchen table. Her body begins to tremble as she sobs. *Why didn't I give him a chance? My love ... my sweetheart is gone. I've lost him.*

She raises her head and closes her eyes. She places her face in her hands. The silence of Stanley's home becomes a deafening blow to her heart and soul. She lays her forehead on his table lamenting. Lamenting that she allowed this to go on for so long. He tried to see her; tried to talk to her. But pride has always been a rigid stone she's stumbled over all her life. Her body shakes as the dam holding back her tears begins to crumble. She cries bitter tears of regret. Her heart shatters into tiny bits of sorrow. *I love him ... I love him. I can't do this. I can't say goodbye.*

A small click and the squeak of a door. She opens her eyes and lifts her head. Stunned and confused Stanley is motionless, hovering in the doorway. His mouth agape. No words come out. He closes his eyes and opens them again. How can this be?

EmmaMae leaps from her chair and rushes into his arms. She wraps her arms around his neck and buries her face in his chest, allowing her tears to flow freely.

Stanley raises his tear-filled eyes to the ceiling and whispers. "Thank you, God." He cradles her face in his hands and gently kisses her lips. "I thought I lost you, my love. I thought I lost you forever."

She rests her head on his chest. He squeezes her tighter. "EmmaMae, I would never betray you, sweetheart. I had no idea ..."

She looks deep into his adoring eyes. Her hand caresses his cheek. "I know dear, I know. I was a fool not to let you explain. I was stubborn and blind not to see what my heart already knew."

Stanley swiftly sweeps her off of her feet and cradles her in his arms. She hangs onto his neck. She can feel the tightness in his broad shoulders and the firm muscles in his biceps contracting as he carries her effortlessly up the stairs. He swings the bedroom door shut with his foot and gently places her on the bed.

They gaze into each other's eyes. Neither one sure of what comes next. She opens her arms and surrenders herself to him, body mind and soul.

When does that rare moment in time occur when two lovers come together as one? When their hearts join and their spirits unite? When their love becomes an unbreakable bond that nothing in heaven or earth can ever tear apart? *This* was that moment.

EPILOGUE

MONDAY, SEPTEMBER 27, 1926 - Saint Peter's Catholic Church. Black suit, black shoes, white shirt and black bow tie. Neatly clipped to his jacket pocket is his vintage Mudder timepiece. His hair is slicked back and shiny. His head is spinning. His heart races. It's impossible to catch a breath. His stomach churns and tightens, twisting into knots and cramping. Never underestimate the level of stress of your wedding day.

He looks out across the pews and the crowd. Frances smiles at him while Koz crosses his burly arms glaring at him with that old Polish scowl. Their eyes meet and Koz breaks into a big smile, nodding his approval.

Max sits behind Mama. He holds his wrists together like he's handcuffed. He mouths the word, *run.*

In the first row sits Mama, Sophie and Sophie's husband Michael. Annie sits next to Michael squirming in her chair and sticking out her tongue at him. A dapper Frank and Billy stand to the left as Best Men.

The organ blasts chords of compressed air sending them vibrating through the walls and the ears of every person in the church. The doors swing open.

EmmaMae walks towards him, escorted by her brother Charles. An angel wearing a beautiful white wedding gown with an exquisite long white veil, white nylons and white shoes. She carries a large bouquet of fall flowers. Golds, oranges, pinks and browns. She gazes deep into his eyes, searching for any sign of fear. Her eyebrows raise and her eyes widen, glistening and sparkling with tears.

"We all are gathered here today to join this young man and this young woman in Holy Matrimony ..." The priest's words fade to muffled echoes.

Life is surreal and is constantly moving forward towards unrealized dreams and the hopes and promises of the future. No matter how deep a tragedy, no matter how unbearable the pain, all of these challenges lead us on a journey. A journey only the traveler can fully understand.

It requires sacrifice and unselfishness and the courage to look oneself in the mirror and confront all the demons of one's past. To learn to forgive yourself and embrace yourself for who you are. To make peace with and say goodbye to those who hurt us. And in that process, we learn to let go of our own anger and our own fears. We learn to truly forgive our past and look ahead.

Rest in peace, Papa. I will never understand the demons that drove you to cause us so much pain. Demons that tormented you for so many years. But I surrender my anger to my God and in that act of humility, I am healed through His limitless mercy and love.

Stanley feels a nudge. The priest is staring at Him and pointing at his ring finger. Stanley fumbles around in his pocket. *Where is it? Oh ... here it is.*

Hands shaking, he slides the glittering diamond gently onto her finger.

"I now pronounce you man and wife. You may kiss your bride, son."

***

JULY 14, 1985, CANTON, OHIO - He gasps as he awakens. Finding himself in a hospital bed. Overtaken by fear and sadness, brought on by the reality of the nightmare that awoke him. He takes deep breaths to slow his fluttering heart.

Hours to live, he fights for more time. Struggling for more breaths, he fumbles with a control button and presses it. A surge of euphoria and sedation enter his bloodstream, easing his intense pain. Gaunt and weak, he's a shadow of the strong proud man he once was.

A clipboard hangs at the bottom of the hospital bed with the name Stanley William Miller and a prognosis of Stage IV-B Colon Cancer. Lying on a wooden table next to the bed sits his vintage stainless-steel Mudder timepiece. The silvery-worn case sits open as the hands steadily tick, marking each precious second. The lights glow dimly in the room overshadowed by a gray threatening sky revealed by the room's only window. The window overlooks a park with a variety of trees. Browns, golds and oranges all slumbering from Autumn's touch. The soft pitter-patter of rain drops tapping the glass adds a droning, almost musical effect to the small room.

His son Rick sits next to him. He's a tall, burly man in his mid-forties. Stanley stares through glossy tired eyes, and manages a feeble smile. His aged eyes beam with a twinkle of respect and love. They maintain eye contact, neither speaking. After a time, his son breaks the gloomy silence. "Tell me about your life, Pops."

Stanley struggles to sit up and raises a scolding finger. "Don't ever ask me about my life, son." Images of a farmhouse in Southington, Ohio fill his mind. *I can never tell you about my life.* Pain rattles through his chest as he draws a deep breath. Sensing his hand is trembling he rests it atop his son's. "Where's your mother?"

"She's on her way."

Words are powerful. Knowing she'll be here soon, he sighs. *Help me hang on Lord, until she gets here.*

He closes his eyes and visualizes her face. *I need to hear your voice. I need to feel your touch. I can't do this without you, my love. You say I am your rock, but in truth you have always been mine. The one heart I could always fall into and feel safe.*

His eyes grow heavy. He rests them for a moment.

Her gentle touch is unmistakable. His eyes open. The surroundings are a sobering reminder of where he is. He glances to his left. EmmaMae pats his hand. His heart floods with unconditional love for her. A surge of strength courses through his body knowing she is here with him.

"I've always adored you. You filled my life with happiness, sweetheart." He points a trembling finger to her heart. "My love for you will live on forever, inside here."

He turns to his son with a deep sadness. "I knew when we drove your brother Robert to the airport, it would be the last time I would ever see him." He raises a feeble finger. "Rick, make sure you and your brother take care of each other. Respect each other. Always make time for each other. There is nothing more important than family. Never neglect those relationships in your life."

He turns to EmmaMae, gazing into her eyes. He softly smiles. He squeezes her hand. With the deepest humility and greatest of dignity, he let's go of his life and exhales his final breath.

His son sits quiet staring at his father. His eyes tear. He stands and gently butts his forehead against his father's. "Goodbye Pops. I love you. Rest in peace. Your suffering is over now." He walks around the bed and softly kisses his mother on the head, then leaves the room.

The rain pounds the window like a thousand tears. She glances at the table next to his bed. His old timepiece lies face open. It has stopped ticking—no longer tracking time.

She stands, clinging to his hand. Her chin trembles. Her eyes well. She presses her lips to his ear. "Rest now my darling. My protector. My love." She kisses his forehead, then gently lies her head on his chest. She holds the man who rescued her so many years ago. The man who changed her life forever and fiercely protected her. Her heart is utterly broken. She clings to him and closes her eyes and sobs.

***

EmmaMae is seated in the front row of a beautiful lush garden, dressed in black. A Catholic Priest delivers the eulogy for Stanley William Miller. A black veil covers her face and hides her tears. She holds a bracelet made of bone, blue seashell beads, and leather between her fingers. The central bead has a pale-blue pearly sheen shaped like the moon.

A white German Shepard wanders into the funeral ceremony. It was the oddest thing. Nobody knew where the animal had come from. The dog sat by her side, placing his head under her hand. It remained by her side until the end of the funeral.

Afterward it trotted off toward a wooded area close to the garden. It stopped and glanced back at her, then disappeared into the woods never to be seen again.

The Irish are a superstitious bunch. She knew in her heart, it was her Stanley, saying goodbye and letting her know he was at peace.

Family and friends place roses on the casket. EmmaMae sits patiently waiting for the crowd to leave.

"It's time now ma'am."

She approaches the casket and places her hand on the shiny pearly-white box. She whispers. "I'll see you again, my darling." She places his timepiece next to the roses covering the casket. She watches as her husband is lowered into his final resting place.

Stanley and EmmaMae Miller had three sons. Bill, Robert and Rick. None of his children ever knew the real story of their father, Stanley William Puchalski and the family tragedy that defined his life and the lives of his siblings. They never knew of the oath of silence they swore in 1921. It would be many years before the truth would reveal itself.

Stanley and EmmaMae remained married for fifty-nine years. She never remarried and in 1997 she joined her beloved in Paradise and was laid to rest next to him, beneath the same headstone in Canton, Ohio.

Stanley William Miller left his legacy through a passionate *Heart of Steel*. A heart that knew no limit of love or sacrifice. Nothing was more important to him than his family and eventually his love and acceptance of Jesus Christ.

The Miller clan lives on through all the generations that follow the young farm boy from Southington, Ohio. Remembering and honoring the Patriarch who gave them all their name, their family history, and their legacy.

The End.

Made in the USA
Las Vegas, NV
23 December 2021

39279422R00135